THE ISLAM
DEBATE

OTHER BOOKS BY JOSH McDOWELL

THE ISLAM DEBATE

by

Josh McDowell

and

John Gilchrist

CAMPUS CRUSADE FOR CHRIST

Published by

HERE'S LIFE PUBLISHERS, INC.

San Bernardino, California 92414

THE ISLAM DEBATE
by Josh McDowell and John Gilchrist

A Campus Crusade for Christ Book

Published by
HERE'S LIFE PUBLISHERS, INC.
P.O. Box 1576
San Bernardino, CA 92402

ISBN 0-86605-104-X
HLP Product No. 403097
Library of Congress Catalogue Card 83-070193
© 1983 by Campus Crusade for Christ, Inc.

FOR MORE INFORMATION, WRITE:

L.I.F.E.–P.O. Box A399, Sydney South 2000, Australia
Campus Crusade for Christ of Canada–Box 368, Abbottsford, B.C., V25 4N9, Canada
Campus Crusade for Christ – 103 Friar Street, Reading RG1 1EP, Berkshire, England
Campus Crusade for Christ–28 Westmoreland St., Dublin 2, Ireland
Lay Institute for Evangelism–P.O. Box 8786, Auckland 3, New Zealand
Life Ministry–P.O. Box/Bus 91015, Auckland Park 2006, Republic of So. Africa
Campus Crusade for Christ, Int'l–Arrowhead Springs, San Bernardino, CA 92414, U.S.A.

THE ISLAM
DEBATE

CONTENTS

INTRODUCTION

WHY THE DEBATE?

In an age which is increasingly relativistic and syncretistic, one might ask—why debate about Islam? Why not "bury the hatchet" in a spirit of mutual trust and respect?

Christians believe firmly in respecting members of other faiths but believe equally firmly that the salvation of the world remains vested in the work of Jesus Christ who died for the sins of men at the cross of Calvary.

The Qur'an affirms various things revealed about Jesus Christ in the Bible, but it denies His divinity, crucifixion and resurrection. In so doing it has negated the heart of the gospel, that is, the crucifixion and resurrection of Jesus Christ. For the apostle Paul said: "...and if Christ has not been raised, your faith is worthless; you are still in your sins" (1 Corinthians 15:17 NASB). The Qur'an, in denying these all-important events in the life of Jesus, enters strongly into debate with Christianity.

Islam is committed to challenging the claims of Christianity. In many situations what is looked at is a false Christianity. What is needed is not an abandonment of the contest, but for discussion to be greatly increased in a spirit of amicability, love and mutual understanding.

Such a debate took place between Josh McDowell and Ahmed Deedat, President of the Islamic Propagation Centre in Durban, South Africa,

THE ISLAM
DEBATE

during August 1981. The subject struck at the roots of the dilemma between Islam and Christianity: "Was Christ crucified?" It was conducted in a spirit of warmth and tolerance without either speaker being expected to dilute his message or refrain from debating the issues head-on. Even though it was one of the wettest periods in the history of Durban, a large crowd of about 6,000 filled the outdoor tennis stadium. Both Muslim and Christian participated spiritedly in the occasion. The text of the debate is recorded at the end of this book and the open, frank, but charitable manner in which the speakers gave account of themselves is clear for all to see.

The debate was initiated from the Muslim side. Ahmed Deedat, a well-known Muslim public speaker in South Africa, had read Josh McDowell's book, *Evidence That Demands a Verdict*, and during 1980 wrote to him, challenging him to come to South Africa to debate the issues regarding the Christian and Muslim views on the crucifixion and resurrection of Jesus Christ. This Muslim leader had held similar debates in South Africa with other Christians, including one with the co-author of this book, John Gilchrist, before a similar crowd six years earlier.

Josh accepted the challenge, seeing it as an opportunity to clarify to thousands of Muslims the essence and heart of the gospel—the crucifixion and resurrection of Jesus Christ—and to clarify many issues that divide Muslims and Christians over the person of Jesus Christ. Before the debate was ended, many, many Muslims were to hear, perhaps for the first time, a clear proclamation of the gospel of God.

"You be the judge!" the posters advertising the symposium boldly claimed. Such a debate as this could not produce a "winner" in one sense of the word, as the issues under discussion had divided many nations for long ages and it was hardly likely that one side would be so successful in presenting its case that all the adherents of the other would summarily abandon their heritage and change their religion.

The great advantage of a dialogue such as this is that the adherents of both religions gained an excellent opportunity to hear both points of view. An atmosphere was created where each individual could examine the claims of another religion freely while evaluating those claims against the arguments for his own position.

As Christians, we believe that the case for the biblical gospel is the right one, and it is our firm conviction that the arguments set forth by

Mr. McDowell, though limited by time, were convincing proof that our case is a sound one. In this book the entire debate is reproduced without bias. Accordingly, all readers, whether Christian or Muslim, are free to judge for themselves.

We are convinced that the debate furthered the cause of the Christian gospel among the Muslims of South Africa. With such a conviction, we have published this book. It is our firm persuasion that it will do much to further the ministry of the gospel to Muslims throughout the whole world.

Josh McDowell   John Gilchrist, Esquire
Julian, California   South Africa
December 1982   December 1982

WHY THIS BOOK?

The debate has stirred a great deal of interest, in both the United States and South Africa, in the differences between Islam and Christianity. Therefore, we have not only published the text of the debate in this book, but we have also included significant background material on many of the issues that surfaced during the debate. For example, an entire chapter deals with the issue of the Christian New Testament not being a reliable historical document today about the life and claims of Christ. Accusations about Christian misinterpretations of various biblical passages concerning the crucifixion and resurrection of Jesus Christ are treated in more detail in this book than time allowed for during the debate. Various Islamic issues raised against Christians and their Bible were not directly addressed in the debate, and a Christian response is given here.

Most Christians are unaware of arguments usually used by Muslim apologists against Christianity, and, when confronted by them, often are caught off guard. How many Christians have ever heard of the Gospel of Barnabas? How many would know how to deal with confident Muslim claims that the Gospel of Barnabas is the only reliable record of the life of Jesus Christ? Now knowing that this so-called gospel is a forgery of a much later age, the average Christian may find himself ill-equipped to give an adequate Christian response when challenged on this point.

How many Christians could refute the bold claims made by Muslims regarding certain biblical texts which allegedly foretell the coming of

THE ISLAM
DEBATE

Muhammad? Muslims who raise such issues are usually well prepared with their arguments. How many Christians could give an equally confident Christian response?

The above issues might seem obscure to most Christians, but they form an integral part of the Muslim polemic against Christianity.

The purpose of publishing this material is threefold.

(1) To help Muslims and Christians alike to better understand the similarities and differences between Islam and Christianity.

(2) To help Christians better relate to Muslims as a result of a greater knowledge of the Christian/Islam conflict through understanding some of the answers to Islamic accusations against the Christian Bible, the crucifixion and resurrection of Christ.

(3) To encourage a bolder Christian witness and expression of love to Muslims. One result of the preparation and research that went into preparing for the debate and for this book is a greater respect for Islam. It is a profound faith that has the capacity to captivate totally a person's mind, will and emotions.

I have greatly benefited personally from my involvement and dialogue with many Muslims. This has enhanced my love for those of the Islamic persuasion and given me a greater desire to share Christ's love and gospel with them.

CHAPTER ONE

HISTORICAL BACKGROUND OF ISLAM

IN RECENT YEARS Islam has been in the spotlight, partly because of the heightened tension in the Middle East. This tension has put Islamic culture under the microscope of world attention. The Muslim faith is a major driving force in nations in the Middle East, Asia, and North Africa. Indonesia and Malaya are 85-100 percent Muslim. The impact of this faith on the world has been increasing steadily. Today Islam claims to be the fastest-growing religion in the world with an estimated 750-800 million believers or adherents dominating more than three dozen countries on three continents.

Even the Arab-Israeli tension can be traced back to the Islam-Judaism conflict. Not only does Islam collectively wield a strong sword as Muslims threaten war with Israel, but Islamic sects also threaten even greater unrest in other areas of the fragile Middle East and could be catalysts for still wider conflict. For example, right-wing militant Islamic fundamentalists were responsible for both the takeover of Iran and the assassination of Egyptian President Anwar Sadat.

The vast majority of Muslims, however, are not militant. The contrast between the moderate, progressive, and constructive Islam of Egypt and Turkey and the fundamentalistic and reactionary Islam of, for example, Iran is well-marked. Islam has had a great deal of positive impact on many countries where it is a strong force. But positive influence is insufficient reason to commit one's life to any religion. One must examine objectively the teachings of Islam (or any other religion) to ascertain its validity.

THE ISLAM
DEBATE

The impact of Islam on history also makes it worthy of study. Professor of Islamic law Sir Norman Anderson, a Christian, summarizes it in this way:

> The religion of Islam is one of the outstanding phenomena of history. Within a century of the death of its founder, the Muslim Empire stretched from Southern France through Spain, North Africa, the Levant and Central Asia to the confines of China; and, although Islam has since been virtually expelled from Western Europe and has lost much of its political power elsewhere, it has from time to time made notable advances in Eastern Europe, in Africa, in India, and in Southeast Asia. Today it extends from the Atlantic to the Philippines and numbers some (eight) hundred million (believers or) adherents drawn from races as different as the European from the Bantu, and the Aryan Indian from the primitive Philippine tribesmen; yet it is still possible to speak of the "World of Islam" (Sir Norman Anderson, ed., *The World's Religions*, Grand Rapids, MI: William B. Eerdmans Publishing Company, 1976, p. 52).

HISTORY

The early history of Islam revolves around one central figure: Muhammad (var. sp.: Muhammed, Mohammed). Although Islam is an interesting mixture of different religions, the origin of the faith is found in the one person of Muhammad.

Muhammad

Muhammad was born around A.D. 570 in the city of Mecca in Arabia. Muhammad's father, Abdullah, died before his birth. His mother, Amina, died when he was six. He was raised first by his grandfather, Abd al-Muttalib, and later by his uncle, Abu Talib. Muhammad's background is not well known. Some scholars believe he came from a well-respected family, but this is not certain. What is clear is that he was of the Hashimite clan of the *Al Qu'raysh* tribe. At 25, he married a wealthy, respected 40-year-old widow named Khadijah. Of his life Anderson relates:

> There is evidence in a tradition which can scarcely have been fabricated that Muhammad suffered in early life from fits. Be that as it may, the adult Muhammad soon showed signs of a markedly religious disposition. He would

retire to caves for seclusion and meditation; he frequently practiced fasting; and he was prone to dreams. Profoundly dissatisfied with the polytheism and crude superstitions of his native Mecca, he appears to have become passionately convinced of the existence and transcendence of one true God. How much of this conviction he owed to Christianity or Judaism it seems impossible to determine. Monophysite Christianity was at that time widely spread in the Arab Kingdom of Ghassan; the Byzantine Church was represented by hermits dotted about the Hijaz with whom he may well have come into contact; the Nestorians were established at al Hira and in Persia; and the Jews were strongly represented in al Madina, the Yemen and elsewhere. There can be no manner of doubt, moreover, that at some period of his life he absorbed much teaching from Talmudic sources and had contact with some form of Christianity; and it seems overwhelmingly probable that his early adoption of monotheism can be traced to one or both of these influences (ibid., p. 54).

The character of Muhammad was quite a mosaic, as Anderson summarizes:

For the rest, his character seems, like that of many another, to have been a strange mixture. He was a poet rather than a theologian: a master improvisor rather than a systematic thinker. That he was in the main simple in his tastes and kindly in his disposition there can be no doubt; he was generous, resolute, genial and astute: a shrewd judge and a born leader of men. He could, however, be cruel and vindictive to his enemies; he could stoop to assassination; and he was undeniably sensual (ibid., p. 60).

Robert Payne also brings this out in his book, *The Holy Sword:*

It is worthwhile to pause for a moment before the quite astonishing polarity of Muhammad's mind. Violence and gentleness were at war within him. Sometimes he gives the appearance of living simultaneously in two worlds, at one and the same moment seeing the world about to be destroyed by the flames of God and in a state of divine peace; and he seems to hold these opposing visions only at the cost of an overwhelmingly sense of strain. Sometimes the spring snaps and we see him gazing with a look of bafflement at the world around him, which is neither the world in flames nor the world in a state of blessedness, but the ordinary day-to-day world in which he was rarely at home (Robert Payne, *The Holy Sword*, New York: Collier Books, 1962, p. 84).

The Call

Muhammad rejected the idolatrous polytheism of those around him. At the age of 40, the religious and monotheistic Muhammad had his first vision. This and subsequent revelations are recorded in the Qur'an.

Muhammad was at first unsure of the source of these visions, whether divine or demonic. His wife, Khadijah, encouraged him to believe they had come from God. Later she was his first convert. However, his most important early convert was a wealthy merchant named Abu Bakr, who eventually was one of his successors.

The authoritative *Cambridge History of Islam* comments on Muhammad's revelations:

> Either in the course of the visions or shortly afterwards, Muhammad began to receive "messages" or "revelations" from God. Sometimes he may have heard the words being spoken to him, but for the most part he seems simply to have "found them in his heart." Whatever the precise "manner of revelation"—and several different "manners" were listed by Muslim scholars—the important point is that the message was not the product of Muhammad's conscious mind. He believed that he could easily distinguish between his own thinking and these revelations.

> The messages which thus came to Muhammad from beyond his conscious mind were at first fairly short, and consisted of short verses ending in a common rhyme or assonance. They were committed to memory by Muhammad and his followers, and recited as part of their common worship. Muhammad continued to receive the messages at intervals until his death. In his closing years the revelations tended to be longer, to have much longer verses and to deal with the affairs of the community of Muslims at Medina. All, or at least many, of the revelations were probably written down during Muhammad's lifetime by his secretaries (P.M. Holt, ed., *The Cambridge History of Islam*, Vol. II, London: Cambridge University Press, 1970, pp. 31, 32).

Popular commentator on Islam, Alfred Guillaume, recounts Muhammad's first vision:

> Now if we look at the accounts of his call, as recorded by the early biographers, some very interesting parallels with Hebrew prophets come to light. They say that it was his habit to leave the haunts of men and retire to the mountains to give himself up to prayer and meditation. One night as he was asleep the angel Gabriel came to him with a piece of silk brocade whereon words were written, and said "Recite!" He answered "What shall I recite?" The order was repeated three times, while he felt continually increasing physical pressure, until the angel said:

Historical Background
of Islam

> Recite in the name of thy Lord who created
> Man from blood coagulated.
> Recite! Thy Lord is wondrous kind
> Who by the pen has taught mankind
> Things they knew not (being blind).

When he woke these words seemed to be written on his heart (or, as we should say, impressed indelibly on his mind). Then the thought came to him that he must be a *sha'ir* or possessed, he who had so hated such people that he could not bear the sight of them; and he could not tolerate the thought that his tribesmen would regard him as one of them—as in fact they afterwards did. Thereupon he left the place with the intention of throwing himself over a precipice. But while on his way he heard a voice from heaven hailing him as the Apostle of God, and lifting up his eyes he saw a figure astride the horizon which turned him from his purpose and kept him rooted to the spot. And there he remained long after his anxious wife's messengers had returned to report that they could not find him (Alfred Guillaume, *Islam*, London: Penguin Books, 1954, pp. 28, 29).

Sir Norman Anderson discusses how Muhammad at first thought he was possessed by the demons, or *Jinn*, as they were called, but later dismissed the idea:

It seems, however, that Muhammad himself was at first doubtful of the source of these revelations, fearing that he was possessed by one of the Jinn, or sprites, as was commonly believed to be the case with Arab poets and soothsayers. But Khadijah and others reassured him, and he soon began to propound divine revelations with increasing frequency (Anderson, *Religions*, p. 55).

These visions marked Muhammad's prophetic call by Allah. Muhammad received visions during the next 22 years, until his death in A.D. 632.

The Hijrah

The new faith encountered opposition in Muhammad's hometown of Mecca. Because of his rejection in Mecca and the ostracism of his views, Muhammad and his companions migrated, in response to an invitation, to the city now known as *Medina*, which means in full, "City of the Prophet," renamed from its original *Yathrib*.

The Hijrah, which means "flight," marks the turning point in Islam. All Islamic calendars mark this date, July 16, 622, as their beginning.

THE ISLAM
DEBATE

Thus, A.D. 630 would be 8 A.H. (in the year of the Hijrah).

In his early years in Medina, Muhammad was sympathetic to both the Jews and the Christians. But they rejected him and his teaching. Because of that rejection, Muhammad turned from Jerusalem as the center of worship of Islam to Mecca. Muhammad denounced all the idols which surrounded the Ka'aba in Mecca and declared it a shrine for the one true God, Allah.

With this new emphasis on Mecca, Muhammad realized the importance of returning to his home there. The rejected prophet soon returned in triumph, conquering the city.

John B. Noss details some of Muhammad's actions upon his return to Mecca:

> One of his first acts was to go reverently to the Ka'aba; yet he showed no signs of yielding to the ancient Meccan polytheism. After honoring the Black Stone and riding seven times around the shrine, he ordered the destruction of the idols within it and the scraping of the paintings of Abraham and the angels from the walls. He sanctioned the use of the well Zamzam and restored the boundary pillars defining the sacred territory around Mecca. Thenceforth no Muslim would have cause to hesitate about going on a pilgrimage to the ancient holy city.

> Muhammad now made sure of his political and prophetic ascendency in Arabia. Active opponents near at hand were conquered by the sword, and tribes far away were invited sternly to send delegations offering their allegiance. Before his sudden death in 632 he knew he was well on the way to unifying the Arab tribes under a theocracy governed by the will of God (John B. Noss, *Man's Religions*, New York: MacMillan Publishing Company Inc., 1974, p. 517).

Between the return to Mecca and Muhammad's death, the prophet zealously and militantly propagated Islam, and the new faith quickly spread throughout the area.

After Muhammad's Death

When Muhammad died he had not revealed any plan which the leadership in Islam could use to determine his successor. Sir Norman Anderson comments:

Historical Background
of Islam

Muhammad died, according to the best-supported view, without having designated any successor (*Khalifa* or Caliph). As the last and greatest of the Prophets he could not, of course, be replaced. But the community he had founded was a theocracy with no distinction between Church and State, and someone must clearly succeed, not to give but to enforce the law, to lead in war and to guide in peace. It was common ground, therefore, that a Caliph must be appointed: and in the event 'Umar ibn al Khattab (himself the second Caliph) succeeded in rushing the election of the aged Abu Bakr, one of the very first believers. But the question of the Caliphate was to cause more divisions and bloodshed than any other issue in Islam, and almost from the first three rival parties, in embryo at least, can be discerned. There were the Companions of the Prophet, who believed in the eligibility of any suitable "Early Believer" of the tribe of Quraysh; there was the aristocracy of Mecca, who wished to capture the Caliphate for the family of Umayya; and there were the "legitimists," who believed that no election was needed, but that 'Ali, the cousin and son-in-law of the Prophet, had been divinely designated as his successor (Anderson, *Religions*, p. 64).

Abu Bakr died less than two years after his designation as Caliph. Upon his death, Umar became successor, and under him the borders of the Islamic empire were considerably expanded.

Eventually a power struggle developed as different factions promoted their own successors over their rivals. The major division came between those who believed the Caliph should be elected by the Islamic leadership and those who believed the successor should be hereditary, through 'Ali, Muhammad's son-in-law, who was married to his daughter, Fatima. This struggle, along with others, produced the two main divisions of Islam known as the Sunnis (followers of the prophet's way), and the Shi'ites (followers of the 12 Imams descended from the prophet) as well as numerous sects, within these two major groups. The Sunni/Shi'ite conflict remains to this day a center of international controversy. (More on this in other chapters.)

ISLAMIC TEACHINGS

Faith and Duty

The teachings of Islam are comprised both of faith *(imam)* and practice or duty *(din)*. Sir Norman Anderson explains:

THE ISLAM
DEBATE

The faith and practice of Islam are governed by the two great branches of Muslim learning, theology and jurisprudence, to both of which some reference has already been made. Muslim theology (usually called "Tawhid" from its central doctrine of the Unity of the Godhead) defines all that a man should believe, while the law (Shari'a) prescribes everything that he should do. There is no priesthood and no sacraments. Except among the Sufis, Islam knows only exhortation and instruction from those who consider themselves, or are considered by others, adequately learned in theology or law.

Unlike any other system in the world today the Shari'a embraces every detail of human life, from the prohibition of crime to the use of the toothpick, and from the organization of the State to the most sacred intimacies—or unsavory aberrations—of family life. It is "the science of all things, human and divine," and divides all actions into what is obligatory or enjoined, what is praiseworthy or recommended, what is permitted or legally indifferent, what is disliked or deprecated, and what is forbidden (Anderson, *Religions*, p. 78).

These practices are true of Sunni and Shi'ite Islam, but not always of the divergent sects.

Islamic law *(Shari'a)* plays a central role in all Islamic culture. The structure of the law is that of civil law rather than common law as generally practiced in England and the United States.

It must be emphasized that the *Shari'a* has been central to Islamic doctrine:

The most important and fundamental religious concept of Islam is that of the *shari'a* which literally means a "path to the watering place" but in its religious application means the total way of life as explicitly or implicitly commanded by God. The word has been used in the Koran, which sometimes suggests that different religions have different shari'as but at other times that all religions have fundamentally one shari'a.

The concept as formulated by Muslim religious teachers, includes both the doctrine or belief, and practice or the law. But historically the formulation and systemization of the law took place earlier than the crystalization of the formal theology. This, as shown below, had far-reaching consequences for the future development of Islam (*Encyclopaedia Britannica*, s.v. "Islam," Chicago: William Benton Publishing Company, 1967, p. 664).

The controversy surrounding the law and theology and the fourfold division of the *Shari'a* led to the formulation of various divisions within Sunni Islam.

Guillaume explains:

> In certain countries certain matters have been taken out of the purview of the shari'a and now come within the scope of secular courts; but, broadly speaking, no change comparable with that which has taken and is taking place in Islamic countries today has been seen within Islam for a thousand years or more. Turkey, as everyone knows, has abolished the shari'a altogether. Officially it is a secular State, though actually the influence of Islam on the population, especially in Asia, is very considerable, and shows signs of becoming stronger under the new democratic government.
>
> In a series of articles in *The Moslem World* and elsewhere my colleague, Mr. J.N.D. Anderson, has shown how in the Arab countries, too, the shari'a is undergoing revision. Egypt, the Sudan, Syria, Lebanon, Jordan, and Iraq are all on the move. The changes which are being made illustrate how a definite attempt to relate the shari'a to the conditions of modern life and to a more liberal view of human relations is being realized in positive legislation (Guillaume, *Islam*, pp. 166, 167).

He then comments on one of the differences of the Shi'ites and the Sunnis:

> In theory, the Shi'ite conception of the supreme authority in law is utterly different from that of the Sunnis, though in practice the difference does not amount to very much. They reject the four schools and the doctrine of *ijma* because their Hidden Imam has the sole right of determining what the believer shall do and believe. Therefore their duly accredited doctors can still exercise the power of *ijtihad* or personal opinion. This power the Sunnis lost a thousand years ago or more (ibid., p. 103).

Qur'an (var. sp. Koran)

The basis for Islamic doctrine is found in the Qur'an. Christian author Kenneth Boa describes the central place of the Qur'an in the Islamic faith as well as the supplementary works:

> The Koran is the authoritative scripture of Islam. About four-fifths the length of the New Testament, it is divided into 114 surahs (chapters). Parts were (recorded) by Muhammad, and the rest, based on his oral teaching, was written from memory by his disciples after Muhammad's death.

THE ISLAM
DEBATE

Over the years a number of additional sayings of Muhammad and his early disciples were compiled. These comprise the *Hadith* ("tradition"), the sayings of which are called *sunna* ("custom"). The Hadith supplements the Koran much as the Talmud supplements the Law in Judaism (Kenneth Boa, *Cults, World Religions, and You*, Wheaton, IL: Victor Books, 1977, p. 52).

The Qur'an is the word of God in Islam, the holy scriptures. As the supreme and authoritative scripture, it is the main guide for all matters of faith and practice. Muslims believe that the Qur'an was revealed to Muhammad as the final word of God for mankind.

Other revelations include the *Torah* (of Moses), the *Suhuf* (books of the prophets), *Zabur* (psalms of David), and *Injil* (gospel of Jesus). The Qur'an supercedes all other revelations and Muslims allege that it is the only one of which we still have the original text. They believe that all the others have been corrupted, almost beyond recognition.

Islam, for example, would not consider our New Testament to be the Injil (gospel of Jesus). It is not the book given to Jesus, it is others' words *about* Jesus. Islam holds that His original words have been corrupted and many have been lost. Only the Qur'an is believed to be pure and infallible. Muhammad and the Qur'an are those which Islam is to follow.

However, one point that most authors on this subject unfortunately overlook is the fact that while the Qur'an directly states that the Taurat, Zabur and Injil were definitely revealed by Allah (Surah 35:27-31; 4:163,164; 5:44; 32:24; 46:11,12; 2:87), it also states that God's revelations are incorruptible and changeable by no one (Sura 6:115). Thus, not only is the charge of a corrupted gospel text indefensible logically from a Muslim's perspective, it is also a denial of Allah's power to insinuate that He cannot keep His word pure, as He says He will.

Christian author Stephen Neill comments:

It is well known that at many points the Qur'an does not agree with the Jews and Christian Scriptures. Therefore, from the Muslim point of view, it follows of necessity that these Scriptures must have been corrupted. Historical evidence makes no impression on the crushing force of the syllogism. So it is, and it can be no other way. The only valid picture of Jesus Christ is that which is to be found in the pages of the Qur'an (Stephen Neill, *Christian Faith and Other Faiths*, London: Oxford University Press, 1970, p. 64).

Historical Background
of Islam

The 114 *surahs,* or chapters of the Qur'an, are all attributed ultimately to Allah. The surahs are arranged in the Qur'an by length—the longer in front, the shorter in back.

For the Muslims, the Koran (q.v.) is the Word of God, confirming and consummating earlier revealed books and thereby replacing them; its instrument or agent of revelation is the Prophet Mohammed, the last and most perfect of a series of messengers of God to mankind—from Adam through Abraham to Moses and Jesus, the Christian claims for whose divinity are strongly rejected. Indeed there is no people to whom a prophet has not come. Although Mohammed is only a human creature of God, he has nevertheless an unequaled importance in the Koran itself which sets him only next to God as deserving of moral and legal obedience. Hence, his sayings and deeds (Sunna) served as a second basis, besides the Koran, of the belief and practice of Islam.

The Koran (which, for the Muslim, is the miracle par excellence of Mohammed, unsurpassable in form as well as in content) is a forceful document basically expressing an *elan* of religious and social justice. The early chapters (suras) of the Koran, reflecting Mohammed's grim struggle against the Meccans, are characterized by grave warnings of the imminent judgment, while the later suras, of the Medina period, are chiefly directed to regulating the internal and external affairs of the young Muslim community—state, besides narrating the stories of the earlier prophets.

The koranic theology is rigorously monotheistic: God is absolutely unique—"there is nothing like him"—omnipotent, omniscient, merciful. Men are exhorted to obey his will (i.e., to be Muslim) as is necessarily done by all inorganic objects. Special responsibility is laid on man who willingly, although with his characteristically foolish pride, accepted "the thrust," refused by all creation. Besides human beings and angels, the Koran speaks of the jinn, both good and evil, to whom sometimes the devil is represented as belonging *(Encyclopaedia Britannica,* p. 663).

In modern times, the Qur'an has faced many of the same critiques as has the Bible. A major issue is the inspiration of the Qur'an. Some progressive Islamic scholars do not agree as a whole on how the Qur'an came to be or how much is true, although conservative Islamic scholars accept it *all* as literally true. John Alden Williams comments:

The Qur'an, then, is the Word of God, for Muslims. While controversies have raged among them as to the sense in which this is true—whether it is the created or uncreated Word, whether it is true of every Arabic letter or only of the message as a whole, that it *is true* has never been questioned by them (John Alden Williams, *Islam,* New York: George Braziller, 1962, p. 15).

THE ISLAM
DEBATE

The Qur'an was revealed and written in the Arabic language. Because of this, and since it allegedly was revealed by God, Muslims refuse to approve translations of the Qur'an into other languages. There is, then, no *authoritative* translation of the Qur'an. Anyone familiar with the reading of translations of any work would be sympathetic to this demand. However, as rich as Arabic is, the translations still provide significantly accurate meanings which must be evaluated.

The Qur'an came into written form shortly after Muhammad's death.

> All the surahs of the Koran had been recorded in writing before the Prophet's death, and many Muslims had committed the whole Koran to memory. But the written surahs were dispersed among the people; and when, in a battle which took place during the Caliphate of Abu Bakr—that is to say, within two years of the Prophet's death—a large number of those who knew the whole Koran by heart were killed, a collection of the whole Koran was made and put in writing. In the Caliphate of Othman, all existing copies of surahs were called in, and an authoritative version, based on Abu Bakr's collection and the testimony of those who had the whole Koran by heart, was compiled exactly in the present form and order, which is regarded as traditional and as the arrangement of the Prophet himself, the Caliph Othman and his helpers being Comrades of the Prophet and the most devout students of the Revelation. The Koran has thus been very carefully preserved (Mohammed Marmaduke Pickthall, trans., *The Meaning of the Glorious Koran*, New York: Mentor Books, n.d., p. xxviii).

On the origin of the Qur'an, Guillaume comments:

> From the books of tradition we learn that the prophet was subject to ecstatic seizures. He is reported to have said that when inspiration came to him he felt as it were the painful sounding of a bell. Even in cold weather his forehead was bathed in sweat. On one occasion he called to his wife to wrap him in a veil. At other times visions came to him in sleep. Religious ecstasy is a world-wide phenomenon in one stage of human society, and in its early stages Muhammad's verses were couched in the Semitic form of mantic oracular utterance. The veiling of the head and the use of rhymed prose were marks of the Arabian soothsayer, while the feeling of physical violence and compulsion, and the outward appearance of "possession" which seemed to the onlookers to indicate madness or demonic possession were sometimes recorded by, or observed in, the Hebrew prophets.

> The Qur'an as we have it now is a record of what Muhammad said while in the state or states just mentioned. It is beyond doubt that his hearers recognized the symptoms of revelation, otherwise his *obiter dicta* which the

literature of tradition purports to record would be included in the Qur'an (Guillaume, *Islam*, p. 56).

Six Articles of Faith

The six articles of faith are the fundamental doctrines of Islam. All Muslims are expected to believe in and submit to these tenets.

1. *God.* There is only one true God and his name is Allah. Allah is all-knowing, all-powerful and the sovereign judge. Yet Allah is not an interacting personal God, for he is so far above man in every way that he is not personally knowable. Noss states:

> In the famous Muslim creedal formula the first part reads: *la ilaha illa Allah*, "(There is) no god but God." This is the most important article in Muslim theology. No statement about God seemed to Muhammad more fundamental than the declaration that God is one, and no sin seemed to him so unpardonable as associating another being with God on terms of equality. God stands alone and supreme. He existed before any other being or thing, is self-subsistent, omniscient, omnipotent ("all-seeing, all-hearing, all-willing"). He is the creator, and in the awful day of judgment he is the sole arbiter who shall save the believer out of the dissolution of the world and place him in paradise (Noss, *Religions*, p. 517).

This doctrine, which makes God different from His creatures, is strong in Islam. Allah is so different that it makes it (1) difficult to know very much about him, and (2) unlikely that he is directly affected by his creatures' attitudes or actions. Although Allah is said to be loving, this aspect of his nature is almost ignored, and the demands of his supreme attribute of justice are thought to supercede those of love (see Anderson, *Religions*, p. 79).

The God of Islam is the God of judgment, not grace, power, nor love. He is the source of all (both good and evil) and his will is supreme.

2. *Angels.* The existence of angels is important to Islamic teaching. Gabriel, the leading angel, appeared to Muhammad and was instrumental in delivering the revelations in the Qur'an to Muhammad. Al-Shaytan is the devil and most likely a fallen angel or jinn. Jinn are those creatures between angels and men which can be either good or evil.

Angels do not perform any bodily functions (sex, eating, etc.) since they are created from light. All angels have different purposes, such as Gabriel, or Jibril, who is the messenger of inspiration. Each man or woman also has two recording angels—one who records his good deeds, the other, his bad deeds.

3. *Scripture.* There are four inspired books in the Islamic faith. They are the *Torah* of Moses, the Psalms *(Zabur)* of David, the Gospel of Jesus *(Injil)* and the *Qur'an.* Muslims believe the former three books have been corrupted by Jews and Christians and little of the originals are extant today. Also, since the Qur'an is God's most recent and final word to man, it supercedes all the other works.

4. *Prophets.* In Islam God has spoken through numerous prophets down through the centuries. The six greatest are: Adam, Noah, Abraham, Moses, Jesus and Muhammad. Muhammad is the last and greatest of all Allah's messengers.

5. *Last Days.* The last day will be a time of resurrection and judgment. Those who follow and obey Allah and Muhammad will go to the Islamic heaven, called *Jannah* (Paradise), a place of pleasure. Those who oppose them will be tormented for a time in hell.

> The last day (the resurrection and the judgment) figures prominently in Muslim thought. The day and hour is a secret to all, but there are to be twenty-five signs of its approach. All men will then be raised; the books kept by the recording angels will be opened; and God as judge will weigh each man's deeds in the balances. Some will be admitted to Paradise, where they will recline on soft couches quaffing cups of wine handed them by the Huris, or maidens of Paradise, of whom each man may marry as many as he pleases; others will be consigned to the torments of Hell. Almost all, it would seem, will have to enter the fire temporarily, but no true Muslim will remain there forever (Anderson, *Religions*, p. 81).

6. *Belief in the Decrees of God.* He decides the fate of men and angels and is responsible for good and evil.

Five Pillars of Faith

Besides the six major beliefs or doctrines in Islam, there are also "five pillars of faith." These are observances in Islam which are foundational practices or duties every Muslim must observe. The five are: The Creed, Prayers, Almsgiving, Fasting and the Pilgrimage to Mecca.

1. *The Creed. (Kalima).* "There is no God but Allah, and Muhammad is the Prophet of Allah," is the confession of faith in Islam. One must state

this aloud publicly in order to become a Muslim. It is repeated constantly by the faithful.

2. *Prayer (Salat)*. Prayer as ritual is central to a devout Muslim. Boa comments:

> The practice of prayer *(salat)* five times a day (upon rising, at noon, in midafternoon, after sunset and before retiring). The worshipper must recite the prescribed prayers (the first surah and other selections from the Koran) in Arabic while facing the Ka'aba in Mecca. The Hadith (book of tradition) has turned these prayers into a mechanical procedure of standing, kneeling, hands and face on the ground, and so forth. The call to prayer is sounded by the *muezzin* (a Muslim crier) from a tower called a *minaret* which is part of the *mosque* (the place of public worship), (Boa, *Cults*, p. 53).

3. *Almsgiving (Zakat)*. Muhammad, himself an orphan, had a strong desire to help the needy. The alms originally were voluntary, but all Muslims are now required to give one-fortieth of their income for the destitute. There are other rules and regulations for donating produce, cattle, etc. Freewill offerings also can be exercised.

Since those to whom alms are given are helping the giver to salvation, they feel no sense of debt to the giver. On the contrary, it is the giver's responsibility and duty to give and he is to consider himself lucky he has someone to whom he may give.

4. *Fasting (Ramadan)*. Faithful Muslims fast from dawn (before sunrise) to sundown each day during the holy month of Ramadan. The fast develops self-control, devotion to God and identity with the destitute. No food or drink may be consumed during the daylight hours; no smoking or sexual pleasures may be enjoyed, either. Many Muslims eat two meals a day during Ramadan, one before sunrise and one shortly after sunset.

5. *The Pilgrimage (Hajj)*. The pilgrimage is expected of all Muslims (preferably in person but also by proxy) at least once in their lifetimes. It can be extremely arduous on the old or infirm, so they may send someone in their place. The trip is an essential part in Muslims' gaining salvation. It involves a set of ceremonies and rituals, many of which center around the Ka'aba shrine, to which the pilgrimage is directed. Of the Ka'aba, Muhammad M. Pickthall comments in *The Meaning of the Glorious Koran*:

THE ISLAM
DEBATE

The Meccans claimed descent from Abraham through Ishmael, and tradition stated that their temple, the Ka'aba, had been built by Abraham for the worship of the One God. It was still called the House of Allah, but the chief objects of worship there were a number of idols which were called daughters of Allah and intercessors (Pickthall, *Glorious Koran*, p. ix).

The idols were destroyed by Muhammad on his return to Mecca in power following the *Hijrah* (exile).

When the pilgrim is about six miles from the holy city, he enters upon the state of *ihram:* he casts off, after prayers, his ordinary clothes and puts on two seamless garments; he walks almost barefooted and neither shaves, cuts his hair nor cuts his nails. The principle activity consists of a visit to the Sacred mosque *(al-Masjid al-Haram);* the kissing of the Black Stone *(al-Hajar al-Aswad),* seven circumambulations of the Ka'aba three times running and four times slowly; the visit to the sacred stone called Maqam Ibrahim; the ascent of and running between Mt. Safa and Mt. Marwa seven times; the visit to Mt. Arafat; the hearing of a sermon there and spending the night at Muzdalifa; the throwing of stones at the three pillars at Mina and offering sacrifice on the last day of Ihram, which is the *'id* of sacrifice *('Id al-Adha)* (*Encyclopaedia Britannica*, p. 664).

This Muslim pilgrimage is to heighten and solidify individual Islamic faith.

There is a sixth religious duty often associated with the five pillars. This is *Jihad*, the Holy War. This duty requires that when the situation warrants, men are required to go to war to spread Islam or defend it against infidels. One who dies in a *Jihad* is guaranteed eternal life in Paradise (heaven) and is considered a *Shahid*, a martyr for Islam.

CULTURAL EXPRESSION

Islam, like Judaism, is both a religion and a cultural identity which cannot be separated from its adherents. In many countries the Islamic faith, though not strictly practiced, is woven into the web of society and government.

The Cambridge History of Islam comments on this phenomenon:

Islam is a religion. It is also, inseparably from this, a community, a civilization and a culture. It is true that many of the countries through which the Qur'anic faith spread already possessed ancient and important cultures. Islam absorbed these cultures, and assimilated itself to them in various ways, to a far greater extent than it attempted to supplant them. But in doing this, it provided them with attributes in common, with a common attitude toward God, to men and to the world, and thus ensured, through the diversities of language, of history and of race, the complex unity of the *dar al-Islam*, the "house" or "world" of Islam.

The history of the Muslim peoples and countries is thus a unique example of a culture with a religious foundation, uniting the spiritual and the temporal, sometimes existing side by side with "secular" cultures, but most often absorbing them by becoming very closely interlinked with them (Holt, ed., *Cambridge History*, Vol. I, p. 569).

Language and the Arts

To doctrine which serves as both a religious and social foundation, the Arabic language can be added as another unifying factor which helps weld Islamic peoples together.

There is an abundance of Arabic poetry and prose which glorifies the Islamic faith. Muslim art and architecture also have great religious significance. Many of the mosques and minarets are tremendous works of art decorated with intricate arabesque ornamentation.

The Family

The family unit is very important to the social economy of Islam. Marriage is recommended for every Muslim. Muhammad commanded men to marry and propagate the race. Traditionally men may not have more than four wives at a time. (Many progressive Muslims teach monogamy.) A Muslim may divorce his wife at any time and for any reason. On the whole, women in Islamic culture do not enjoy the status or the privileges of men and are often dependent on their husbands. This is quite an understatement in very strict Islamic cultures. Consider the prophet's words in the Sura dealing with women:

Men have authority over women because Allah has made the one superior to the others, and because they spend their wealth to maintain them. Good women are obedient. They guard their unseen parts because Allah has guarded them. As for those from whom you fear disobedience, admonish them and send them to beds apart and beat them. Then if they obey you, take no further action against them. Allah is high, supreme (4:34).

Sexual relations for men and women are not exactly equal either. Women may indulge only with their husbands of course. Men, however, may also indulge with all of their female servants (see page 183).

While this sounds cruel and sexist to Westerners, it was a humane innovation in Muhammad's time. Islamic law required what was then unheard of, that each wife was to be treated equally.

Other practices include the veiling of women, circumcision, abstention from alcohol, gambling and certain foods. Many of the above, such as alcohol and gambling, are seen as vices of the West.

CONTEMPORARY INFLUENCE

The crescent of Islam has recently cast its shadow over far more territory than the geography of its native area. Its ideological influence expands its borders daily. Nationalism, coupled with the Islamic faith, has served as a *raison d'etre* for many in the Arab world as they stand against Israel, their enemy. At various times in the recent past, Arab alliances have been conceived, discussed and then have died. There was the United Arab Republic and later an alliance discussed between Egypt, Libya and Syria.

Scholar G.E. von Grunebaum comments:

> The spectacular success of the Arab Muslims in establishing an empire by means of a small number of campaigns against the great powers of the day has never ceased to stimulate the wonderment and the admiration of the Muslim world and Western scholarship (G.E. von Grunebaum, *Modern Islam*, Berkeley: University of California Press, 1962, p. 1).

Neill amplifies:

> It is not surprising that the Islamic world has caught the fever of nationalism that is raging everywhere among the peoples of Asia and Africa. The special intensity and vigour of Islamic, and especially Arab, nationalism springs from a complex of causes—memories of past splendour, resentment over Muslim weakness and Christian strength, above all that obscure

sense of malaise, the feeling that in some way history has gone awry, that somehow the purposes of God are not being fulfilled as the Muslim has a right to expect.

The achievements of the post-war period have been considerable. Egyptian self-assertion has made the Middle East one of the chief problem areas in the world. Libya became independent after the war. Morocco and Tunis have since won their independence. In Algeria the story of detachment from France was long and painful. But here too, in 1962, the goal of total independence was attained. And so the story goes on (Neill, *Faith*, pp. 43, 44).

The Camp David accords, which saw a peace between Israel and Egypt, are an exception to the generally anti-Israeli attitudes of most Muslim nations. But elsewhere committed and radical Islamic fundamentalists have drawn world attention to Iran, and also to Egypt, where many attributed to them the assassination of former President Anwar Sadat. Nationalism is a strong sweeping movement in nations with Muslim populations in the majority.

However, secularism has increased in Muslim countries as the practices of the West infiltrated those nations. Some of the Western transfusions have been sudden—many Arab countries are accumulating new and previously unknown wealth in the form of petro-dollars. Yet, the secularism has also had a backlash effect as some Muslim countries, in an attempt to preserve their distinct Islamic identity, reject most imported Western customs.

Since Islam embraces not only religion but also culture, the future of the faith will be very much dependent on the state of the nations in which it thrives today. With Arab nations prospering, this could turn out to be both a curse and a blessing to the Islamic faith. It may be good for its social growth, but its faith could be seriously compromised.

Islam is a rapidly spreading religion for several reasons. It is the state religion of Moslem countries and this gives it a strong cultural and political base. It has the appeal of a universal message because of its simple creed and tenets. Anyone can enter the *Ummah*, the community of faithful Muslims. There are no racial barriers and thus it spreads quickly among the black communities of Africa, and more recently, of America. Its five doctrines and five pillars can be easily communicated. In the West it is making appeals to the universal brotherhood of man, world peace, temperance, and the uplifting of women (Boa, *Cults*, p. 56).

THE ISLAM
DEBATE

The supremacy of Islam in the political and social (as well as religious) arenas is prefigured in the following quote from the Qur'an:

> Believers, have fear of Allah and stand with those who uphold the cause of truth. No cause have the people of Medina and the desert Arabs who dwell around them to forsake Allah's apostle or to jeopardize his life so as to safeguard their own; for they do not expose themselves to thirst or hunger or to any ordeal on account of the cause of Allah, nor do they stir a step which may provoke the unbelievers. Each loss they suffer at the enemy's hands shall be counted as a good deed in the sight of Allah: He will not deny the righteous of their recompense. Each sum they give, be it small or large, and each journey they undertake, shall be noted down, so that Allah may requite them for their noblest deeds.

> It is not right that all the faithful should go to war at once. A band from each community should stay behind to instruct themselves in religion and admonish their men when they return, so that they may take heed.

> Believers, make war on the infidels who dwell around you. Deal courteously with them. Know that Allah is with the righteous (N.J. Dawood, trans., *The Koran*, London: Penguin Books, 1956, p. 333).

With 750 to 800 million now claiming the Muslim faith, Christians need to have an answer for the hope within us (1 Peter 3:15). The impact of Islam in world affairs is steadily on the upswing, and in order to present the gospel effectively, we must have a good background knowledge of Islam.

Muslim countries presently (1) through OPEC have a great deal to say about world economy, (2) play a powerful role in the social stability (or instability) of various governments, (3) are the political focal point for numerous potentially serious situations for war, and (4) are growing in their religious influence.

Politically, economically, religiously, and socially Islam affects the world on several fronts: Most important for the Christian is Islam's spiritual impact, which has been great in recent years. To this Christians are called to respond in love, and with the truth, realizing Christ loves Muslims and desires them to come to salvation.

CHAPTER TWO

TEACHINGS OF ISLAM

A COMPARATIVE STUDY OF THE TEXTUAL HISTORY OF THE QUR'AN AND THE BIBLE

Christians should be willing to subject their Scriptures to the closest scrutiny to verify their authenticity. They are not to believe blindly that the Bible is the Word of God but are to seek to be sure, after thorough tests of its composition and contents, that it is indeed the Word of God. The Christian must be prepared to examine not only those assertions which tend to support this view, but particularly any assertions which are brought in opposition to it. If he is persuaded that the Bible is indeed the Word of God after sincerely considering all the evidence at hand, he then possesses a fair and objective faith. Such full assurance of faith cannot come to a heart that is unwilling to inquire objectively into the evidence both for and against what he believes is God's Word. Likewise, Muslims believe that the Qur'an is authentic. Yet they generally shun critical inquiry or examination of its composition and origins. To the Christian, the Bible may not validly be revered as the Word of God unless it can withstand an assault on its integrity and authenticity. Once he has discovered that the Bible is a solid anvil on which many critical hammers have been broken, the Christian is able with a clear conscience to vest all his confidence in this book as the genuine Word of God. In these circumstances he has very sound reasons for believing in the divine origin of his Scriptures.

THE ISLAM
DEBATE

In the Muslim world today numerous assaults have been made on the Bible in an effort to disprove its claim to be the Word of God. At the same time, however, the Qur'an has been exempt from any substantial historical examination of its origins and development. Muslims generally believe that the Bible has been changed and corrupted and is untrustworthy while only the Qur'an, being perfect in every detail, can be considered the Word of God:

> *The most important element of the Moslem view of Christianity is that the Bible lacks authenticity.* The Koran is the only book of authentic revealed scripture. Moslems believe that every religious group in the world has had a divine messenger who was a human being. All of these messengers (including Jesus) taught the same message—submission to the will of God. The Moslems regard all these messengers as great prophets. However, they believe that their messenger, the Prophet Mohammed, was the last of all such messengers and that he perfected all religion and scripture in the Koranic revelation. *Although Moslems believe in all revealed scripture, they follow the Koran first because they believe that it alone contains the authentic teachings given in all former scripture and because none of the former scriptures exists in original and pure form.* (Nasser Lotfi, *Iranian Christian*, Waco, TX: Word Books, 1980, p. 116).

When the Bible and the Qur'an are approached openly and objectively, God will grant to the sincere inquirer knowledge of that which is genuinely His Word and truth. No genuine assurance that the Qur'an is the Word of God can come to any Muslim who retreats from considering serious problems both from the Qur'an and from Islamic tradition which challenge the claim that the Qur'an is the unaltered Word of God.

Since the Qur'an speaks so highly of the Bible, the Muslim faces a dilemma about the teaching that the Bible is corrupted:

> The outstanding fact emerging from this old controversy, a fact of which we shall have occasion to speak repeatedly in this volume, is that there is marked disagreement on several vital matters between the Qur'an and the Bible. This is something which cannot, and does not, escape the notice of the earnest, educated Muslim of today. The more he thinks of it, the more embarrassing he feels the dilemma to be. *"Is he to believe in the Qur'an's witness to the Bible and deny the Qur'an itself—his own Book. Or is he to deny the witness of the Qur'an and so the Qur'an itself?"* His way out of a hopeless position is to assert that one of the Books must have been corrupted and is, therefore, now untrustworthy. This, he argues, cannot be the Qur'an for it belongs (so he persuades himself) to an altogether superior category; therefore it must be the Bible; accordingly, he accuses

the Christians with having corrupted it. (L. Bevan-Jones, *Christianity Explained to Moslems*, Calcutta, India: Baptist Mission Press, 1964, p. 15).

Muslims recognize the Qur'an as well as sections of the Bible as Scripture. Even though hypothetically the Bible can carry equal weight with the Qur'an, the Qur'an is always venerated more highly than the Bible in the Islamic community. This apparent discrepancy is because Islam regards the Bible as having been corrupted, especially at those points where it disagrees with the Qur'an. One problem Muslims have with this approach is that often the sections of Scripture they need to reject because they contradict the Qur'an also contain teachings found in the Qur'an.

The Muslims' high regard for the Qur'an and their full assurance of its authenticity and accuracy are not based on a critical examination of its veracity and historicity. They accept its truth by blind faith. They assume that neither God nor Muhammad would lie. Yet most of what they know about the characters of God and Muhammad stems from Qur'anic teaching.

Muslims attempt to discredit the Bible on a number of fronts. These are: 1) textual variants and differences in translations found in the Bible; 2) the transmission of the Bible through the years which allowed many errors; 3) numerous contradictions found in the Bible; 4) the soundness of the Qur'an on the above issues, showing its superiority. All of these points are concerned with one topic—the reliability of the Bible vs. the reliability of the Qur'an.

CONSIDERING THE BIBLE

In a booklet, *Is The Bible God's Word?* (Islamic Propagation Centre, Durban, South Africa, March 1980), Muslim apologist Ahmed Deedat attempts to discredit the Bible's reliability. His thinking is representative of the Islamic anti-biblical argument.

Variant Readings in the Qur'an and the Bible

One of the most frequent Muslim objections to the Bible is that it is beset by variant readings. On the other hand, they believe the Qur'an to be exactly the same today as it was when it was first handed down by Muhammad to his companions. This is offered as proof that the Qur'an must be the Word of God.

However, even if it were true that the Bible has a number of variant readings while the Qur'an has none, this in no way proves that the Qur'an is the Word of God. If a book were not the Word of God in the first place, no amount of faithful transmission would ever make it the Word of God. Conversely, if a book in its original form were indeed the Word of God, variant readings and copyist errors would not negate the divine authority of its ascertainable teachings—especially when these errors and readings can be identified and when they do not alter the general message and thrust of the book as a whole.

Concerning the alteration of the Bible, Muslim scholars judge the Bible to be defective on two points. In *Sharing Your Faith*, the author states

> The technical term used by Muslim scholars to signify corruption of the Bible is "Tahrif." It is believed to be of two kinds; namely, "Tahrif-I-Lafzi," a corruption of words, and "Tahrif-I-Manawi," corruption of the meaning only. The early commentators of the Koran and doctors of Islam who did not have a firsthand knowledge of the Bible believed in "Tahrif-I-Manawi" only (p. 38).

Patrick Cate, as a result of his research for his doctoral dissertation on the Bible and the Qur'an, notes the Islamic allegations about:

> The corruption of the Bible takes two basic forms: corruption of the text and corruption of the interpretation of the Bible. *The corruption of the text has three facets: (1) changing the text, (2) omission of part of the Bible, and (3) interpolating new material into the text* (Patrick O'Hair Cate, *Each Other's Scripture—The Muslims' Views of the Bible and the Christians' Views of the Qur'an*, submitted to the faculty of the Hartford Seminary Foundation, New Hartford, Connecticut, May, 1974, p. 90).

Sharing Your Faith gives a further explanation:

> The Koran contains a large body of material in common with the Bible. But often it does not tally in exact detail with its Biblical counterpart. So long as the Muslims did not have a firsthand knowledge of the Bible, they were not quite concerned about this issue. But when they began to learn from the Bible directly or through knowledgeable Jewish and Christian proselytes, they felt the need to account for its divergence from the Koran. Understandably, it was taken for granted that in each case of difference

between the two Scriptures, the Koranic version was authentic. Hence the Biblical version was considered inauthentic. On the basis of the Koran itself, God never sent inauthentic Scripture. It was concluded, therefore, that the Jews and Christians are responsible for corrupting their Scriptures.

Of "Tahrif," *Moslem World* comments in their article, "Tahrif or the Alteration of the Bible According to the Moslems":

> Razi says that, according to Qaffal, *tahrif* means to bend something from its natural condition (Mafatih, i, 379). The word is also defined as mispronouncing a word or a sentence so as to change the sense (Zamakhshari's Kashshaf on Kor. iv, 367); as erroneously changing a vowel-sign or a letter in writing or in uttering it (Qaffal in Razi's Mafatih, ii, 479); as the condition of the writing pen when the point is not cut straight but somewhat inclined.

> Moslem polemists ascribe *tahrif* in general to the Jews and the Christians in reference to the Holy Scriptures, interpreting the word sometimes as a material change of the text and at other times, as a change in the sense (V. 14, 1924, p. 61).

However, the main support for corruption or alteration of the Bible by the Muslims comes not so much from the idea of corruption of the interpretation but rather corruption of the text.

They believe that the Bible has been changed many times, altered, corrected, and edited down through the centuries. They then criticize the various textual readings for different passages in the Bible, arguing that if the Bible has not been altered, then there should not be any differences. They accept the liberal school of biblical criticism without ever investigating its faulty foundation.

Christians freely admit that there are variant readings in the biblical manuscripts available to us (they are often listed in footnotes in many modern English translations of the Bible) but no one has ever been able to show that these small and usually obvious variants affect the message of the Bible as a whole.

Muslims know that the Bible not only agrees with all major Christian doctrines but in fact is the source of all Christian doctrines. Due to this, they argue that the Bible must have been changed because Islam teaches that the prophets prior to Muhammad, all of whom are recorded in the Bible, were all Muslims in creed, thought and message.

THE ISLAM
DEBATE

History shows that there is no evidence whatsoever to support the claim that the Bible has been changed from a Muslim book to a Christian book. Frankly, the contrary is strongly supported. It is the Bible which is the foundation—the Qur'an takes its background from both the Old and New Testament Scriptures and other sources. When the Muslim tries to prove his point, we believe his evidence is found wanting. Let us examine his claims.

The "Multiple" Bible Versions

Deedat denies that the Jewish and Christian Scriptures constituting the Holy Bible are those honored by the Qur'an as the *Taurat* and *Injil* respectively (the Law and the Gospel—i.e., the Old and New Testaments). Instead he suggests that the real Taurat and Injil were different books entirely which were allegedly revealed to Moses and Jesus.

This attempt to distinguish between the books of the Bible and those referred to in the Qur'an has little evidence to support it. At no time in history has there ever been any proof that any Taurat (Law) or Injil (Gospel) other than the books of the Old and New Testaments ever existed. Furthermore, as we shall show, the Qur'an itself does not distinguish these books from the Scriptures of the Jews and the Christians, but, on the contrary, clearly testifies that they are those books which the Jews and Christians themselves hold to be the Word of God. (See *Why I Believe the Scripture* at the end of this chapter.)

In passing, we must comment that, in the light of Deedat's claim that the Qur'an has been *perfectly preserved and protected from human tampering* by God Himself for 14 centuries (see p. 7), it is rather astonishing to discover that the same God proved incapable of preserving even a record of the fact that such a Taurat or an Injil ever even existed—let alone preserve the books themselves! We find such a paradox incredible. That the Eternal Ruler of the universe ought to act consistently at all times is found to be incredible by Muslims. God cannot be limited by consistency.

In any event, the Qur'an itself unambiguously confirms that the Taurat of the Jews at the time of Muhammad was what we know as the Old Testament. The Injil likewise was the book in the possession of the Christians at that time and was what we know today as the New Testament. At no time in history have Jews and Christians ever regarded any books other than those constituting the Old and New Testaments as we know them today as the sacred Word of God. Useful Qur'anic texts proving the point are:

> How come they (i.e. the Jews) turn unto thee for judgment when *they have the Torah* (Taurat in the original Arabic) wherein Allah hath revealed judgment? (Surah 5:43)

> Let the People (i.e. the Christians) of the Gospel (Injil in the original Arabic) judge by that which Allah hath revealed therein. (Surah 5:47)

It is difficult to consider how the Christians of Muhammad's time could ever judge by the Injil if they were not in possession of it. In Surah 7:157 the Qur'an again admits that the Taurat and Injil were in the possession of the Jews and Christians at the time of Muhammad and that they were those books which these two groups themselves accepted as the Law and the Gospel respectively.

Distinguished commentators like Baidawi and Zamakshari openly admit that Injil is not an original Arabic word but is *borrowed* from the Syriac word used by the Christians themselves to describe the gospel. Indeed, whereas some early Qur'anic scholars tried to find an Arabic origin for it, these two men of authority reject the theory (Arthur Jeffery, *The Foreign Vocabulary of the Qur'an*, Lahore: Al-Biruni, 1977, p. 71). This substantiates the conclusion that the Injil was not a phantom book revealed as such to Jesus, all trace of which has strangely disappeared, but rather the New Testament itself precisely as we know it today. The same can be said for the Taurat as the word is obviously of Hebrew origin and is the title which the Jews themselves have always given to the books of the Old Testament as we know it today.

Therefore, the Qur'an claims that the Bible itself is the true Word of God. Deedat realizes the validity here, and thus tries to circumvent the implications by suggesting that there are "multiple" Bible versions in circulation today. He speaks of the King James Version (KJV), Revised Version (RV) and Revised Standard Version (RSV) but it is not clear that these are not conflicting editions of the Bible but simply different English translations of it. All three versions are compatible with the original Hebrew and Greek texts of the Old and New Testaments which have been preserved intact by the Christian Church since centuries before the time of Muhammad.

THE ISLAM
DEBATE

The Apocrypha

Deedat then charges that the *Protestants have bravely expunged seven whole books* from the Bible (p. 9), the books being those which constitute the *Apocrypha*. It seems that there is very poor information about the Bible at Deedat's disposal for these books are of *Jewish* origin. The Jews as a body never accepted them as Scripture. Therefore, they have not been "expunged" from the Bible as Deedat concludes. Only the Roman Catholic Church, at a much later time, gave them the authority of Scripture. And this authority was only given by the pope following the Protestant Reformation. At the Council of Trent (1260s A.D.), the Church had adopted these books in order to legitimize some doctrines the Protestants were taking issue with.

The "Grave Defects"

In his booklet, Deedat challenges the believing Christian to prepare himself for the unkindest blow of all. He quotes these words from the preface to the RSV and underlines them in his booklet:

> Yet the King James Version has grave defects…these defects are so many and so serious as to call for revision (p. 11).

These "defects" are nothing but a number of insignificant variant readings which were generally unknown to the translators who composed the KJV early in the seventeenth century. The RSV of this century has identified these readings and they are noted as footnotes on the relevant pages of its text. We must again point out that the KJV and RSV are *English translations* of the original Greek texts and that these texts, as they are preserved for us, have in no significant way been changed. (We have over 5,000 Greek texts, some dating back to more than 500 years before Muhammad and Islam).

Second, there is no material alteration of any doctrine of the Bible in the translations referred to. Throughout the translations, the essence and substance of the Bible is totally consistent and unchanged.

Third, these are not differing versions of the Bible. These "versions" are compatible English translations of the original Hebrew and Greek texts, and a cursory comparison of these will immediately show that we have just one Bible. There are many such English translations of the

Qur'an as well but no one suggests that these are "different versions" of the Qur'an.

Fifty Thousand Errors?

Deedat produces a reproduction of a page from a magazine entitled *Awake* dating back some 23 years (published by the Jehovah's Witnesses, a non-Christian cult), which quotes a secular magazine *Look* to the effect that there are some "modern students" who "say" that there are probably "50,000 errors in the Bible."

Very significantly no mention is made of the identity of these so-called modern students, nor is any evidence given of these alleged errors.

We find Deedat hard to believe when he says:

> We do not have the time and space to go into the tens of thousands of—grave or minor—defects that the authors of the Revised Standard Version (RSV) have attempted to revise (p. 14).

Of these alleged 50,000 defects, he produces just four for our consideration, without even listing the others or giving his primary source. Now, it would follow, with so many errors, that in the four cases presented the best evidence of corruption should be cited. Let us examine them.

The first—and presumably foremost—"error" in the Bible is found in Isaiah 7:14 which reads in the King James Version:

> Therefore the Lord himself shall give you a sign; Behold, a virgin shall conceive, and bear a son, and shall call his name Immanuel.

In the RSV we read instead of the word *virgin* that a *young woman* shall conceive and bear a son. According to Deedat, this is supposed to be one of the foremost defects in the Bible.

The word for virgin in the original Hebrew is *almah*—a word found in every Hebrew text of Isaiah. Therefore there is no change of any nature in the original text. The issue is purely one of interpretation and translation. The common Hebrew word for virgin is *bethulah* whereas *almah* often refers to a young woman—and always an unmarried one. So the RSV translation is a perfectly good literal rendering of the word. But, as there

DEBATE

are always difficulties translating from one language to another, and as a good translator will try to convey the real meaning of the original, almost all English translations translate the word as *virgin*. The reason is that the context of the word demands such an interpretation. (Muslims who have translated the Qur'an into English have often experienced similar problems with the original Arabic text. A literal rendering of a word or text may lose the implied meaning in the original language.)

The conception of the child was to be a sign to Israel. Now there would be no sign in the simple conception of a child in the womb of an unmarried woman. Such a thing is commonplace throughout the world. The sign is clearly that a *virgin* would conceive and bear a son. That would be a real sign—and so it was when Jesus Christ fulfilled this prophecy by being conceived of the Virgin Mary.

Isaiah uses the word *almah* rather than *bethulah* because the latter word not only means a virgin but also a chaste widow (as in Joel 1:8). Those who translate it as a young woman (so the RSV) give a literal rendering of the word whereas those who translate it as virgin (so the KJV, NIV, etc.) give its meaning in its context. Either way the young woman was a virgin as Mary duly was when Jesus was conceived. The issue is purely one of translation and interpretation from the original Hebrew into English. It has absolutely nothing to do with the textual integrity of the Bible as such.

His next text is John 3:16 which reads in the King James Version as follows:

> For God so loved the world, that he gave his only begotten Son, that whosoever believeth in him should not perish, but have everlasting life.

In the RSV we read that he gave his "only Son" and Deedat charges that the omission of the word "begotten" proves that the Bible has been changed. Once again, however, this is purely a matter of interpretation and translation for the original Greek word properly means *unique*. Either way there is no difference between "only Son" and "only begotten Son" for both are fair translations of the original Greek and make the same point: *Jesus is the unique Son of God*. We need to emphasize once again that there is *no change* in the original Greek text and that the issue is purely one of interpretation and translation.

To illustrate our point further we can refer to Deedat's quote from Surah 19:88 where we read that Christians say that God *Most Gracious has begotten a Son*. He has taken this from Yusuf Ali's translation of the Qur'an. Now in the translations of Pickthall, Muhammad Ali and Maulana Daryabadi we do not find the word *begotten* but rather *taken*. If Deedat's line of reasoning is to be believed, then here is evidence that the Qur'an, too, has been changed and corrupted.

We know our Muslim readers will immediately tell us that these are only English translations and that the original Arabic has not been changed even though the word "begotten" is not found in the other versions of the Qur'an. So we in turn plead with you to be quite realistic about this as well—nothing can be said against the integrity of the Bible just because the word "begotten," as in the Qur'an, is only found in one translation and not in another when both translations represent the same Greek.

Deedat's third example is one of the defects the RSV set out to correct. In 1 John 5:7 in the KJV we find a verse outlining the unity of the Father, Word and Holy Ghost which is omitted in the RSV. It might have been that this verse was originally set out as a marginal note in an early text and that it was mistaken by later transcribers as part of the actual text. It is often omitted by many modern translations, or usually placed in the margin, because we now have older texts where it is not found. However, it should be noted that many reputable Christian scholars believe it does belong in the text. And although the oldest manuscripts omit it in the main text, the majority of all our manuscripts do include it.

Deedat suggests that *this verse is the closest approximation to what the Christians call their Holy Trinity in the encyclopaedia called the BIBLE* (p. 16). If it was, or alternatively, if the whole doctrine of the Trinity was based on this one text alone, then indeed this would be a matter for very serious consideration. However, any honest expositor of biblical theology will admit—as all Catholics, Protestants and other Christians uniformly do—that the doctrine of the Trinity is the only doctrine of God that can be obtained from the teaching of the Bible as a whole. Indeed the following verse is a good illustration of the Trinity:

> Go therefore and make disciples of all nations, baptizing them in the name of the Father and of the Son and of the Holy Spirit (Matthew 28:19).

Only one singular name of the three persons is referred to. In the Bible the word "name" used in such a context refers to the nature and character of the thing so described. So Jesus speaks of only *one* name of the Father, Son and Holy Spirit—implying unity of essence but a plurality of persons. This verse is thoroughly Trinitarian in content and emphasis. An important point here is that even if 1 John 1:7 were not in the original text, what it clearly teaches is the doctrine of the Trinity, which was the belief of the Early Church, and is taught throughout the Bible.

His fourth point contains an interesting fallacy. He suggests that the "inspired" authors of the canonical gospels did not record a single word about the ascension of Jesus (p. 19). This claim is made pursuant to a reference to two statements about the ascension of Jesus in the Gospels of Mark and Luke which the RSV has identified as being among the variant readings we have referred to earlier. Apart from these verses the gospel writers allegedly make no reference of any nature whatsoever to the ascension. On the contrary we find that all four Gospel writers acknowledged it. John has 11 references to it, of which this text, where Jesus is speaking, serves as a good example:

> ...I am ascending to my Father and your Father, to my God and your God (John 20:17).

Luke not only wrote his Gospel but also the Book of Acts and in the latter book the first thing he mentions is the ascension of Jesus to heaven:

> And when (Jesus) had said this, as they were looking on, he was lifted up, and a cloud took him out of their sight (Acts 1:9).

Matthew and Mark regularly speak of the second coming of Jesus from heaven (e.g., Matthew 26:64 and Mark 14:62). It is difficult to see how Jesus could come from heaven if He had not ascended there in the first place!

In conclusion we must point out that the passages Mark 16:9-20 and John 8:1-11 have not been expunged from the Bible and later restored as Deedat suggests. In the RSV *translation* they are now included in the text because scholars are persuaded that they are indeed part of the original text. The truth of the matter is that in our oldest scripts they are found in some texts and not in others. The RSV editors are not tampering with the Bible as Deedat has suggested—they are merely trying to bring our English translations as close as possible to the original texts.

Finally it proves nothing to state that all the original manuscripts—those on which the books of the Bible were written for the first time—

are now lost and have perished, for the same is true of the very first texts of the Qur'an. The oldest text of the Qur'an still extant dates from the second century after the Hijrah and is written on vellum in the early *al-mail* Arabic script. All the other old texts of the Qur'an are in *Kufic* script and date from the late second century (after the Hijrah) as well.

"Allah" in the Bible?

Deedat reproduces a pamphlet which attempts to show that the Arabic word for God, *Allah*, is found in the Scofield edition of the Bible. Fortunately the evidence, in this case, is set before us to consider. A copy of a page from a Scofield Bible is reproduced and in a *footnote* there we find that the Hebrew word for God, Elohim, is derived from two words, *El* (strength) and *Alah* (to swear). This last word is supposed to be proof that the Arabic word *Allah* is found in the Bible!

A more fanciful effort to prove a point can hardly be imagined. The word in Hebrew is *alah*, a common word meaning "to swear." How this is supposed to be proof that the word *Allah* in Arabic, meaning God, is found in the Bible is altogether unclear to us. Deedat's effort to twist the facts further in suggesting that *Elah* in Hebrew (meaning God) has been spelled by the Scofield edition *alternatively as Alah* (p. 21) taxes our credulity to extreme. These editors clearly identify the latter word as another one meaning "to swear."

There is nothing unique about the word *Allah*, nor must it be regarded as coming originally from the pages of the Qur'an. On the contrary, it is derived from the Syriac word *Alaha* (meaning "God") which was in common use among Christians in pre-Islamic times (Cf. the authorities cited by Arthur Jefferey in *The Foreign Vocabulary of the Qur'an*, p. 66). It was also in common use among the Arabs before Islam. An example is the name of Muhammad's own father, Abdullah (i.e., servant of God from *abd*, meaning "servant," and *Allah*, meaning "God"). It is also certain that *Allah* was the name used for God in pre-Islamic poetry (Bell, *The Origin of Islam in Its Christian Environment*, London: Frank Cass and Company, Ltd., 1968, p. 53). Accordingly there is nothing unique about the name at all. In these circumstances, we really fail to see the significance of what Deedat is trying to prove.

THE ISLAM
DEBATE

Alleged Contradictions in the Bible

Deedat begins his seventh chapter, "The Acid Test," with a claim that there is a contradiction between 2 Samuel 24:1, where we read that the Lord moved David to number Israel, and 1 Chronicles 21:1, which says it was Satan who provoked him to do so. Anyone with a reasonable knowledge of the Scriptures and the Qur'an will immediately perceive that what is in view here is an inadequate understanding of a feature of the theology of both books. In the Qur'an we read:

> Seest thou not that We have set the devils on the disbelievers to confound them with confusion? (Surah 19:83).

Here we read that Allah sets devils on unbelievers. Therefore, while it is God who moves them to confusion, He uses the devils to provoke them toward it. In precisely the same way God moved against David and used Satan to provoke him to number Israel. Similarly, in the book of Job in the Bible, we read that Satan was given power over Job (*Ayub* in the Qur'an) to afflict him (Job 1:12) but that God later spoke as if it were He who was moved against him (Job 2:3). Whenever Satan provokes men the action also can be described indirectly as the movement of God since without His permission Satan could achieve nothing. This quote from Zamakhshari's commentary on Surah 2:7 (*Allah hath sealed their hearing and their hearts*) should suffice as the final word on this matter:

> It is now in reality Satan or the unbeliever who has sealed the heart. However, since it is God who has granted to him the ability and possibility to do it, the sealing is ascribed to him in the same sense as an act which he has caused (Helmut Gatje, *The Qur'an and Its Exegesis*, London: Routledge and Kegan Paul, 1976, p. 223).

Parallel Passages in the Qur'an and the Bible

Occasionally it is alleged that certain parallel passages in the Bible (e.g. 2 Kings 18:13-20:11 and Isaiah 36:1-38:8, 21-22) reflect on its integrity as the Word of God. Although this final point is not explicitly brought out by Deedat, it nevertheless is implicit and is one which Muslims often raise. It has been argued that a man cannot be writing under divine inspiration if he borrows from another work. If the passage was originally written under divine inspiration, that inspiration can hardly be affected when the passage is repeated in another book!

When one knows the background of the parallel passages in the Bible it is very easy to understand and accept the repetition of one section in another book. We freely concede that Mark's Gospel could have been written before Matthew's Gospel and that Matthew could have used the Gospel of Mark as a foundation for his own and repeated many of the narratives of the life of Jesus in this Gospel. But he would have done so for very sound reasons.

Mark gained his information from the apostle Peter: "Mark, having been the interpreter of Peter, wrote down accurately all that he mentioned, whether sayings or doings of Christ....So then Mark made no mistake, writing down in this way some things as he (Peter) mentioned them; for he paid attention to this one thing, not to omit anything that he heard nor to include any false statement among them" (written by Papias, traditionally considered as a disciple of the apostle John).

The apostle Peter probably had more first-hand information of the life of Christ than the apostle Matthew. Often we find Peter with Jesus when Matthew is not present (e.g., the transfiguration, Gethsemane, etc.) but never the other way around. Matthew was one of the last apostles to be called. In his own gospel he records the call of Peter in Chapter 4 and his own call in Chapter 9. If he recognized Peter's accurate knowledge of the life of Christ in Mark's records, obviously he would be wise to use this as a basis and build around it other discourses and incidents known to him. He could hardly have found a more reliable source!

Generally, narratives in the Bible do not have parallels in extra-biblical works. Therefore, the parallels within the Bible obviously do not affect its claim to be a divinely inspired book. What is rather astonishing, however, is that many of the Qur'anic narratives of the lives of the prophets of old have parallels not only in the Bible but also in Jewish books of folklore, myths and fables. There are many passages in the Qur'an which are characterized by this feature and two of them will be considered here.

Cain and Abel. The biblical story of the murder of Abel by Cain after the former had offered a more acceptable sacrifice than the latter is repeated in the Qur'an (Surah 5:27-32). But in verse 31 we read that God showed him how to hide his brother's corpse:

> Then Allah sent a raven scratching up the ground, to show him how to hide his brother's naked corpse.

THE ISLAM
DEBATE

This phenomenon is not found in the Book of Genesis in the Bible. But in a book of Jewish folklore we read:

> Adam and his companion sat weeping and mourning for him (Abel) and did not know what to do with him, as burial was unknown to them. There came a raven, whose companion was dead, took its body, scratched in the earth and hid it before their eyes; then Adam said, I shall do as this raven has done (Pirke Rabbi Eliezer, Ch. 21).

It is very interesting that what is purported to be revealed to Muhammad by God in the Qur'an finds its parallel not in the Old Testament, but in a book of Jewish folklore composed before the time of Muhammad. Minor differences aside, the uncanny similarity between the two cannot be overlooked. It cannot be suggested that the Jews had turned historical truths from the Torah into folklore. The Qur'an accuses the Jews of declaring their folklore to be Holy Scripture (Surah 2:79). It nowhere accuses them of taking Holy Scripture and making it folklore. What we wish to know, however, is why that same folklore is Holy Scripture in the Qur'an. If Muhammad did not borrow the story of the raven from Jewish sources, not knowing that it was only part of their traditions (he could not read their Scriptures, which were not written in Arabic), how is this phenomenon explained? And here is a further anomaly:

> For that cause We decreed for the Children of Israel that whoever killeth a human being for other than manslaughter or corruption in the earth, it shall be as if he had killed all mankind, and whoso saveth the life of one, it shall be as if he had saved the life of all mankind" (Surah 5.32).

This statement appears to have no connection with the preceding story. Why the life or death of one should be as if it were the salvation or destruction of all mankind is not at all clear.

When we turn to another Jewish tradition in the Mishnah, we read:

> We find it said in the case of Cain who murdered his brother, The voice of thy brother's bloods crieth (Genesis 4:10). It is not said here blood in the singular, but bloods in the plural, that is, his own blood and the blood of his seed. Man was created single in order to show that to him who kills a single individual it shall be reckoned that he has slain the whole race; but to him who preserves the life of a single individual it is counted that he hath preserved the whole race (*Mishnah*, Sanhedrin 4:5).

Here is where we find the trend of thought that is the source of the Qur'an's observation. The Jewish rabbi, centuries later than Genesis but before Muhammad, has drawn this interpretation from the plural "bloods" in the Bible. Whether he is correct in his interpretation or not is not of importance here. What does concern us is that Surah 5:32 in the Qur'an is a repetition of the rabbi's beliefs! How is it that the alleged revelation of God is substantially a repetition of an already existing rabbinical interpretation of a biblical verse?

Abraham. The story of Abraham in the Qur'an also follows the biblical narrative in many respects but when it deviates from it, much of its contents can be traced to Jewish myth. The Qur'an narrates a story about the idolatry of Abraham's father and his community. Abraham, the monotheist, allegedly destroyed all the idols except the main one and when questioned whether he had done it, he blamed the main idol and suggested that they consult it about who had destroyed the others. Then the infuriated mob threw Abraham into the fiery furnace but God made it cool for him and saved him from their evil designs. The story is found in Surah 21:52-70. Now a strikingly similar story is told in Jewish folklore. (It stems from a misunderstanding of Genesis 15:7 where God said "I am the Lord who brought you from Ur of the Chaldeans." Ur was a place which archaeology has proved existed in the land of Abraham and is referred to elsewhere in the Bible (Genesis 11:31). But a Jewish scribe, Jonathan Ben Uzziel, mistook "Ur" for "Or," meaning fire, and wrote the verse "I am the Lord who brought you from the fire of the Chaldees" and the fable was wound around this error.)

A short narration of this story in the *Midrash Rabbah* will show how strikingly similar is the Qur'anic story. Bearing in mind the origin of the Jewish fable, any sincere reader must realize that this example of a parallel passage in Jewish folklore reflects very seriously against the Qur'an and its claim to be the Word of God.

> Abraham broke all the idols with one axe except the biggest one and then placed the axe in the hand of the idol he spared. Now his father heard the commotion and ran to investigate and saw Abraham leaving as he arrived. When he was accused by his father, he said he gave them all meat to eat but the others went for the meat without waiting for the biggest one to do so first so the biggest one took the axe and shattered them all! Then his father, enraged by Abraham's reply, went to Nimrod who threw Abraham into the fire but God then stepped in and saved him from it.

DEBATE

The similarity between the stories is unmistakable. That it found its way into the Qur'an as a story true to history should cause Muslims to doubt its divine origin.

In conclusion, there is no valid evidence for the historical alteration of the Bible. It has not been changed and should be accepted as a reliable account of God's revelation to man over the ages. There is no reliable corroborative evidence for the Qur'an, especially when it contradicts the Bible in facts of history (e.g., the crucifixion of Christ, which is denied by the Qur'an nearly 600 years after the event but which is nevertheless confirmed by history through the evidence available to us).

As a result of this study, we believe the Muslim world, in spite of its strong faith, should initiate a more critical study of the origins of the Qur'an. Unless a book can withstand assaults to its authority, it is difficult for its claim to be the Word of God to be credible.

CONSIDERING THE QUR'AN

We have shown that in a comparison between the textual transmission of the Qur'an and the Bible, the Bible's text can be identified and affirmed. But now we propose to show that the Qur'an's transmission is not free from errors and variant readings in significant points.

There is concrete evidence in the best works of Islamic tradition (e.g. the *Sahih of Muslim*, the *Sahih of Bukhari*, the *Mishkat-ul-Masabih*), that from the start the Qur'an had numerous variant and conflicting readings. That these are no longer found in the Qur'an is only because they have been discreetly removed—not by direction of God but by human discretion.

There is abundant evidence that, when the Qur'an was first collated by the Caliph Uthman into one standard text, there were numerous texts in existence which all contained a host of variant readings. During his reign reports were brought to him that, in various parts of Syria, Armenia and Iraq, Muslims were reciting the Qur'an in a way different than those in Arabia were reciting it. Uthman immediately called for the manuscript of the Qur'an which was in the possession of Hafsah (one of the wives of Muhammad and the daughter of Umar) and ordered Zaid-b-Thabit and three others to make copies of the text and to correct it wherever necessary. When these were complete Uthman took drastic action regarding the other manuscripts of the Qur'an in existence:

> Uthman sent to every Muslim province one copy of what they had copied, and ordered that all the other Qur'anic materials, whether written in fragmentary manuscripts or whole copies, be burnt (*Sahih Bukhari*, Vol. 6, p. 479).

At no time in Christian history has a major Christian movement attempted to standardize just one copy of the Bible as the true one while attempting to have all the others destroyed. Why did Uthman make such an order regarding the other Qur'ans in circulation? We can only presume that he believed that they contained grave defects—so many and so serious as to call not for revision but for wholesale destruction. In other words, if we assess the textual history of the Qur'an at this point, we find that the Qur'an standardized as the correct one is that which a man (and not God), according to his own discretion (and not by revelation), decreed to be the true one. We fail to see on what grounds this copy was justified as the only perfect one available.

There is incontrovertible evidence that even this one "Revised Standard Version" of the Qur'an was not perfect. In the most accredited works of Islamic tradition we read that even *after* these copies were sent out the same Zaid recalled a verse which was missing. He testified:

> A verse from Surat Ahzab was missed by me when we copied the Qur'an and I used to hear Allah's Apostle reciting it. So we searched for it and found it with Khuzaima-bin-Thabit al Ansari (*Sahih Bukhari*, Vol. 6, p. 479).

The verse was Surah 33:23. Therefore, there was *not one Qur'an* at the time of Uthman's reclension which was perfect.

Secondly, there is similar evidence that, to this day, verses and, indeed, whole passages are still missing from the Qur'an. We are told that Umar in his reign as Caliph stated that certain verses prescribing stoning for adultery were recited by Muhammad as part of the Qur'an in his lifetime:

> God sent Muhammad and sent down the Scripture to him. Part of what he sent down was the passage on stoning, we read it, we were taught it, and we heeded it. The apostle stoned and we stoned them after him. I fear that in time to come men will say that they find no mention of stoning in God's book and thereby go astray in neglecting an ordinance which God has sent

THE ISLAM
DEBATE

down. Verily stoning in the book of God is a penalty laid on married men and women who commit adultery (Ibn Ishaq, *Sirat Rasulullah*, p. 684).

Here is clear evidence that the Qur'an as it stands today is still not "perfect." Elsewhere in the Hadith we find further evidence that certain verses and passages once formed part of the Qur'an but are now omitted from its text. It is quite clear, therefore, that the *textus receptus* of the Qur'an in today's world is not the exact *textus originalis*.

Going back to the texts which were marked for the fire, we find that in every case there were considerable differences between these and the text which Uthman decided, according to his own discretion, to standardize as the best text of the Qur'an. In many cases we find that they were "real, textual variants and not mere dialectal peculiarities as is often suggested" (Arthur Jeffery, *The Qur'an As Scripture*, New York: Books for Libraries, 1980, p. 97).

A difference between the Qur'an and the Bible today is that the Christian Church has carefully preserved the variant readings that exist in the biblical texts whereas the Muslims at the time of Uthman deemed it expedient to destroy as far as possible all evidences of different readings of the Qur'an in the cause of standardizing one text for the whole of the Muslim world. There may well be only one text of the Qur'an in circulation today, but no one can honestly claim that it is exactly that which Muhammad handed down to his companions. And no one has ever shown why Hafsah's text deserved to be regarded as infallible.

It does not help to say that all Qur'ans in the world today are the same. A chain is only as strong as its weakest link—and the weak link in the chain of the textual history of the Qur'an is found right at this point where, in those crucial early days, different and differing codices of the Qur'an existed and evidence has been shown that the text finally standardized as the best one was still far from being complete or in any way perfect.

Muslims believe that Jews and Christians have corrupted the biblical text in order to achieve their own ends, yet the textual history of the Bible as we have seen, does not bear this out. The above can be summarized as follows:

1. There is little physical manuscript evidence of alteration to substantiate Islam's claims. In fact, the opposite is true. The incredible

devotion of the Jewish people to the Torah and the meticulous copying of text by the Massoretes runs against Muslim charges. (See *Family Handbook of Christian Knowledge, The Bible*, by Josh McDowell and Don Stewart, published by Here's Life Publishers, Inc., San Bernardino, California, © 1983, pp. 44-48.)

2. There is no satisfactory answer to why Jews and Christians would change their text.

3. At the supposed time of textual corruption, it would have been impossible for Jews and Christians to have changed the text; they were spread all over the world.

4. Also, at the time of corruption, there would be too many copies in circulation to change—not to mention the diversity of language.

5. Jews and Christians were hostile to each other. Little agreement could have been achieved.

6. Differing new sects would have disagreed with mainline groups over changes. Thus no uniform set of alterations could be made as the Muslim claims.

7. Former Jews and Christians who became Muslims never mentioned any possibility of deliberate corruption—something we could definitely expect if it were true (cf. *Christianity Explained to Muslims*, p. 20-21).

The evidence supports the idea that both the Qur'an and the Bible are reliable in their representation of what was originally written. The Muslim claim that the Bible was corrupted does not bear out the facts. However, there is sound reason to question much of the Qur'an's use of the Bible in its scripture.

EVIDENCE FOR THE RELIABILITY OF THE NEW TESTAMENT

While I was lecturing at Arizona State University, a professor who was accompanied by students from his graduate seminar on world literature approached me after a "free-speech" lecture outdoors. He said, "Mr. McDowell, you are basing all your claims about Christ on a second-century document that is obsolete. I showed in class today how the New

Testament was written so long after Christ that it could not be accurate in what it recorded." His opinion about the records concerning Jesus found their source in the conclusions of various critics who assume that most of the New Testament Scriptures were not written until late in the second century A.D. They concluded that these writings came basically from myths or legends that had developed during the lengthy interval between the lifetime of Jesus and the time these accounts were set down in writing.

I replied, "Sir your opinions or conclusions about the New Testament are 25 years out of date."

Since the New Testament provides the primary historical source for the majority of the information about Jesus, it is important to determine its accuracy concerning what it reports.

When you have a religious faith that appeals to truth and is based upon the searching out of truth and the preserving of that knowledge, you have a built-in plus factor for preserving its integrity over the years. Biblical Christianity has such a plus factor for researching and preserving truth.

For example, John 8:32 says, "You shall know the truth." It doesn't say to ignore it. It says, "You shall know the truth, and the truth shall make you free" (NASB). In 2 Timothy 2:15, the apostle Paul admonishes the believer to "be diligent to present yourself approved to God as a workman who does not need to be ashamed, handling accurately the word of truth" (NASB). All the way through the entire New Testament there is an emphasis on truth, and the preserving of that truth. When you compare the Bible to other literature of antiquity, the evidence for the Bible is overwhelming. If other literature had the same evidence, no one would question its authenticity and reliability. But with the Bible you encounter two objections. First, it's a religious book and therefore it can't be trusted. Second, it assumes existence of the supernatural. For many people, the historical evidence is not the key. The issue for many (not all) involved in New Testament criticism is, if there's any element of the supernatural, then it's unhistorical.

Because of this, many critics during the 19th and 20th centuries attacked the reliability of the biblical documents. There seems to be a constant barrage of accusations that have no historical foundation or that have now been outdated by archaeological discoveries and research.

Many of these opinions about the records concerning Jesus are based on the conclusions of a German critic, F.C. Baur. Baur assumed that most of the New Testament Scriptures were not written until late in the second century A.D. He concluded that these writings came basically from myths or legends that had developed during the lengthy interval between the lifetime of Jesus and the time these accounts were set down in writing.

By the 20th century, however, archaeological discoveries had gone a long way in confirming the historical accuracy of the New Testament manuscripts, and their first-century origin. Discoveries of early papyri manuscripts (the John Ryland manuscript, A.D. 130; the Chester Beatty Papyri, A.D. 155; and the Bodmer Papyri II, A.D. 200) helped bridge the gap between the time of Christ and existing manuscripts from a later date.

Archaeologist Millar Burrows of Yale has said that one result of comparing New Testament Greek with the language of the papyri is an increase of confidence in the accurate transmission of the text of the New Testament (Millar Burrows, *What Mean These Stones*, New York: Meridian Books, 1956, p. 52).

William F. Albright, who was one of the world's foremost biblical archaeologists, writes: "We can already say emphatically that there is no longer any solid basis for dating any book of the New Testament after about A.D. 80, two full generations before the date between 130 and 150 given by the more radical New Testament critics of today (William F. Albright, *Recent Discoveries in Bible Lands*, New York: Funk and Wagnall, 1955, p. 136).

Sir William Ramsey was regarded as one of the greatest geographers who ever lived. He was a student of the German historical school which taught that the Book of Acts was a product of the mid-second century A.D. and not the first century as it purports to be. After reading modern criticism about the Book of Acts, he became convinced that it was not a trustworthy account of the facts of the time just after Christ (A.D. 50) and therefore was unworthy of consideration by a historian. So in his research on the history of Asia Minor, Ramsey paid little attention to the New Testament. His archaeological investigation, however, eventually compelled him to consider the writings of Luke. He observed the meticulous accuracy of its historical details, and gradually his attitude toward the Book of Acts began to change. The evidence forced him to conclude that "Luke is a historian of the first rank...this author should be placed along

THE ISLAM
DEBATE

with the very greatest of historians" (Sir William Ramsey, *The Bearing of Recent Discoveries on the Trustworthiness of the New Testament*, London: Hodder and Stoughton, 1915, p. 222). Because of the accuracy of Luke, Ramsey finally conceded that Acts could not be a second-century document but was rather a mid-first-century historical account.

Dr. John A.T. Robinson, lecturer at Trinity College, Cambridge, has been for years one of England's more distinguished critics. Robinson at first accepted the consensus typified by German criticism that the New Testament was written years after the time of Christ at the end of the first century. But, as "little more than a theological joke," he decided to investigate the arguments on the late dating of all the New Testament books, a field largely dormant since the turn of the century.

The results stunned him. He said that owing to scholarly "sloth," the "tyranny of unexamined assumptions" and "almost willful blindness" by previous authors, much of the past reasoning was untenable. He concluded that the New Testament is the work of the apostles themselves or of contemporaries who worked with them and that all the New Testament books, including John, had to have been written before A.D. 64 (John T. Robinson, *Redating the New Testament*, London: SCM Press, 1976, p. 221).

Robinson challenged his colleagues to try to prove him wrong. If scholars reopen the question, he is convinced, the results will force "the rewriting of many introductions to—and ultimately, theologies of— the New Testament" (ibid).

One can also make a strong case for the reliability of the Scriptures from a legal perspective. The "ancient document" principle under the *Federal Rules of Evidence* (published by West Publishing Co., St. Paul, 1979, Rule 901 (b) (8)) permits the authentication of a document to be made by showing that the document (1) is in such condition as to create no suspicion concerning its authenticity; (2) was in a place where, if authentic, it would likely be; and (3) has been in existence 20 years or more at the time it is offered.

Dr. John Warwick Montgomery, a lawyer and theologian, and dean of the Simon Greenleaf School of Law, comments about the application of the "ancient document" rule to the New Testament documents: "Applied to the gospel records, and reinforced by responsible lower (textual) criticism, this rule would establish competency in any court of law" (John

Warwick Montgomery, "Legal Reasoning and Christian Apologetics," *The Law Above the Law*, Oak Park, IL: Christian Legal Society, 1975, pp. 88, 89).

Some critics argue that information about Christ was passed by word of mouth until it was written down in the form of the Gospels. Even though the period was much shorter than previously believed, they conclude that the Gospel accounts took on the forms of tales and myths.

But the period of oral tradition (as defined by the critics) is not long enough to have allowed the alterations in the tradition that these critics have alleged. Dr. Simon Kistemaker, professor of Bible at Reformed Seminary, writes: "Normally, the accumulation of folklore among people of primitive culture takes many generations; it is a gradual process spread over centuries of time. But in conformity with the thinking of the form critic, we must conclude that the Gospel stories were produced and collected within little more than one generation. In terms of the form-critical approach, the formation of the individual Gospel units must be understood as a telescoped project with accelerated course of action" (Simon Kistemaker, *The Gospels in Current Study*, Grand Rapids, MI: Baker Book House, 1972, pp. 48, 49).

A.H. McNeile, former Regius Professor of Divinity at the University of Dublin, points out that form critics do not deal with the tradition of Jesus' words as closely as they should. A careful look at 1 Corinthians 7:10, 12, 25 shows the careful preservation and the existence of a genuine tradition of recording these words. In the Jewish religion it was customary for a student to memorize a rabbi's teaching. A good pupil was like "a plastered cistern that loses not a drop" (*Mishna*, Aboth, 2:8) (A.H. McNeile, *An Introduction to the Study of the New Testament*, London: Oxford University Press, 1953, p. 54).

Moreover, if we rely on C.F. Birney's theory (in *The Poetry of Our Lord*, 1925), we can assume that much of the Lord's teaching is in Aramaic poetical form, making it easy to be memorized.

There is strong internal testimony that the Gospels were written at an early date. The Book of Acts records the missionary activity of the early Church and was written as a sequel by the same person who wrote the Gospel according to Luke. The Book of Acts ends with the apostle Paul being alive in Rome, his death not being recorded.

This would lead us to believe that it was written before he died, since the other major events in his life have been recorded. We have some reason to believe that Paul was put to death in the Neronian persecution of A.D. 64, which means the Book of Acts was composed before this time.

If the Book of Acts was written before A.D. 64, then the Gospel of Luke, to which Acts was a sequel, had to have been composed some time before that, probably in the late fifties or early sixties of the first century. The death of Christ took place around A.D. 30, which would make the composition of Luke at the latest within 30 years of the events.

The early Church generally taught that the first Gospel composed was that of Matthew, which would place us still closer to the time of Christ. This evidence leads us to believe that the first three Gospels were all composed within 30 years from the time these events occurred, a time when unfriendly eyewitnesses were still living who could contradict their testimony if it was not accurate (Josh McDowell and Don Stewart, *Answers to Tough Questions,* San Bernardino, CA: Here's Life Publishers, 1980, pp. 7, 8).

Facts involved in the issue led W.F. Albright, the great biblical archaeologist, to comment:

"Every book of the New Testament was written...between the forties and the eighties of the first century A.D. (very probably sometime between about A.D. 50 and 75" (William F. Albright, *Christianity Today,* Vol. 7, Jan. 18, 1963, p. 3).

The historical reliability of the Scripture should be tested by the same criteria used to test all historical documents. Military historian C. Sanders lists and explains three basic principles of historiography: the bibliographical test, the internal evidence test, and the external evidence test (C. Sanders, *Introduction to Research in English Literary History,* New York: MacMillan Company, 1952, pp. 143ff).

The bibliographical test is an examination of the textual transmission by which documents reach us. In other words, not having the original documents, how reliable are the copies we have in regard to the number of manuscripts and the time interval between the original and extant copies?

A common misconception is that the text of the Bible has not come down to us as it was originally written. Accusations abound of zealous monks changing the biblical text throughout Church history.

Fortunately, the problem is not a lack of evidence. When research into biblical reliability was completed and we released *Evidence That Demands a Verdict* in 1973, we were able to document 14,000 manuscripts and portions of manuscripts in Greek and early versions of the New Testament alone. Recently we updated and reissued *Evidence* because of the vast amount of new research material available. Now we are able to document 24,633 manuscripts and portions of the New Testament alone.

The significance of the number of manuscripts documenting the New Testament is even greater when one realizes that in all of history the second book in terms of manuscript authority is *The Iliad*, by Homer. It has only 643 surviving manuscripts.

The New Testament was originally composed in Greek. There are approximately 5,500 copies in existence that contain all or part of the New Testament. Although we do not possess the originals, copies exist from a very early date. The earliest fragment dates about A.D. 120, with about 50 other fragments dating within 150-200 years from the time of composition.

Two major manuscripts, Codex Vaticanus (A.D. 325) and Codex Sinaiticus (A.D. 350), a complete copy, date within 250 years of the time of composition. This may seem like a long time span, but it is minimal compared to most ancient works. The first complete copy of the *Odyssey* is from 2,200 years after it was written. The New Testament Greek scholar J. Harold Greenlee adds:

> Since scholars accept as generally trustworthy the writings of the ancient classics even though the earliest MSS were written so long after the original writings and the number of extant MSS is in many instances so small, it is clear that the reliability of the text of the New Testament is likewise assured (J. Harold Greenlee, *Introduction to New Testament Textual Criticism*, Grand Rapids, MI: William B. Eerdmans Publishing Co., 1964, p. 15).

Many ancient writings have been transmitted to us by only a handful of manuscripts (Catullus—three copies; earliest one is 1,600 years after he wrote; Herodotus—eight copies and 1,300 years).

Many people consider Thucydides one of the most accurate of ancient historians, and only eight manuscripts survived. Of *Aristotle*, it was 37, but they found 12 more, so now 49 *manuscripts* survived. What about the New Testament?

Not only do the New Testament documents have more manuscript evidence and closer time interval between the writing and earliest copy, but they were also translated into several other languages at an early date. Translation of a document into another language was rare in the ancient world, so this is an added textual verification for the New Testament. The number of copies of these versions is in excess of 18,000, with possibly as many as 25,000. This is further evidence that helps us establish the New Testament text.

Less than 10 years ago, 36,000 quotations of the Scriptures by the early church fathers could be documented. But more recently, as a result of some research done at the British Museum, we are now able to document in early church writings, 89,000 quotations from the New Testament. Without any Bibles or manuscripts—they could all be thrown away or burned—one could reconstruct all but 11 verses of the entire New Testament from material written within 150 and 200 years of the time of Jesus Christ.

New Testament scholar F.F. Bruce makes the following observation:

> The evidence for our New Testament writings is ever so much greater than the evidence for many writings of classical authors, the authenticity of which no one dreams of questioning.

He also states,

> And if the New Testament were a collection of secular writings, their authenticity would generally be regarded as beyond all doubt (F.F. Bruce, *The New Testament Documents: Are They Reliable?* Rev. ed., Grand Rapids, MI: William B. Eerdmans Publishing Co., 1977, p. 15).

Sir Frederic Kenyon, former director and principal librarian of the British Museum, was one of the foremost experts on ancient manuscripts and their authority. Shortly before his death, he wrote this concerning the New Testament:

> The interval between the dates of original composition (of the New Testament) and the earliest extant evidence becomes so small as to be in fact negligible, and the last foundation for any doubt that the Scriptures have come down to us substantially as they were written has now been

removed. Both the authenticity and the general integrity of the books of the New Testament may be regarded as finally established (Sir Frederic Kenyon, *The Bible and Archaeology*, New York: Harper and Row, Publishers, 1940, pp. 288, 289).

Of the *Iliad* by Homer, Bruce Metzger observes:

In the entire range of ancient Greek and Latin literature, the *Iliad* ranks next to the New Testament in possessing the greatest amount of manuscript testimony (Bruce Metzger, *Chapters in the History of New Testament Textual Criticism*, Grand Rapids, MI: William B. Eerdmans Publishing Co., 1963, p. 144).

He adds:

Of all the literary compositions by the Greek people, the Homeric poems are the best suited for comparison with the Bible (ibid, p. 145).

WORK	WHEN WRITTEN	EARLIEST COPY	TIME SPAN	NO. OF COPIES
Homer (Iliad)...........	900 BC	400 BC	500 yrs	643
New Testament	AD 40-100	AD 125	25 yrs	over 24,000

Of course, we must apply the same bibliographical test to the Qur'an. There are no original manuscripts available today of the text of the Qur'an dating from the time of Muhammad. Muslims allege that the Qur'an standardized by the third Caliph Uthman still exists, though there are at least 20 early Qur'an manuscripts which claim this coveted origin! One is on display at the Topkapi Museum in Istanbul, another is in the Soviet State Library, and yet others are preserved elsewhere in the Muslim world. All are written in early kufic script, but if even one could be attributed to Uthman, this still leaves a gap of over a generation between the demise of Muhammad and the oldest Qur'an manuscript. In fact there is only one manuscript of the Qur'an surviving in the Medinan al-mail script (Medina being the city where Muhammad spent his last years) and this text is known to date from the eighth century—at least 150 years after the death of Muhammad. It is preserved in the British Museum and is on permanent display. Neither Christians nor Muslims have *original* copies of their Scriptures and the test of reliability has to be applied in the same way to both books in respect of the transcribed copies that have survived. In both cases the result is the same—the Bible and the Qur'an each has been remarkably preserved in its earliest known form.

THE ISLAM
DEBATE

The bibliographical test determines only that the text we have now is what was originally recorded. One still has to determine whether that written record is credible and to what extent it is credible.

Internal criticism, which is the second test of historicity listed by C. Sanders, deals with the credibility of the text.

There are two factors that must guide the application of this test. The first is that in the event of an apparent inaccuracy or discrepancy, the literary critic follows Aristotle's dictum that "The benefit of the doubt is to be given to the document itself, and not arrogated by the critic to himself." In other words, as John W. Montgomery often summarizes in his lectures: "One must listen to the claims of the document under analysis, and not assume fraud or error unless the author disqualifies himself by contradictions or known factual inaccuracies" (John Warwick Montgomery, *History and Christianity*, Downers Grove, IL: InterVarsity Press, 1971, p. 29). As a person is innocent until proven guilty, so a document is innocent, until, by an absolute discrepancy, or inaccuracy or error, it's shown to be not trustworthy.

But when alleged discrepancies or a problem or an error are discovered, there are certain questions that should be asked. First, have we correctly understood the passage; the proper use of the numbers or the words? Second, do we possess all the available knowledge in that matter? Third, can any further light possibly be thrown on it through textual research, archaeology or historical investigation? All three considerations contribute to investigating textual veracity.

Dr. Robert Horn put it this way:

> Difficulties are to be grappled with and problems are to drive us to see clear light. But until such time as we have total and final light on any issue, we are in no position to affirm there is a proven error, an unquestionable objection to an infallible Bible. It is common knowledge that countless objections have been fully resolved since this century began (Robert M. Horn, *The Book That Speaks for Itself*, Downers Grove, IL: InterVarsity Press, 1970, pp. 86, 87).

When faced with an alleged contradiction, you appeal to the manuscript evidence, the internal biblical evidence, the documented linguistic evidence, and the canons of textual criticism. Space does not permit the luxury of amplifying each of these areas.

The second factor of the internal evidence test is that the nearness of the witness both geographically and chronologically to the events recorded greatly affects the writers' credibility. How does this affect the New Testament? The New Testament accounts of the life and teachings of Jesus were recorded by men who either had been eyewitnesses themselves or who related the accounts of eyewitnesses.

Dr. Louis Gottschalk, former Professor of History at the University of Chicago, outlines his historical method in *Understanding History*, a guide used by many for historical investigation. Gottschalk points out that the ability of the writer or the witness to tell the truth is helpful to the historian to determine credibility, "even if it is contained in a document obtained by force or fraud, or is otherwise impeachable, or is based on hearsay evidence, or is from an interested witness" (Louis R. Gottschalk, *Understanding History.* New York: Knopf, 1969, 2nd ed., p. 150).

This "ability to tell the truth" is closely related to the witness's nearness both geographically and chronologically to the events recorded. The New Testament accounts of the life and teachings of Jesus were recorded by men who had been either eyewitnesses themselves or who related the accounts of eyewitnesses of the actual events or teachings of Christ.

> Luke 1:13—Inasmuch as many have undertaken to compile an account of the things accomplished among us, just as those who from the beginning were eyewitnesses and servants of the Word have handed them down to us, it seemed fitting for me as well, having investigated everything carefully from the beginning, to write it out for you in consecutive order, most excellent Theophilus (NASB).

> 2 Peter 1:16—For we did not follow cleverly devised tales when we made known to you the power and coming of our Lord Jesus Christ, but we were eyewitnesses of His majesty (NASB).

> 1 John 1:3—What we have seen and heard we proclaim to you also, that you also may have fellowship with us; and indeed our fellowship is with the Father, and with His Son Jesus Christ (NASB).

> John 19:35—And he who has seen has borne witness, and his witness is true; and he knows that he is telling the truth, so that you also may believe (NASB).

Luke 3:1—Now in the fifteenth year of the reign of Tiberius Caesar, when Pontius Pilate was governor of Judea, and Herod was tetrarch of Galilee, and his brother Philip was tetrarch of the region of Ituraea and Trachonitis, and Lysanias was tetrarch of Abilene (NASB).

This closeness to the recorded accounts is an extremely effective means of certifying the accuracy of what is retained by a witness. The historian, however, also has to deal with the eyewitness who consciously or unconsciously tells falsehoods even though he is near the event and is competent enough to tell the truth.

The New Testament accounts of Christ were being circulated within the lifetimes of His contemporaries. These people could have confirmed or denied the accuracy of the accounts. In advocating their case for the gospel, the apostles had appealed (even when confronting their most severe opponents) to common knowledge concerning Jesus. They not only said, "Look, we saw this" or "We heard that..." but they turned the tables around and right in front of adverse critics said, "You also know about these things...you saw them; you yourselves know about it." One had better be careful when he says to his opposition, "You know this also," because if he isn't right in the details, he will be exposed.

In Acts 2:22, Peter was before the Jewish people. He said: *"Men of Israel, listen to these words: Jesus the Nazarene, a man attested to you."* Not just to us. But a man "attested to you *by God with miracles and wonders and signs which God performed through Him."* Notice this: *"In your midst, just as you yourselves know" (NASB).* Now, if they hadn't seen those miracles and signs, Peter would never have gotten out of there alive, let alone have thousands come to Christ. Paul did the same thing. In Acts 26:24-26 Paul was brought before the king, and he said, in my own loose paraphrase, I'm glad I'm brought before you, because you know of my life from childhood up, and you know the customs of the Jews. And he started to present the evidence for Christianity. And he was interrupted. And while Paul was saying this in his defense, King Festus said in a loud voice, "Paul, you're out of your mind! Your great learning's driving you mad." They knew he had great learning. He'd studied under Gamaliel, he'd studied in Tarsus. But Paul said, "I'm not out of my mind, most excellent Festus. But I had words of sober truth." And that phrase of "sober truth" in the Greek literally says, of "truth and rationale." And then notice what Paul does: he said, "I am persuaded that none of these things escape his notice for this has not been done in a corner."

Teachings of
Islam

When I study history, and I want to check out the accuracy of the writer, there are several things I ask. First, does he have a good character? Second, is there a consistency in his writing—a consistency of accuracy? Third, is there confrontation? In other words, was the material written down or presented at a time when there were those alive who were aware of the facts surrounding the events or statements recorded?

Concerning the primary-source value of the New Testament records, the British New Testament scholar of Manchester University, F.F. Bruce, says:

> And it was not only friendly eyewitnesses that the early preachers had to reckon with; there were others less well disposed who were also conversant with the main facts of the ministry and death of Jesus. The disciples could not afford to risk inaccuracies (not to speak of willful manipulation of the facts) which would at once be exposed by those who would be only too glad to do so. On the contrary, one of the strong points in the original apostolic preaching is the confident appeal to the knowledge of the hearers; they not only said, 'We are witnesses of these things,' but also, 'As you yourselves also know' (Acts 2:22). Had there been any tendency to depart from the facts in any material respect, the possible presence of hostile witnesses in the audiences would have served as a further corrective (Bruce, *Documents*, p. 33).

New Testament scholar Robert Grant of the University of Chicago concludes:

> At the time they [the synoptic gospels] were written or may be supposed to have been written, there were eyewitnesses and their testimony was not completely disregarded....This means that the gospels must be regarded as largely reliable witnesses to the life, death and resurrection of Jesus (Robert Grant, *Historical Introduction to the New Testament*, New York: Harper and Row, 1963, p. 302).

While the multiple number of New Testament eyewitnesses are not a 100% guarantee of reliability, it would be extremely difficult to argue that each one made the same mistake in identification. The eyewitness accounts of having seen Christ alive after his resurrection would be very convincing in a court of law, especially in view of the extensive testimony.

McCormick's *Handbook of the Law of Evidence*, an excellent treatise on analyzing evidence, observes that the legal system's insistence upon

THE ISLAM
DEBATE

using only the most reliable sources of information is manifested best in the rule requiring that a witness who testifies to a fact which can be perceived by the senses must actually have observed the fact (McCormick's *Handbook of the Law of Evidence*, Edward W. Cleary, ed., St. Paul: West Publishing Co., 1972, pp. 586, 587).

The emphasis of this *hearsay rule* is that "hearsay" is not admissible as evidence in a court of law. *The Federal Rules of Evidence* declares that a witness must testify concerning what he has firsthand knowledge of, not what has come to him indirectly from other sources *(Federal Rules of Evidence, Rule 801 and 802).*

Concerning the value of one testifying "of his own knowledge," Dr. John Montgomery points out that from a legal perspective the New Testament documents meet the demand for "primary-source" evidence. He writes that the New Testament record is:

> fully vindicated by the constant assertions of their authors to be setting forth that which we have heard, which we have seen with our eyes, which we have looked upon and our hands have handled (John Warwick Montgomery, "Legal Reasoning and Christian Apologetics," (pp. 88, 89).

In the New Testament, it comes from firsthand knowledge. For example, when Mary went to the tomb, the angel appeared to her and said, "He is not here, He has risen." When Mary repeated that, it was because she hadn't seen Him; she just had heard about it. But then later, Jesus appeared to Mary. That took it out of hearsay, and made it a primary source.

Now, along with the eyewitnesses, we need to get in a little bit of the psychological perspective. In law today, there's a whole new field opening up of the psychological make-up of the witness, and what he can remember and what he can't. Dr. Elizabeth Loftus, who is a professor of psychology of the University of Washington, wrote in a journal, "people who witness fearful events, remember the details of them less accurately than they recall ordinary happenings. Stress or fear disrupts perception and therefore memory. Stress can also affect the person's ability to recall something observed or learned during that period of relative tranquility" (Elizabeth S. Loftus, "The Eyewitness on Trial," *Trials*, Vol. 16, No. 10, Oct. 1980, pp. 30-35).

Her observations actually strengthen the eyewitness accounts of the New Testament. You do not find there any fleeting glimpse of a stranger in the darkness of an alley, wielding a knife or a gun. The followers of Christ spent time with someone they knew and loved. Several times Jesus said, "Don't be afraid," so there must have been stress there. And fear. But there was also the repetition of appearances—for over 40 days He appeared with them. As eyewitnesses for 40 days they became much more certain in their memories.

The multiple number of New Testament eyewitnesses, and all the appearances, 500 at one time for instance, do not give 100 percent assurance that the witnesses were accurate. However, it would be extremely difficult, and just about contrary to everything we know in history, to argue that each one of them made the same mistake in identification. For example, you have 500 witnesses at one time. Let's take them to a court of law. *We'll only give them six minutes each.* Now, when was the last time you were in a court, and you only had an eyewitness given six minutes. Only give them six minutes. Take 500, *multiply it by six minutes, that's three thousand minutes* of eyewitness testimony. *Divide that by 60 minutes, an hour, and it comes out to 50 hours of eyewitness testimony.* Just for the resurrection.

There is an area of the internal evidence test relating to the apostles that is often overlooked—the resurrection and its effect on their lives. This is written and documented quite extensively in *More Than a Carpenter* (published by Tyndale House Publishers, Wheaton, IL, 1977) and *Evidence That Demands a Verdict* (published by Here's Life Publishers, San Bernardino, California, 1979). But because the resurrection is unique and foundational to Christianity, let's explore it briefly here.

There are two crucial questions that relate to the reliability of the biblical record we have today: (1) Is what we have now what actually was written down 2,000 years ago? In other words, has the original message been changed down through the centuries? (2) Was what was recorded or written down true? Or was it distorted, stretched, embellished or tailored by His followers to coincide with their own theology or understanding? The following deals with the second question.

Good historical tradition shows us 12 Jewish men, 11 of whom died martyrs' deaths as a tribute to one thing: an empty tomb, and the appearances of Jesus of Nazareth alive after His death by crucifixion. For 40 days after His resurrection, these men walked with Him and lived with Him and ate with Him (Acts 1:3). His resurrection was accompanied by

THE ISLAM
DEBATE

many convincing proofs. That phrase "convincing proofs" is a phrase, meaning overwhelming, compelling evidence, which was used in law courts of that day.

The critic will say that the apostles died for a lie, but if the resurrection were a lie, there were 12 men who knew it was a lie.

Andre Kole is considered the world's leading illusionist, often called the magician's magician. He has never been fooled by another illusionist or magician. He has created and sold more than 1,400 illusionary magical effects.

When Andre was a non-Christian, he studied psychology. And he was trained in illusion and magic. He was challenged to apply his proficiency to the miracles of Jesus Christ, to explain them away. He accepted that challenge. He can explain several of them away, but most of them he cannot. And he said to me, "One, Josh, I couldn't even come near to explaining away."

I said, "What was that?"

He said, "The resurrection of Jesus Christ." He said that there is no way through modern illusionary effects or magic that Jesus could have deceived His apostles. There are too many built-in safety factors. And he said if the resurrection was a lie, they had to know it.

While it's true that thousands of people throughout history have died for a lie, they did so only if they thought it to be the truth. And if the resurrection was a lie, then these men not only died for a lie, but they knew it was a lie.

As the early Church Father Tertulian said, "No man would be willing to die unless he knew he had the truth." What happened to these people? Author Dr. Michael Green of England points out that "the resurrection was the belief that turned heart-broken followers of a crucified Rabbi into the courageous witness and martyrs of the early church. This is the one belief that separated the followers of Jesus from the Jews, and turned them into the community of the Resurrection. You can imprison them, flog them, but you could not make them deny their conviction that on the third day, He rose again" (Michael Green, "Editor's Preface," *I Believe in the Resurrection of Jesus* by George Eldon Ladd, Grand Rapids, MI: William B. Eerdmans Publishing Co., 1975, p. 3).

Kenneth Scott Latourette, the man who for years held the chair of history at Yale, observed that "from discouraged, disillusioned men and women, who sadly looked back upon the days when they had hoped that Jesus was here, and would redeem Israel, they were made over into a company of enthusiastic witnesses" (Kenneth Scott Latourette, *A History of Christianity*, New York: Harper and Row, Publishers, 1937, 1:59).

Dr. Simon Greenleaf was one of the great legal minds of our country. He was the famous Royal Professor of Law at Harvard. His proficiency was in the area of reducing the credibility of a witness in a court of law, to show that he was lying. After examining Christianity and the resurrection, he became a Christian and went on to write a book explaining the evidence that led him to the conclusion that the resurrection is a well-established historical event (Simon Greenleaf, *An Examination of the Testimony of the Four Evangelists by the Rules of Evidence Administered in the Courts of Justice*, Grand Rapids, MI: Baker Book House, reprinted 1965 [first edition, 1874], p. 29).

Greenleaf made this observation in support of the veracity and integrity of the testimony of the disciples: "The annals of military warfare, afford scarcely an example of the like; heroic constancy, patience, and unflinching courage. They had every possible motive to review carefully the ground of their fate, and the evidences of the great facts and truths they asserted" (ibid).

Critics also assert that dying for a great cause doesn't prove the truth of that cause.

Yes, a lot of people have died for great causes. But the apostles' great Cause died on the cross. Let me take you back in history before the time of Christ to see why many Jews who were Jesus' contemporaries denied Him as Messiah. The Jews taught that there would be two Messiahs, not one. One would be the suffering Messiah who would die for the sins of Israel. The other would be the reigning political Messiah, who would relieve them from oppression, the son of David. Jesus denied this, asserting that there were not to be two Messiahs; there would be one Messiah coming twice. Jesus said, "I'm coming to die for your sins, and I'm coming back again, to reign throughout the world."

Before the time of Christ, the hierarchy of Judaism had become very self-righteous. Christ accused them of being white-washed sepulchers. They were under the oppression of the Romans, so, to hold the allegiance of the people, they taught them they didn't need the suffering Messiah, and that when the Messiah came, he'd be the reigning political Messiah. He would bring the chariots and the cavalry down out of the mountains; he would use every weapon possible, and he would throw the Romans out. And that's what the people believed. That is why it was so hard for the apostles to understand what Jesus was saying. He said, "I have to die. I have to go to Jerusalem. I'm going to suffer. I'm going to be crucified and buried." They couldn't understand it. Why? From childhood it had been ingrained into them that when the Messiah came, he'd reign politically. They really thought they were in on something big. They were going to rule with Him. They believed that.

Professor E.F. Scott points this out when he says that "for the people at large, their Messiah remained what He had been to Isaiah and His contemporaries, the Son of David, who would bring victory and prosperity to the Jewish nation. In the light of the Gospel references, it can hardly be doubted that the popular conception of the Messiah was mainly national and political" (Ernest Findlay Scott, *Kingdom and the Messiah*, Edinburgh: T and T Clark, 1911, p. 55).

Dr. Joseph Klausner, a Jewish scholar, observed "that the Messiah became more and more not only a pre-eminent political ruler, but also a man of pre-eminent moral qualities" (Joseph Klausner, *The Messianic Idea in Israel*, New York: Macmillan Co., 1955, p. 23).

Another Jewish gentleman, Dr. Jacob Gardenhus, says that the Jews awaited the Messiah as the one who would deliver them from Roman oppression. The Temple with its sacrificial service was intact, and the Romans did not interfere in the Jewish religious affairs, and the Messianic hope, was basically for national liberation. A redeemer of the country that was being oppressed.

The Jewish Encyclopedia records that the Jews "yearned for the promised deliverer of the house of David who would free them from the yoke of the hated foreign ursurper, who would put an end to the impious world, and rule, and would establish his own reign of peace and justice in its place" (*The Jewish Encyclopedia*, New York: Funk and Wagnalls Co., 1906, Vol. 8, p. 508).

This was also the attitude of the disciples. Were they awaiting a suffering Messiah? No! They were expecting a reigning, political Messiah. And so when Christ died, not having set up a reign of power, they became discouraged. Their great cause was literally crucified. They went back to their own homes discouraged.

But then something happened. In a matter of a few days, their lives were turned upside down. All but one became a martyr for the cause of the man who left the tomb empty and appeared after death. The resurrection is the only thing that could have changed these frightened, discouraged men into men who would dedicate their lives to spreading His message. Once they were convinced of it, they never denied it. Twelve different men, and 11 of them died martyrs, never once having denied it through all the agony, the pain and torture of martyrs' deaths.

Harold Mattingly, in his history, writes: "The apostles, St. Peter and St. Paul, seal their witnesses with their blood" (Harold Mattingly, *Roman Imperial Civilization*, London: Edward Arnold Publishers, Ltd., 1967, p. 226). Tertullian wrote that "no man would be willing to die unless he knew he had the truth" (Gaston Foote, *The Transformation of the Twelve*, Nashville: Abingdon Press, 1958, p. 12). They went through the test of death to determine their veracity. I would rather trust them than most people I meet today who are not willing to walk across the street for what they believe, let alone be persecuted and die for the truth of what they wrote.

The internal evidence points out that the documents were not written long after the events recorded, and they were written during the period when many eyewitnesses were alive. The inescapable conclusion of the internal evidence for me is that the New Testament picture of Christ can be trusted. I can stake my life on it.

The late historian Will Durant, who was trained in the discipline of historical investigation and spent his life analyzing records of antiquity, writes:

"Despite the prejudices and theological preconceptions of the evangelists, they record many incidents that mere inventors would have concealed—the competition of the apostles for high places in the Kingdom, their flight after Jesus' arrest, Peter's denial, the failure of Christ to work miracles in Galilee, the references of some authors to his possible insanity, his early uncertainty as to his mission, his confessions of ignorance as to the future, his moments of bitterness, his despairing cry on the cross; no one reading these scenes can doubt the reality of the figure behind them. That a few simple men should in one generation have invented so powerful and appealing a personality, so lofty an ethic, and so inspiring a vision of human brotherhood, would be a miracle far more incredible than any recorded in the Gospels. After two centuries of Higher Criticism the outlines of the life, character, and teaching of Christ remain reasonably clear, and constitute the most fascinating feature in the history of Western man" (Will Durant, "Caesar and Christ," *The Story of Civilization*, New York: Simon and Schuster, 1944, 3:557).

The third test is that of *external evidence*. The issue here is whether other historical material confirms or denies the internal testimony of the documents themselves. In other words, what sources are there, apart from the literature under analysis, which substantiate its accuracy, reliability and authenticity?

Two friends of the apostle John affirm the internal evidence from John's accounts. The historian Eusebius preserves writings of one, Papias, bishop of Hierapolis (A.D. 130):

> "The Elder (Apostle John) used to say this also: 'Mark, having been the interpreter of Peter, wrote down accurately all that he (Peter) mentioned, whether sayings or doings of Christ, not, however, in order. For he was neither a hearer nor a companion of the Lord; but afterwards, as I said, he accompanied Peter, who adapted his teachings as necessity required, not as though he were making a compilation of the sayings of the Lord. So then Mark made no mistake, writing down in this way some things as he mentioned them; for he paid attention to this one thing, not to omit anything that he had heard, nor to include any false statement among them' " (Eusebius, *Ecclesiastical History*, 3:39).

The second, Irenaeus, Bishop of Lyons (A.D. 180), preserves the writings of Polycarp, Bishop of Smyrna, who had been a Christian for 86 years and was a disciple of John the apostle:

> So firm is the ground upon which these Gospels rest, that the very heretics themselves bear witness to them, and, starting from these, each one of them endeavours to establish his own particular doctrine (Irenaeus, *Against Heresies*, 3:1:1).

Polycarp was saying that the four gospel accounts about what Christ said were so accurate (firm) that even the heretics could not deny their record of events. Instead of attacking the scriptural account, which would have proven fruitless, the heretics started with the very teachings of Christ and developed their own heretical interpretations. Since they weren't able to say, "Jesus didn't say that..." they instead said, "This is what He meant..." You are on pretty solid ground when you get those who disagree with you to do that.

Archaeology also often provides powerful external evidence. It contributes to biblical criticism, not in the area of inspiration and revelation, but by providing evidence of accuracy about events that are recorded. Archaeologist Joseph Free writes: "Archaeology has confirmed countless passages which have been rejected by critics as unhistorical or contradictory to known facts" (Joseph Free, *Archaeology and Bible History*, Wheaton, IL: Scripture Press, 1969, p. 1).

Part of their message was, "We were eyewitnesses of it." Notice in Luke 3, verse 1, that there are 15 references given by Luke that can be checked for accuracy. "Now in the fifteenth year (that's one historical reference) of the reign of Tiberius Caesar (that's two references), when Pontius Pilate (three) was governor (four) of Judea (five) and Herod (six) was tetrarch (seven) of Galilee (eight) and his brother Philip (nine) was tetrarch (ten) of the region of Ituraea and Trachonitis (that's eleven and twelve), and Lysanias (thirteen), was tetrarch (fourteen) of Abilene (fifteen)."

Fifteen historical references in one verse, and they all can be checked for historical accuracy.

Luke at one time was considered incorrect for referring to the Philippian rulers as *praetors*. According to the "scholars," two *duumuirs* would have ruled the town. However, as usual, Luke was right. Findings have shown that the title of *praetor* was employed by the magistrates of a Roman colony.

Luke's choice of the word *proconsul* as the title for Gallio also has been proven correct, as evidenced by the Delphi inscription which states in part: "As Lucius Junius Gallio, my friend, and the proconsul of Achaia...."

The Delphi inscription (A.D. 52) gives us a fixed time period for establishing Paul's ministry of one and one-half years in Corinth. We know this by the fact, from other sources, that Gallio took office on July 1, that his proconsulship lasted only one year, and that that same year overlapped Paul's work in Corinth.

Luke gives to Publius, the chief man in Malta, the title "leading man of the island." Inscriptions have been unearthed which also give him the title, "first man."

Still another case for Luke's reliability is his usage of *politarchs* to denote the civil authorities of Thessalonica. Since *politarch* is not found in classical literature, Luke again was assumed to be wrong. However, some 19 inscriptions now have been found that make use of the title. Interestingly enough, five of these refer to leaders in Thessalonica.

Archaeologists at first questioned Luke's implication that Lystra and Derbe were in Lycaonia and that Iconium was not. They based their belief on the writings of Romans such as Cicero who indicated that Iconium was in Lycaonia. Thus, archaeologists said the book of Acts was unreliable. However, Sir William Ramsay found a monument that showed Iconium to be a Phrygian city. Later discoveries confirmed this.

Among other historical references made by Luke is that of "Lysanias the Tetrarch of Abilene" at the beginning of John the Baptist's ministry in 27 A.D. The only Lysanias known to ancient historians was the one who was killed in 36 B.C. However, an inscription found near Damascus speaks of the "Freedman of Lysanias the Tetrarch" and is dated between 14 and 29 A.D.

It is no wonder that E.M. Blaiklock, professor of classics at Auckland University, concludes that "Luke is a consummate historian, to be ranked in his own right with the great writers of the Greeks."

A True Picture

F.F. Bruce, of the University of Manchester, notes:

"Where Luke has been suspected of inaccuracy, and accuracy has been vindicated by some inscriptional evidence, it may be legitimate to say that archaeology has confirmed the New Testament record."

Bruce comments on the historical accuracy of Luke:

"A man whose accuracy can be demonstrated in matters where we are able to test it is likely to be accurate even where the means for testing him are not available. Accuracy is a habit of mind, and we know from happy (or unhappy) experience that some people are habitually accurate just as others can be depended upon to be inaccurate. Luke's record entitles him to be regarded as a writer of habitual accuracy" (Josh McDowell, *The Resurrection Factor*, San Bernardino, CA: Here's Life Publishers, 1981, pp. 34, 35).

There was a time in my life when I tried to shatter the historicity and validity of the Scriptures. But I have come to the conclusion that they are historically trustworthy. If a person discards the Bible as unreliable in this sense, then he or she must discard almost all the literature of antiquity. One problem I constantly face is the desire on the part of many to apply one standard or test to secular literature and another to the Bible. We need to apply the same test, whether the literature under investigation is secular or religious. Having done this, I believe we can say, "The Bible is trustworthy and historically reliable in its witness about Jesus."

I now understand why the classical Roman historian, Dr. A.N. Sherwin-White, writes, "For the New Testament book of Acts, the confirmation of historicity is overwhelming....Any attempt to reject its basic historicity, even in matters of detail, must now appear absurd. Roman historians have long taken it for granted" (A.N. Sherwin-White, *Roman Society and Roman Law in the New Testament*, Oxford: Clarendon Press, 1963, p. 189).

Dr. Clark Pinnock, professor of interpretations at McMasters University in Canada, after thorough research concluded, "There exists no document from the ancient world, witnessed by so excellent a set of textual and historical testimonies and offering so superb an array of historical data on which an intelligent decision may be made. An honest person cannot dismiss a source of this kind. Scepticism regarding the historical credentials of Christianity is based upon an irrational bias" (Clark Pinnock, *Set Forth Your Case*, Nutley, NJ: Craig Press, 1968, p. 58).

One can conclude that the New Testament gives an accurate portrait of Christ. This historical account of Him cannot be rationalized away by wishful thinking, historical manipulation or literary maneuvering.

IS MUHAMMAD FORETOLD IN THE BIBLE?

Muslims contend that the coming of Muhammad was foretold in the Bible. The scripture in the Qur'an used to support their claim is found in Surah 7:157:

> "Those who follow the Messenger, the Prophet of the common folk, whom they find written down with them in the Torah and the Gospel."

If these words are correct, then we should find reference to Muhammad the Prophet in the prophecies of Moses and the Gospels. The Islamic community has searched diligently to find the prophecies which support their belief that Muhammad's coming was indeed foretold. The Qur'an implies that these prophecies would be found in the Torah and the Gospel without much difficulty but Muslims have been surprised to discover that it is Jesus Christ who appears to be the subject of the many prophecies and not Muhammad.

THE ISLAM
DEBATE

There are divergent opinions in the Muslim world as to which prophecies of the Bible are the correct ones. The great majority of Muslims hold to Deuteronomy 18:18 as the reference from the Torah (the Jewish name for the first five books of Moses). The New Testament references to the "Comforter" in John 14-16 are believed to be the major Gospel reference to Muhammad.

Patrick Cate comments:

As there is a spectrum of Muslim's views concerning *tahrif* so there is also a wide variety of Muslim's views of the Bible's predictions of Muhammad. Some find many predictions, some find few and some find no predictions. The less corrupt one believes the Bible to be, the fewer predictions he tends to find (Cate, *Dissertation*, p. 78).

OLD TESTAMENT REFERENCE

I will raise up for them a prophet like you from among their brethren; and I will put my words in his mouth, and he shall speak to them all that I command him (Deuteronomy 18:18).

Muslims hold this to be a clear reference to the coming of Muhammad as predicted by Moses. The following reasons are given for believing the promised prophet is Muhammad:

1. The Qur'an is believed to be the Word of God and therefore, as Muhammad recited each passage that was delivered to him, he had the words of God put in his mouth in accordance with the words of this prophecy.

2. The prophet to come was to be from among the brethren of the Israelites, hence the Ishmaelites, because Israel (Jacob) and Ishmael were both descended from Abraham and the tribes who descended from the 12 sons of Ishmael are therefore "brethren" of the tribes who descended from the 12 sons of Israel. As Muhammad was the only Ishmaelite to claim prophethood in the line of the Old Testament prophets, they declare that the prophecy can only refer to him.

3. Muhammad was supposedly like Moses in so many ways that the prophecy can only refer to him.

However, when one considers any passage of Scripture, it must not be isolated from its context. The passage claims that the prophet would be raised up—

"From among their brethren."

The Muslim contention is that the identity of their brethren is the Ishmaelites. Ishmael was the half-brother of Isaac, who was born of Hagar to Abraham. The Arab race descends from Ishmael.

Technically, although the Israelite nation is descended from Isaac, the name of Israel was applied to Jacob, not Isaac. So, Israel and Ishmael are not related as brothers, but rather as uncle and nephew.

To understand the true identity of "their brethren" one must examine the context. Deuteronomy 18:1-2 reveals who is being described as "brethren":

"The *Levitical priests*, that is, all the tribe of *Levi*, shall have no portion or inheritance with *Israel...they* shall have no inheritance among *their brethren*" (Deuteronomy 18:1-2)

From this passage, one sees that "brethren" refers to the tribes of Israel (excluding Levi in this case). "Their brethren" is always seen not as the brother of Isaac, but the brothers from Jacob's house, or the 12 tribes of Israel. This is clear from other passages of Scripture as well, where the term "brethren" is used to delineate one tribe of Israel from the other 11. Let us consider this verse as an example:

"But the children of Benjamin would not harken to the voice of their brethren the children of Israel" (Judges 20:13 KJV).

Here "their brethren" is specifically stated to be the other tribes of Israel as distinct from the tribe of Benjamin. (Further Scriptures proving the point are Judges 21:22; 2 Samuel 2:26; 2 Kings 23:9; I Chronicles 12:32; 2 Chronicles 28:15; Nehemiah 5:1.)

An important passage to note in this discussion is Deuteronomy 17:14-15:

When you enter the land which the Lord your God gives you, and you possess it and live in it, and you say, "I will set a king over me like all the nations who are around me," you shall surely set a king over you whom the

DEBATE

Lord your God chooses, one from among your countrymen you shall set as king over yourselves; you may not put a foreigner over yourselves who is not your countryman (NASB).

The word "countryman" here is actually "brethren." No foreigner could be set as king. Clearly here, "brethren" refers to an Israelite; be he prophet, priest or king. Strong national unity and identity are characteristic of Judaism both spiritually as expressed in Scripture and traditionally, as expressed through customs. The context of "brethren" shows that this is to be understood as the tribes of Israel.

Secondly, the passages claims the fulfilment concerning the identity would be—

"In a prophet like you."

The prophet foretold by Moses was to be like Moses. The Muslim world claims that Muhammad was far more similar to Moses than was Jesus Christ, whom Christians hold to have fulfilled this prophecy.

Some of the similarities between Moses and Muhammad are:

1) Moses and Muhammad were lawgivers, military leaders, and spiritual guides of their peoples and nations.

2) Moses and Muhammad were at first rejected by their own people, fled to exile, but returned some years later to become the religious and secular leaders of their nations.

3) Moses and Muhammad made possible the immediate and successful conquests of the land of Palestine after their deaths by their followers, Joshua and Umar respectively.

At the same time, it is alleged in the Islamic Propagation Centre's publications that Jesus and Moses were so different that Jesus cannot be the prophet referred to. Such differences are:

1) Moses was only a prophet but Jesus is the Son of God.

2) Moses died naturally but Jesus died violently on a cross.

3) Moses was the national ruler of Israel which Jesus was not at any time during His ministry on earth.

We ask ourselves—do these similarities and contrasts in any way prove that Muhammad is the prophet like Moses? In actuality this reasoning does not assist us in discovering the real identity of the prophet. First, none of the alleged differences between Moses and Jesus are of vital importance. The Bible often calls Jesus a prophet as well as the Son of God (cf. Matthew 13:57, 21:11, John 4:44). The fact that Jesus died violently is not relevant to the issues at hand. Many prophets were killed by the Jews for their testimonies (cf. Matthew 23:31; Surah 2:91). Furthermore the Bible teaches that the Christian Church as a whole has replaced the nation of Israel in this age as the collective object of God's special favors. Likewise, whereas Moses led that nation during his life on earth, so Jesus today heads the Church of God from His throne in heaven above. In this respect, therefore, Jesus is really *like* Moses.

Second, if we reverse the process we can show many similarities between Moses and Jesus where Muhammad at the same time can be contrasted with them. Some of these are:

1) Moses and Jesus were Israelites—Muhammad was an Ishmaelite. (This is, as we have seen, a crucial factor in determining the identity of the prophet.)

2) Moses and Jesus both left Egypt to perform God's work—Muhammad was never in Egypt. Of Moses we read, "By faith he forsook Egypt" (Hebrews 11:27 KJV). Of Jesus we read, "Out of Egypt have I called my Son" (Matthew 2:15 KJV).

3) Moses and Jesus forsook great wealth to share the poverty of their people, which Muhammad did not. Of Moses we read, "He considered abuse suffered for the Christ greater wealth than all the treasures of Egypt" and that he chose "to share ill-treatment with the people of God" (Hebrews 11:25-26). Of Jesus we read, "For you know the grace of our Lord Jesus Christ, that though he was rich, yet for your sake he became poor, so that by his poverty you might become rich" (2 Corinthians 8:9).

So we have similarities between Moses and Jesus where Muhammad can be contrasted with them. This shows the weakness of trying to compare Moses with Muhammad. How then can we identify the prophet to be like Moses?

As there were numerous prophets down through the ages, it is logical to assume that this prophet would be uniquely like Moses in a way that

DEBATE

none of the other prophets were. Clearly the prophet to come would emulate Moses in the exceptional and unique characteristics of his prophethood. Indeed we would expect that God would give some indication in the prophecy of the distinguishing features of this prophet who was to be like Moses. We only need refer to the *context* of the prophecy to find this striking verse which clearly gives us an indication of the nature of the prophet to follow:

> The LORD your God will raise up for you a prophet like me from among you, from your brethren—Him you shall heed—just as you desired of the LORD your God at Horeb on the day of the assembly, when you said "Let me not hear again the voice of the LORD my God, or see this great fire any more, lest I die" (Deuteronomy 18.15-16).

The two distinguishing features of Moses as a prophet are clearly mentioned: he knew the Lord face to face and did great signs and wonders. The prophet like Moses would obviously have to do the same. Did Muhammad possess these exceptional characteristics by which the prophet was to be recognized?

First, God spoke directly to Moses, so that he was a direct mediator between God and Israel. The Qur'an is alleged to have come at all times from the angel Gabriel to Muhammad and at no time did God directly communicate it to him face to face, as the Muslims themselves admit.

Second, Muhammad performed no signs or wonders. Although the Hadith record some fanciful miracles, these are purely mythical, for the Qur'an clearly says of Muhammad that he performed no signs. In Surah 6:37, when Muhammad's adversaries say, "Why has no sign been sent down to him from his Lord?" Muhammad is bidden to reply merely that God could send one if he wanted to but had not done so. In the same Surah we read that Muhammad said, "I have *not* that for which you are impatient" (6:57), meaning signs and wonders. He goes on to say that if he had had them, the dispute between him and them would have been decided long ago. Again in the same Surah, Muhammad's adversaries say they will believe if signs come from God but he only replies that God has reserved them because they would still disbelieve anyway.

So we find that on earth Muhammad was not a direct mediator between God and man, nor could he do any signs and wonders to confirm his office. Deuteronomy 34:11 makes it essential that the prophet like Moses would do similar signs and wonders to those which Moses did.

Since Muhammad did not, we have a second fatal objection to the theory that he is the prophet foretold in Deuteronomy 18:18.

Jesus Christ has traditionally been recognized as the prophet promised in Deuteronomy 18:15-18. Evidence to support this can be cited from many sources, both biblical and historical. What is important to consider here is that the Jews did see Christ as fulfilling the prophecy as "The Prophet." Their mistake was not seeing the prophet as the Messiah as well.

Another favorite objection is that Jesus died at the hands of the Jews whereas God said, in Deuteronomy 18:20, that only the self-styled prophets would die. However, every prophet died—many violently as the Qur'an and the Bible jointly testify—and the mere physical death of a prophet was certainly no evidence against his divine mission. God certainly did not mean that every true prophet would not die! What he meant was that the false prophet would perish eternally—and all his prophecies with him. Only Judgment Day will reveal all the false prophets of the ages.

What we are ultimately concerned about is this—God gave a definite promise that a prophet would arise like Moses who would mediate another covenant and that signs would accompany this new covenant to confirm its heavenly origin. The Bible clearly affirms that that prophet was Jesus Christ. The apostle Peter, claiming that God had foretold the coming of Jesus Christ through all the prophets, appealed specifically to Deuteronomy 18:18 as proof that Moses had done so (Acts 3:22). Jesus Himself claimed, "Moses wrote of me" (John 5:45) and it is difficult to find elsewhere in the five books of Moses such a direct prophecy of His advent. Peter chose Deuteronomy 18:18 as the one distinctive prophecy of the coming of Jesus Christ in all the writings of Moses.

Likewise in Acts 7:37 Stephen appealed to Deuteronomy 18:18 as proof that Moses was one of those who had "announced beforehand the coming of the Righteous One," Jesus, the one whom the Jews had recently betrayed and crucified.

After witnessing all the things that Jesus had done and after taking part in the new covenant which He had mediated face-to-face between God and His people, the early Christians knew that Jesus was the prophet whose coming was foretold in Deuteronomy 18:18. They also knew that the prophecy of a prophet to come like Moses had been supplemented by

THE ISLAM
DEBATE

God's promise to the prophet Jeremiah that He would mediate a new covenant in the days to come between Himself and His people:

> Behold, the days are coming, says the LORD, when I will make a new covenant with the house of Israel and the house of Judah, not like the covenant which I made with their fathers when I took them by the hand to bring them out of the land of Egypt, my covenant which they broke, though I was their husband, says the LORD. But this is the covenant which I will make with the house of Israel after those days, says the LORD: I will put my law within them, and I will write it upon their hearts; and I will be their God, and they shall be my people. And no longer shall each man teach his neighbor and each his brother, saying, "Know the LORD," for they shall all know me, from the least of them to the greatest, says the LORD; for I will forgive their iniquity, and I will remember their sin no more (Jeremiah 31:31-34).

The covenant was to be different from that given through Moses but the prophet who would mediate it would be like him. And we read "Therefore (Jesus) is the mediator of a new covenant" (Hebrews 9:15). To ratify the first covenant, we read that:

> Moses took the blood and threw it upon the people, and said, "Behold the blood of the covenant which the Lord has made with you in accordance with all these words" (Exodus 24:8).

Unlike the Israelites under the old covenant who fell by the wayside, the people of God through this new covenant have come "to the assembly of the first-born who are enrolled in heaven, and to a judge who is God of all, and to the spirits of just men made perfect, and to Jesus, the mediator of a new covenant, and to the sprinkled blood that speaks more graciously than the blood of Abel" (Hebrews 12:23-24).

When he spoke to God face-to-face, "Moses did not know that the skin of his face shone because he had been talking with God" (Exodus 34:29-30). When the image of the invisible God was directly revealed through the transfigured face of Jesus Christ "his face shone like the sun" (Matthew 17:2). No other prophet could claim such a distinction— no one else knew God face to face in such a way that his face shone while he communed with Him.

So it seems evident that Muhammad is not foretold in Deuteronomy 18:18 but rather that the prophet whose coming was foretold in that verse was Jesus Christ.

We will now see in the New Testament that Jesus Christ is the climax of all prophecy in all the revealed scriptures of God. For all the promises, revelations and blessings of God are vested in Him—the fountain-head of the love and favor of God towards men.

We will also see even more clearly that in the Torah and the Gospels there is only one Savior, one Man through whom alone the favor of God can be obtained. While there were many prophets in ages past—both true and false—yet there is for us only one Lord and one Savior—Jesus Christ. Again it will be seen how deeply God wishes to impress this truth upon all men that they may believe in and follow Jesus Christ into the Kingdom of Heaven.

NEW TESTAMENT REFERENCE

The most familiar New Testament Gospel reference cited by Muslims to support their claim of Muhammad being foretold in the Bible is found in the "Comforter" passages from John's account of the Upper Room Discourse. Whereas the Revised Standard Version of the Bible uses the word "Counsellor" rather than "Comforter," we shall use the word "Comforter" throughout this section. It is more familiar to the Muslims and will help the Christian relate to them better. The references are as follows:

And I will pray the Father, and he will give you another *Comforter*, to be with you for ever, even the *Spirit of truth*, whom the world cannot receive, because it neither sees him nor knows him; you know him, for he dwells with you, and will be in you (John 14:16-17).

But the *Comforter*, the *Holy Spirit*, whom the Father will send in my name, he will teach you all things, and bring to your remembrance all that I have said to you (John 14:26).

But when the *Comforter* comes, whom I shall send you from the Father, even the *Spirit of truth*, who proceeds from the Father, he will bear witness to me (John 15:26).

Nevertheless I tell you the truth: it is to your advantage that I go away, for if I do not go away, the *Comforter* will not come to you; but if I go, I will send him to you (John 16:7).

THE ISLAM
DEBATE

It is generally alleged by the Muslims that the Greek word "paracletos" (meaning Comforter, Counsellor, Advocate, etc. in effect, one who unites men to God) is not the original word but that Jesus in fact foretold the coming of Muhammad by name and that the translation of his name into Greek (or at least the meaning of his name in Greek) is "periklutos," that is, the "praised one."

There is no evidence in favor of the assertion that the original word was "periklutos." We have thousands of New Testament manuscripts pre-dating Islam, none of which contains the word "periklutos." A cursory reading of the texts where the word "paracletos" appears will show that this is the only word that suits the context.

Many Muslims actually admit that "comforter" is the correct translation, and then claim Muhammad was the comforter that Jesus referred to there. The Christian community understands the Comforter to be the Holy Spirit, who comes to dwell in the believers after Pentecost.

In light of the clear references in John to the fact that the Comforter is the Holy Spirit (John 14:17 & 26; 15:26; 16:13), it is hard to draw any other valid conclusion. A careful study of the passage helps identify the Comforter as the Spirit, and not Muhammad.

It does seem clear from the four texts quoted that Comforter, Holy Spirit and Spirit of Truth are interchangeable terms and that Jesus is speaking of the same person in each instance. The one fact that emerges is that the Comforter is a *spirit*. The fact that Jesus always speaks of the Spirit in the masculine gender in no way suggests that the Comforter must be a man as some Muslim publications suggest. God Himself is always spoken of in both the Bible and the Qur'an in the masculine gender and God is spirit—John 4:24. In the same way Jesus always speaks of the Comforter as a *spirit* and not a *man*.

If we apply sound exegesis to John 14.16-17, we will discover no less than eight reasons why the Comforter cannot possibly be Muhammad.

1. "He will give *you* another Comforter."

Jesus promised His disciples that God would send the Comforter to *them*. He would send the Spirit of Truth to Peter, and to John, and to the rest of the disciples—and not to Meccans or Medinans or Arabians.

2. "He will give you *another* Comforter."

If, as Muslims allege, the original word was *periklutos* and that Christians changed it into *paracletos*, then the sentence would have read "He will give you another praised one" and this statement is both out of place in its context and devoid of support elsewhere in the Bible. Jesus is never called the *periklutos* in the Bible (the word appears nowhere in the Bible) so it is grossly unlikely that He would have said "He will give you another praised one" when He never called Himself by that title.

John 16:12-13 makes it clear that the word *paracletos* is the correct one. The text reads "I have yet many things to say to you, but you cannot bear them now. When the Spirit of Truth comes, He will guide you into all the truth." In other words, I have been your Comforter, your *paracletos*, and have many things to tell you, but I send the Spirit of Truth to you, another Comforter, another *paracletos*.

In 1 John 2.1 we read that Christians have an "advocate" with the Father, "Jesus Christ the Righteous" and the word translated "advocate" is *paracletos* in the Greek. So Jesus is our *paracletos*, our advocate.

3. "To be with you *forever*."

When Muhammad came he did not stay with his people forever but died in A.D. 632 and his tomb is in Medina where his body has lain for over 1,300 years. Nevertheless, Jesus said that the Comforter, once He would come, would never leave His disciples but would be with them forever.

4. "The Spirit of truth whom the world *cannot* receive."

The Qur'an says that Muhammad was sent as a universal messenger to men (Surah 34.28). If so, Jesus was not referring to Muhammad for He said that the world as a whole cannot receive the Comforter, the Spirit of Truth.

5. "You *know* him."

It is quite obvious by this statement that the disciples knew the Spirit of Truth. As Muhammad was only born more than 500 years later, it certainly could not be him. The next clause brings out just how the disciples knew Him. Quite clearly we can see at this stage that the Comforter is a spirit who was in the presence of the disciples already.

6. "He dwells *with* you."

Where did the Comforter dwell "with them"? From various verses, especially John 1:32, we can see that the Spirit was in Jesus Himself and so was with the disciples.

7. "He will be *in* you."

Here a strong blow is dealt to the theory that Muhammad is the Comforter, the Spirit of Truth. As the Spirit was *in* Jesus, so He would be *in* the disciples as well. The Greek word here is *en* and this means "right inside." So Jesus was in fact saying, "He will be right inside you."

8. The last reason is really a re-emphasis of the first one. Do you notice how often Jesus addresses His *own disciples* when He speaks of the sphere of influence of the Comforter? "*You* know Him...He dwells with *you*...He will be in *you*." Quite clearly the disciples were to anticipate the coming of the Comforter as a spirit who would come to them just after Jesus had left them. No other interpretation can possibly be fairly drawn from this text.

Let us read of how the Spirit came to Jesus: "The Holy Spirit descended upon him in bodily form, as a dove" (Luke 3:22). We read that the Spirit, the Comforter, came to the disciples in a similar way shortly after the ascension of Jesus (as Jesus had told them He would): "And there appeared to them tongues as of fire, distributed and resting on them. And they were all filled with the Holy Spirit" (Acts 2:3-4). He was *with* the disciples in the person of Jesus (while He was with them) and He was *in* the disciples from the day of Pentecost.

Within only ten days after the ascension of Jesus, the disciples duly received the Comforter as He was promised to them by Jesus. He had told them to wait in Jerusalem until the Holy Spirit, the Comforter, should come (Acts 1:4-8) as indeed He did while they were all together praying for his advent in the city. Muhammad does not seem in view here in any way.

Moving on now to John 16:7 (quoted earlier) the whole meaning of this verse also becomes clear from the statement of Jesus: "I have many things to say to you, but you cannot bear them now" in John 16:12. Jesus said, "It is to your advantage that I go away." The disciples could not bear His teaching now because they were ordinary men devoid of power to comprehend or apply what He said. The Spirit of Truth was indeed in Jesus but was not yet in His disciples, so they were unable to follow the spiritual elements in His teaching. But after the ascension they received the Spirit and could now communicate and understand His teaching because the Spirit of Truth was in them as well. That is why Jesus said "it is to your advantage that I go away." Paul makes this equally clear:

> "…what no eye has seen, or ear heard, nor the heart of man conceived, what God has prepared for those who love him," God has revealed to us through the Spirit. For what person knows a man's thoughts except the spirit of the man which is in him? So no one comprehends the thoughts of God except the Spirit of God. Now we have received not the spirit of the world, but the spirit which is from God, that we might understand the gifts bestowed on us by God (1 Corinthians 2:9-13).

Paul makes it plain that the Spirit had already been given and if He had not, it could not have been to any advantage to the disciples to be without Jesus.

So it appears evident that Muhammad is not the Spirit of Truth, the Comforter, whose coming Jesus foretold. Who is the Comforter then? He is the very Spirit of the Living God as can be seen from some of the quotations already given. On the day when the Comforter came upon the disciples, His coming was accompanied by a tremendous sound "Like the rush of a mighty wind" (Acts 2:2). When the Jews heard this, they rushed to see what was happening. Peter, the disciple, declared to all those gathered together:

> This is what was spoken by the prophet Joel: "And in the last days it shall be, God declares, that I will pour out *my Spirit* on all flesh" (Acts 2:16, 17).

The Comforter, the Spirit of God, had come down on the disciples as promised by Jesus and was to be given to believing Christian men and women from every nation under the sun. But notice how carefully Peter immediately linked the coming of the Spirit, the Comforter, with the ascension of Christ:

> This Jesus God raised up, and of that we are all witnesses. Being therefore *exalted* at the right hand of God, and having received from the Father the

promise of the *Holy Spirit*, he has poured out this which you see and hear (Acts 2:32-33).

Clearly the coming of the Comforter was inseparably linked to the risen, ascended and glorified Jesus in the highest place that heaven affords. The Comforter is also called the "Spirit of Christ" (Romans 8:9) and the reason is plain from what Jesus said:

1. "He will *glorify me*" (John 16:14).

2. "He will bear witness to *me*" (John 15:26).

3. "When he comes he will convince the world concerning sin because they do not believe in *me*" (John 16:8-9).

4. "He will take what is *mine* and declare it to you" (John 16:14).

5. "He will bring to your remembrance all that *I* have said to you" (John 14:26).

Quite obviously the great work of the Comforter is to do the work of bringing people to Jesus, making them see Him as Savior and Lord, and drawing them to Him. The Comforter was given so that the glory of Jesus might be revealed to men and in men. A beautiful example of this is given by John:

His disciples did not understand this at first; but when Jesus was glorified, then they remembered that this had been written of him and had been done to him (John 12:16).

Without the Spirit, they had no understanding, but when they received the Spirit after Jesus was glorified, then they remembered as Jesus said they would. John illustrates this in another passage as well:

On the last day of the feast, the great day, Jesus stood up and proclaimed, "If any one thirst, let him come to me and drink. He who believes in me, as the scripture has said, 'Out of his heart will flow rivers of living water.'" Now this he said about the *Spirit*, which those who believed in him were to *receive;* for as yet the Spirit had *not* been given, because Jesus was not yet *glorified'* (John 7:37-39).

As soon as Jesus was glorified the Spirit was given so that the glory of Jesus in heaven might become real to men here on earth. As Peter said (Acts 2:33), once Jesus was *exalted* at the right hand of God, the Spirit was given freely by God as He had promised to all true believers.

Again Peter said, "The God of our fathers *glorified* Jesus" (Acts 3:13). We cannot see or comprehend this glory of Jesus Christ here on earth (and Jesus Himself said, "I do not receive glory from men"—John 5:41), but He sent the Spirit to us so that we could behold this glory by the eye of faith. As Jesus Himself said to the disciples of the Spirit:

> He will glorify me, for he will take what is mine and declare it to you. All that the Father has is mine, therefore I said he will take what is mine and declare it to you (John 16:14-15).

Jesus Christ spoke to his own disciples of the coming of the Comforter because the Spirit was sent down to comfort and regenerate all true believers in Jesus. This is one of the most significant and consistent elements of the teaching of Jesus about the Comforter. The prime purpose of the coming of the Comforter—immediately after the ascension of Jesus—was to draw men to Him so that those who are influenced by the work of the Comforter will therefore become followers of Jesus.

Far from Muhammad being foretold in the Bible, every prophecy, every agent of God, every true prophet and spirit, rather looks upward toward the radiance of the Father's glory, the one who sits upon the throne, the Lord Jesus Christ.

Jesus Christ ascended to heaven—God the Father took Him to Himself. Jesus alone is the Redeemer of the world. He alone is able to enter the holy presence of the Father's throne and fill it with His own glorious majesty. So likewise He is able to reconcile sinful men to God and will one day be seen again in all His splendor as He comes to call His own—those who eagerly awaited His coming and all those who now look forward to His return from heaven—to be with Him where He is to behold the glory which the Father gave Him before the foundation of the world.

Moses rejoiced when speaking of the prophet to come who was Jesus Christ. The Comforter, the Holy Spirit, still rejoices to reveal His glory and majesty to those in whom He dwells. The angels and departed saints await the day when every knee shall bow and every tongue shall confess that it is Jesus Christ who is Lord—to the everlasting glory of God the Father.

THE ISLAM
DEBATE

THE GOSPEL OF BARNABAS

Muslims hold that the Christian account of the life of Jesus in the gospels is not authentic, but rather that the truth is to be found in the Gospel of Barnabas. This gospel, purportedly written in the first century by the apostle Barnabas, contains prophecies in reference to the coming of Muhammad, a denunciation of Paul and his ministry, and teaching which rejects the deity, messiahship and the uniqueness of Jesus. One can see how influential this issue is on the textual history of the Qur'an and Muhammad being foretold as a prophet.

Islam believes that Christianity deliberately suppressed the teaching of the Gospel of Barnabas with its strong pro-Islamic stance in order to promote the Christian gospel. However, there is no evidence to support the Muslim claim—either for the existence of a historical document written by the apostle Barnabas or for any suppression of such a document by the early Christian community.

This is an important issue to resolve because much of the historical evidence (if not most of it) which Muslims use to support the teaching of the Qur'an over and against the Bible finds its source in the Gospel of Barnabas. The Gospel of Barnabas in recent years has been distributed fairly widely throughout the Muslim world in many languages.

Since 1973 the English translation of the Gospel of Barnabas by Lonsdale and Laura Ragg has been reprinted in large numbers by the Begum Aisha Bawany Wakf in Pakistan.

Muslims have been persuaded that this book tells the ultimate truth about the life and teachings of Jesus Christ. It alleges that Jesus was not the Son of God, that He was not crucified, and that He foretold the coming of Muhammad. As a result some Muslims believe that this is the true *Injil* that was given to Jesus. The Gospel of Barnabas, however, does not claim to be the Injil but actually distinguishes itself from the book allegedly given to Jesus:

> The angel Gabriel presented to him as it were a shining mirror, a book, which descended into the heart of Jesus, in which he had knowledge of what God hath done and what he hath said, and what God willeth insomuch that everything was laid bare and open to him; as he said unto me: "Believe, Barnabas, that I know every prophet with every prophecy, insomuch that whatever I say the whole hath come forth from that book" (Barnabas 10).

Other Muslims believe that the Gospel of Barnabas is the "original testament" and that the Christians have substituted it with the "New Testament." Such an attitude betrays an ignorance, not only of the Gospel of Barnabas, but also of the structure of the Christian Bible as a whole.

This chapter does not purport to be an in-depth analysis of the ongoing scholarly study that is being conducted into the background and origins of the Gospel of Barnabas. For this we are indebted chiefly to the Raggs, who first translated the Gospel into English, and to men like Gairdner, Jomier and Slomp who have gone to great lengths in the cause of truth to provide substantial evidence of the falsehood of the Gospel of Barnabas. Rather we have endeavored to produce here a summary of some of the proofs which have come from these studies to share with our Muslim friends so that they may have a better understanding of the historical background and inaccuracy of the Gospel of Barnabas.

WHO WAS BARNABAS?

Barnabas is first encountered in the Book of Acts. James Cannon, writing in *Muslim World*, gives this account of Barnabas' life:

> The New Testament book of Acts knows a wealthy Cypriot Jew, a Levite, of generous spirit and broad sympathies, the friend and sponsor of Paul, and like the latter, though not one of the original twelve, eventually honored by the title of apostle. Beyond the record of his association with Paul in missionary service, their eventual separation, and incidental mention of him in two of Paul's epistles, the New Testament is silent (James Cannon, "The Gospel of Barnabas," *Moslem World*, III, 1942, 32:167-168).

HISTORICAL BACKGROUND

The next mention of Barnabas is found in a decree which was supposedly given by Pope Gelasius I in the late fifth century. Here, the Gospel of Barnabas is mentioned as forbidden to Christians because of its heretical teaching. The book was of Gnostic origin, which means those who wrote it denied such key teachings as the deity of Christ. The Gnostics taught that matter was evil and that the spiritual world was superior. This view caused them to deny the incarnation of Jesus; that God took on human flesh. Gnostic books also had critical and negative teaching on the apostle Paul and his ministry. All this doctrine would fall well in line with Muslim doctrine.

Concerning this fifth century reference, Cannon comments:

> Special significance attaches here as showing that a Gnostic Gospel of Barnabas might have been in circulation, though condemned by Christian authority, in 550-600 A.D., the approximate time of Mohammed. From such a source some gleams of knowledge of supposedly orthodox Christian tradition might be imagined as filtering into Mohammed's slender stock of Christian information. Indeed the glaring absurdities of the Koran account of Christ can be accounted for only on the ground that Mohammed knew the Christian tradition by hearsay fragments.

> (Of this lost Gnostic gospel but a single unimportant sentence in Greek has come down to us. A tradition asserts that when the alleged body of Barnabas was exhumed it had a copy of the gospel by Matthew clasped to its breast, and that this gospel contained a denunciation of St. Paul.) This could obviously be, not the canonical gospel, but an apocryphal work claiming Matthew's authority. Incidentally, the present text of the Gospel of Barnabas contains in its opening and closing paragraphs a dissent from St. Paul. All Gnostic literature made Paul its object of attack.

> The lost Gnostic "Gospel of Barnabas" would probably have had much greater kinship to a Mohammedan version of the gospel than can be shown between it and the New Testament writings. Such things as the "painless birth," the type of eschatology, the elimination of John the Baptist, and the Docetic Passion, would all seem to be items that would appeal both to Gnostics and to Moslems.

> The next appearance of the name of Barnabas is in the so-called Gelasian Decree. This documents contains a list of permitted and forbidden books, and lists as forbidden "The Gospel of Barnabas." It is safe to assume that the ground of the prohibition was the supposed Gnostic teaching of the book, since the Decree itself was an anti-Gnostic document, and the name of this particular book appears in the list with other better known Gnostic material. Several points engage our attention here:

> 1. The first use of the title, "Gospel of Barnabas."

> 2. The Gnostic background of the book. This is of interest because the denial of the divinity of Jesus found in Gnosticism is in accord with what we might expect in a Moslem account of the life of Christ, since Moslems accept him historically and as a great prophet, denying to him only divinity and Messiahship.

3. The date of the Gelasian Decree. Catholic tradition has assigned this document to Gelasius I, Pope from 492-496, but modern critical scholarship offers conclusive evidence to prove that whatever may have been the connection of Pope Gelasius with this list, or with a shorter and earlier list, the complete Gelasian Decree cannot be earlier (James Montague Rhodes, *The Apocryphal New Testament*, Oxford: The Clarendon Press, 1924, p. 21). (ibid., pp. 168-69).

Before citing the next historical reference to the Gospel of Barnabas, it should be mentioned that beyond the biblical account, there is nothing known of what happened to the apostle Barnabas. Somewhat reliable tradition has Barnabas both in Alexandria and Rome. In fact, another apocryphal book, the Epistle of Barnabas, came from Alexandria. This is *not* to be confused with the Gospel of Barnabas. The Gospel is the one we are concerned with. The apocryphal Epistle has no correlation with the Islamic Community. It is the Gospel of Barnabas the Muslims believe to be a genuine account.

The next mention of the Gospel comes from the 18th century, where an Italian copy of the manuscript was found. This version of the Gospel of Barnabas is undoubtedly a forgery and certainly does not have its origin in the first century.

The manuscript quotes a variety of lines from the Qur'an. This brings up two important points. First, this account of the Gospel of Barnabas must be later than the seventh century, when the Qur'an was written. Second, because of its relation to the Qur'an, it *cannot* be historically related to the original apocryphal Gospel of Barnabas, the one mentioned in the Gelasian Decree, although the author could well have been familiar with its heretical teachings.

Not only does this Italian copy of the Gospel of Barnabas quote from the Qur'an, it takes statements from the Italian author, Dante, who wrote the *Divine Comedy* in the 13th century.

Cannon states:

> *Despite the numerous contacts between Christians and Moslems during the Crusades and the Moslem invasion of Europe, there is no hint that such a book was known to either side. Francis of Assisi, 1182-1286, though residing for a month at the court of the Sultan of Egypt, never heard of it.* Raymond Lull, 1235-1315, the first man to offer a program of intellectual and spiritual approach to Moslems, as contrasted with the

THE ISLAM
DEBATE

program of force, lived a long life devoted to research in all forms of Moslem lore, but gives no hint of having heard of such a work, though he lived in direct contact and controversy with intelligent Moslems at three different periods of his life (ibid., pp. 169-170).

The only known manuscript in existence is the Italian. In 1784 there was said to be a Spanish translation of the Italian, but it has since disappeared. No one has ever mentioned or seen the original copy in Arabic. And there is no evidence to support its existence.

EXAMINATION OF THE GOSPEL

Was Barnabas Really Its Author?

This book professes to be a Gospel and alleges that its author was the apostle Barnabas. To determine this, we must make some comparisons between the knowledge that we have of the real apostle Barnabas in the Bible and the professed author of the Gospel of Barnabas. At the beginning and end of the gospel, two comments appear which immediately assist us in our quest. They are these:

> Many, being deceived of Satan, under pretense of piety, are preaching most impious doctrine, calling Jesus son of God, repudiating the circumcision ordained of God for ever, and permitting every unclean meat: among whom Paul also hath been deceived (Barnabas, Prologue).

> Other preached that he really died, but rose again. Other preached, and yet preach, that Jesus is the Son of God, among whom is Paul deceived (Barnabas 222).

The author of this book uses strong language to denounce the teachings of Paul, especially regarding circumcision; the crucifixion, death and resurrection of Jesus; and the Christian belief that Jesus is the Son of God. The whole book abounds in discourses levelled against those things which the author particularly takes Paul to task for, and there can be no doubt that the author of this book is poles apart from Paul and his doctrine and is diametrically opposed to his preaching and teaching. This is strong evidence against the authenticity of the book.

When examining the history of Barnabas in the Bible we find, as previously mentioned, that he only appears among the apostles *after* the ascension of Jesus to heaven when the early Christian Church was taking root in the land of Palestine. As a gesture of faith and love towards his brethren, he sold a field he owned and gave the proceeds to the apostles for distribution at their discretion to those who were in need among the brethren. This gesture of kindness was a great source of encouragement to the believers and the apostles accordingly named him "Bar-nabas," which means "son of encouragement." Before this he had been known only by his common name Joseph (Acts 4:36).

Here the author of the Gospel of Barnabas makes a serious blunder for he suggests throughout his book not only that Barnabas was actually one of the 12 disciples of Jesus during His ministry on earth, but also that he was known by this name "Barnabas" throughout that period of ministry. On more than one occasion in the book we find that Jesus allegedly addressed him by name and the first occasion, which comes particularly early in the book, is this one:

> Jesus answered: "Be not sore grieved, Barnabas; for those whom God hath chosen before the creation of the world shall not perish" (Barnabas 19).

Now here is an anachronism which destroys the possibility that this book was really written by the apostle Barnabas. The apostles only gave him the name "Barnabas" (son of encouragement) *after* the ascension of Jesus because of the generous act he had done which had heartened the spirits of the early Christians. But the Gospel of Barnabas makes Jesus call him by this name some three years *before* He ascended to heaven. This is a serious objection to the claim that this book was written by the apostle Barnabas.

The next time Barnabas appears in the early events of the Church was on the occasion of Paul's first visit to all the apostles in Jerusalem. Because the apostles knew that Paul had in previous years been a relentless persecutor of the early Christians (primarily because they believed that Jesus was the Son of God), the apostles and other Christians in Jerusalem doubted whether he really was now converted to their faith. It is indeed a revelation to discover, in the light of the vehement attacks made on Paul in the Gospel of Barnabas, just who it was who went to great pains to assure the brethren in Jerusalem that Paul was really a disciple:

> But Barnabas took him, and brought him to the apostles, and declared to them how on the road he had seen the Lord, who spoke to him, and how at

Damascus he had preached boldly in the name of Jesus (Acts 9:27).

We are now confronted with a second serious chain of evidence against the suggestion that Barnabas was the author of the "Gospel" attributed to him. Only seven verses earlier we read that when Paul engaged in public preaching in the synagogue of Damascus, "immediately he proclaimed Jesus, saying, 'He is the Son of God' " (Acts 9:20). When this same Paul came to Jerusalem, it was Barnabas who vigorously defended him as a true disciple of Jesus.

What a contrast we have here with the book we are considering where the author, supposedly Barnabas, takes Paul to task for the very fact that he was proclaiming that Jesus was the Son of God. The true Barnabas was the right-hand man of this very Paul who publicly taught that Jesus was indeed the Son of God. It is this same Barnabas who represented him at Jerusalem and who spared no effort in persuading the disciples there that Paul really was a disciple of Jesus.

In this chapter, we shall attempt to show that the Gospel of Barnabas was first written not earlier than *14 centuries* after Christ and that the author, whoever he was, simply chose to make Barnabas the alleged author of his forgery. The men we referred to earlier, who have made much in-depth study into the origins and sources of the Gospel of Barnabas, have also tried to ascertain why the real author of this book chose to make Barnabas its supposed author.

When the church in Jersalem heard that the church in Antioch was growing well, the apostles decided to send Barnabas there to take over the teaching and instruction of the new believers. But Barnabas, of his own volition, decided that he could not handle this by himself, and decided to obtain the assistance of a fellow believer, well-grounded in the faith, for this work. Without hesitation Barnabas went all the way to Tarsus in Asia Minor to find *Paul.* He brought Paul to Antioch to assist him in the instruction of the church. We read of their ministry:

> For a whole year they met with the church, and taught a large company of people; and in Antioch the disciples were for the first time called Christians (Acts 11:26).

Paul and Barnabas then went to Jerusalem with aid for the brethren because of a famine in the days of the Roman Emperor Claudius (Acts 11:28-30). After this Paul and Barnabas returned to Antioch (Acts 12:25).

They continued to lead the church there and subsequently were sent out by the church to preach the gospel in the provinces of Galatia (part of Turkey as we know it today).

Wherever they went Paul and Barnabas preached that Jesus was the Son of God and that God had raised Him from the dead (cf. Acts 13:33). And yet, the author of the Gospel of Barnabas would have us believe that Barnabas was an arch-enemy of Paul on these matters! We even find them *both* proclaiming that the restrictive ordinances of Judaism (e.g., circumcision) should not be forced upon the Gentiles and that they were unnecessary for salvation. A very interesting event in their joint ministry is recorded in these words:

> But some men came down from Judea and were teaching the brethren, "Unless you are circumcised according to the custom of Moses, you cannot be saved." And when Paul and Barnabas had no small dissension and debate with them, Paul and Barnabas and some of the others were appointed to go up to Jerusalem to the apostles and the elders about this question (Acts 15:1-2).

Certain Judaizers had come among the early Christians stating that circumcision was necessary for salvation. Who do we find debating hotly with them on this point? None other than Paul and Barnabas!

And yet, in the Gospel of Barnabas, we read that one of the "impious doctrines" that Paul was holding to was repudiation of circumcision. That he repudiated it was an essential element of salvation we will readily concede (Galatians 5:2-6)—but his chief partner in this repudiation is none other than Barnabas!

According to the Gospel of Barnabas, Jesus is alleged to have said to His disciples:

> Leave fear to him that hath not circumcised his foreskin for he is deprived of paradise (Barnabas 23).

Thus circumcision is an essential element and a prerequisite of salvation in the Gospel of Barnabas and the author obviously assents to this doctrine. But of the real Barnabas we read that he joined with Paul in debating *against* the doctrine of the Judaizers that circumcision was necessary for salvation. It appears clear that the real Barnabas was not the author of the book that bears his name and that someone else not only forged this book but misrepresented the name of its author as well.

THE ISLAM
DEBATE

The current publishers of the Gospel of Barnabas (Begum Aisha Bawany Wakf) are well aware that the major objective of the Gospel of Barnabas is to counteract "Pauline Christianity." In an appendix entitled "Life and Message of Barnabas" they allege that the passage about the debate on the issue of circumcision reveals a growing rift between Paul and Barnabas. They quote Acts 15:2 (quoted above) and shamelessly comment "After this rift, there was a parting of the ways" between Paul and Barnabas (6th edition, p. 279). But it is quite obvious that the rift was *not* between Paul and Barnabas on the issue, but between the certain men from Judea on the one hand, who were glorifying circumcision, and Paul and Barnabas on the other, who were furiously against perverting the freedom of Christians with legalistic restrictions of no value. Because this sixth edition of the Gospel of Barnabas has become a standard edition of this book, we must say that its whole article in the appendix is a misrepresentation of the true relationship between Paul and Barnabas.

There is no evidence that Paul and Barnabas ever disagreed on a matter of doctrine. They once had a minor personal dispute when Paul did not wish to take John Mark on a missionary journey as he had fallen back on a previous one (Acts 15:38-40). This, however, was purely a personal matter which was clearly resolved as we see in other passages in the Scriptures (Colossians 4:10, 2 Timothy 4:11). On one other occasion, Barnabas was guilty of some religious discrimination with other Jewish Christians in Antioch when they would not eat with the Gentile Christians (Galatians 2:13). Paul censured this strongly but this was also not about a doctrinal matter but one of common fellowship among all Christians no matter what their background. None of these minor disputes had anything to do with the fundamental doctrines Paul and Barnabas so rigidly promoted—the repudiation of circumcision as necessary for salvation, the crucifixion and resurrection of Jesus Christ and the basic doctrine that Jesus is the Son of God. Rather, the evidence shows that Barnabas was the prime vindicator of these doctrines which Paul taught.

Another point from within the Gospel of Barnabas shows that the author could not be the real apostle Barnabas. The Gospel of Barnabas makes Jesus consistently deny that He is the Messiah and yet the same book calls Jesus "the Christ" (Prologue). "Christos" is the Greek translation of Messiah and "Jesus Christ" is an anglicised form of the Greek *Iesous Christos*, meaning "Jesus the Messiah." The very real contradiction that exists here within the Gospel of Barnabas is further evidence that the author was not Barnabas himself. He came from Cyprus, an island where Greek was the common tongue and Greek would have been his home language. The real Barnabas would never have made a mistake like calling Jesus the Christ and then denying that he was the Messiah.

Evidence of Its Medieval Origin

We possess much evidence today that the Gospel of Barnabas was first written in the Middle Ages—more than a thousand years after Christ and many hundreds of years after Muhammad.

The Centenary Jubilee. In the time of Moses God ordained that the Jews were to observe a jubilee year twice a century in these words:

> A jubilee shall that fiftieth year be to you (Leviticus 25:11).

Throughout the centuries this command was observed and the Roman Catholic Church eventually took it over into the Christian faith. About A.D. 1300 Pope Boniface VIII gave a decree that the jubilee should be observed once every hundred years. This is the first occasion that the jubilee year was made to be only once every hundred years. After the death of Boniface, however, Pope Clements VI decreed in 1343 that the jubilee year should revert to once every 50 years, as it was observed by the Jews after the time of Moses. Now we find in the Gospel of Barnabas that Jesus is alleged to have said:

> And then through all the world will God be worshipped, and mercy received, insomuch that the year of jubilee, which now cometh every hundred years, shall by the Messiah be reduced to every year in every place (Barnabas 82).

Only one solution can account for this remarkable coincidence. The author of the Gospel of Barnabas only quoted Jesus as speaking of the jubilee year as coming "every hundred years" because he knew of the decree of Pope Boniface. But he could not know of this decree unless he lived at the same time as the Pope or sometime afterwards. This anachronism leads us to conclude that the Gospel of Barnabas could not have been written earlier than the 14th century after Christ.

This means that the Gospel of Barnabas dates at least 700 years after the time of Muhammad and has no authenticated historical value. Although it often makes Jesus predict the coming of Muhammad by name (which is one major reason it is a best-seller in the world of Islam today), since it was written after the death of Muhammad, the "prophecies" are of no value. The Gospel of Barnabas contains many discourses and practices fully synonymous with the basic teachings of Islam—but these too are of no value because the book was written at least 700 years after the advent of Islam.

Quotations from Dante. Dante was an Italian who, significantly, also lived about the time of Pope Boniface and wrote his famous *Divina Comedia* in the 14th century. Essentially, this was a fantasy about hell, purgatory and paradise according to the Roman Catholic beliefs of his times.

In the Gospel of Barnabas we read that Jesus allegedly said of the prophets of old:

> Readily and with gladness they went to their death, so as not to offend against the law of God given by Moses his servant, and go and serve false and lying gods (Barnabas 23).

The expression "false and lying gods" *(dei falsi e lugiardi)* is found elsewhere in the Gospel of Barnabas as well: in 78 it is Jesus again who allegedly uses these words, in 217 it is the author himself who describes Herod as serving "false and lying gods." Nevertheless this expression is found in neither the Bible nor the Qur'an. What is interesting is that it is a direct quote from Dante! (Inferno 1.72). Many of the descriptions of hell in the Gospel of Barnabas (59-60) are reminiscent of those in the third canto of Dante's *Inferno.*

Likewise the expression "raging hunger" *(rabbiosa fame)* is reminiscent of the first canto of Dante's *Inferno.* Later in the Gospel of Barnabas the descriptions of hell are strikingly similar again to those in Dante's. Both speak of the "circles of hell" and the author of the Gospel of Barnabas also makes Jesus say to Peter:

> Know ye therefore, that hell is one, yet hath seven centres one below another. Hence even as sin is of seven kinds, for as seven gates of hell hath Satan generated it: so are there seven punishments therein (Barnabas 135).

This is precisely Dante's description found in the fifth and sixth cantos of the *Inferno.* We could go on and quote many more examples but space here demands that we press on. One striking quote must be mentioned, however, because in this case the Gospel of Barnabas agrees with Dante while contradicting the Qur'an. We read in the Qur'an that there are seven heavens:

> He it is Who created for you all that is in the earth. Then turned He to the heaven, and fashioned it as seven heavens. And He is the Knower of all things (Surah 2:29).

On the contrary we read in the Gospel of Barnabas that there are nine heavens and that Paradise—like Dante's Empyrean—is the tenth heaven above all the other nine. The author of the Gospel of Barnabas has Jesus say:

> Paradise is so great that no man can measure it. Verily I say unto thee that the heavens are nine...I say to thee that paradise is greater than all the earth and all the heavens together (Barnabas 178).

The author of the Gospel of Barnabas knew Dante's work and did not hesitate to quote from it.

This book often makes Jesus state that He is not the Messiah but that Muhammad would be the Messiah. This is a constant recurring theme in the Gospel of Barnabas. Two quotes show not only that Jesus did not consider Himself the Messiah but preached that Muhammad was to be the Messiah. "Jesus confessed and said the truth, 'I am not the Messiah, I am in descent to the house of Israel as a prophet of salvation but after me shall come the Messiah' " (Barnabas 42, 82).

Other passages in the Gospel of Barnabas contain similar denials by Jesus that He was the Messiah. One of the expressed purposes of the book is to establish Muhammad as the Messiah and to subject Jesus to him in dignity and authority. Here, the author has overreached himself in his zeal for the cause of Islam. The Qur'an plainly admits that Jesus is the Messiah on numerous occasions and in doing so it confirms the teaching of Jesus as the Messiah (John 4:26, Matthew 16:20). One quote from the Qur'an will help to prove the point:

> O Mary! Lo! Allah giveth thee glad tidings of a word from Him, whose name is the Messiah, Jesus, son of Mary, illustrious in the world and the Hereafter (Surah 3:45).

The Gospel of Barnabas was written as an ideal "Islamic" Gospel, setting forth a life of Christ in which He is made to be the *Isa* of the

Qur'an rather than the Lord Jesus of the Christian Gospels. But as it contradicts both the Qur'an and the Bible on the fact that Jesus was the Messiah and does this so often consistently, it should be rejected as a forgery by both Christian and Muslim alike.

Who Actually Composed This Forgery?

There are only two known manuscripts of the Gospel of Barnabas which existed before any copies were made from the texts available to us. The Italian version is in a library today in Vienna whereas only fragments remain of the Spanish version. George Sale, in his comments on the Gospel of Barnabas in his *Preliminary Discourse to the Koran*, speaks of a complete Spanish version which he saw personally. It appears that the Spanish version may well have been the original one. In the introduction to this version it is claimed that it is a translation of the Italian version, but numerous spelling errors in the Italian version—typical of an author using Italian as a second language—certainly show at least that the author was more at home in Spanish than in Italian. Nevertheless this does not negate the possibility of someone from Spain trying his hand at composing an "original" in Italian. This possibility is made all the more real by two considerations. First, the author often quotes the Vulgate (Latin translation of the Bible) and has borrowed many of his stories from the Scriptures. He might well have found it more convenient to use the Italian language medium for his own contrived composition.

Second, he might have thought that his book would look far more authentic if it were written in Italian. It would serve to substantiate the introduction of the Spanish version where it is alleged that the Gospel of Barnabas was originally hidden in the Pope's library before it was discovered in rather questionable circumstances by a certain Fra Marino who allegedly became a Muslim after reading it.

Certain features, however, substantiate the suggestion that this book was first written in Spain by a Spaniard, no matter what language he originally wrote it in. The Gospel of Barnabas makes Jesus say:

> For he who would get in change a piece of gold must have sixty mites (Barnabas 54).

The Italian version divides the golden "denarius" into 60 "minuti." These coins were actually of Spanish origin during the Visigothic period and betray a Spanish background to the Gospel of Barnabas.

No one knows who actually wrote the Gospel of Barnabas, but what is known is that whoever it was, it was not the apostle Barnabas. Most probably it was a Muslim in Spain who, possibly the victim of the reconquest of his country, decided to take private revenge by composing a false Gospel under the assumed name of Barnabas to give his obnoxious forgery some measure of apparent authenticity. He probably first composed the Gospel in Italian to maintain this appearance of genuineness but simultaneously composed (or arranged for such a translation) a Spanish version for distribution in his own country. He may well have been Fra Marino or he may have been the translator Mustafa de Aranda. He was someone far more at home in Spain in the Middle Ages rather than in Palestine at the time of Jesus Christ.

Whatever the Gospel of Barnabas may claim to be, whatever it may appear to be, a general study of its contents and authorship shows that it is an attempt to mold the life of Jesus into the Qur'an and Islamic tradition.

THE CRUCIFIXION AND RESURRECTION IN THE QUR'AN AND THE BIBLE

THE CRUCIFIXION OF JESUS CHRIST IN THE BIBLE

The Scriptures contain the main historical record of the life and teaching of Jesus Christ. They tell us that His life ended when He was 33 years of age and that He was crucified by the hand of the Roman rulers of Israel at the instigation of the Jewish leaders who hated Him because He claimed to be the Messiah and vociferously denounced them as hypocrites. The Bible does not view His death on the cross as the martyrdom of a prophet but rather as the deliberate outworking of God's plan of salvation for mankind. It tells us that Jesus died willingly as an atonement for the sins of men, rose from the dead three days later, and triumphed over sin and death. Forty days later Jesus ascended to heaven and sat down at the right hand of the Majesty on high.

The Christian Church throughout the world for 20 centuries has held a unanimous opinion on the crucifixion, death and resurrection of Jesus Christ and to this day there is no dispute among Christians as to what happened to Him. We all believe He was crucified for our sins and raised for our salvation.

This consensus has resulted from the unambiguous testimony of the Bible to these facts. The following texts are examples of clear statements in the Bible about the crucifixion, death and resurrection of Jesus Christ. Ten days after His ascension to heaven the apostle Peter addressed the Jews, gathered in Jerusalem for one of their major feasts, with these words:

> This Jesus, delivered up according to the definite plan and foreknowledge of God, you *crucified* and *killed* by the hands of lawless men (Acts 2:23).

In these words we find incontrovertible testimony to the crucifixion and death of Jesus Christ. The apostle Paul makes a similar statement about Him in these words:

> He humbled himself and became obedient unto *death*, even death on a *cross* (Philippians 2:8).

Addressing the Jews on another occasion the apostle Peter gave a similar testimony of His resurrection from the dead:

> By the name of Jesus Christ of Nazareth, whom you *crucified*, whom God *raised* from the *dead* (Acts 4:10).

Likewise we read in one of the Gospels that an angel spoke to some of the women who had followed Jesus as they visited His tomb on the day of His resurrection:

> I know that you seek Jesus who was *crucified*. He is not here; for he has *risen*, as he said. Come, see the place where he lay. Then go quickly and tell his disciples that he has risen from the *dead* (Matthew 28:5-7).

In all these texts we find one concurrent theme—that Jesus was crucified, that He died on the cross, and that He was raised to life again by the power of God (cf. 1 Corinthians 15). The Bible is a clear record left to the Christian Church and its testimony has been accepted without dispute in all quarters of the Church throughout history. While some may not believe what it says, it is difficult to deny what it claims.

THE DENIAL OF THE CRUCIFIXION IN THE QUR'AN

In the Qur'an, however, the crucifixion of Christ is mentioned only once and contradicts the biblical account. The Qur'an states:

> They said "We killed Christ Jesus the son of Mary, the Apostle of God," but they killed him not, nor crucified him, but so it was made to appear to them, and those who differ therein are full of doubts with no certain knowledge, but only conjecture to follow. For a surety they killed him not: Nay, God raised him up unto Himself, and God is Exalted in Power, Wise (Surah 4:157-158).

These words are spoken in response to a boast of the Jews that they had killed Jesus Christ. The Qur'an, however, denies either that Christ was crucified *or* that He was killed.

Therefore the Bible and the Qur'an clearly contradict each other on this issue. We should consider that the Bible not only gives an historical record of the crucifixion on the strength of the divine authority of Holy Scripture, but that it does so in clear terms. The Qur'an teaches emphatically that Christ was not crucified, although its explanation appears somewhat ambiguous. We hope to show that the Qur'an does not take into account all the facts of history in its treatment of the crucifixion and resurrection.

In our view, one conclusion unavoidable from the text quoted is that the Qur'an teaches that Jesus was never put on the cross. This fact has become the foundation of the orthodox opinion in Islam on the fate of Jesus. The words that follow this denial, namely *"but so it was made to appear to them,"* tend to suggest that, whereas Christ was not crucified, God made it appear to the Jews that they had in fact crucified Him. This is interpreted by most orthodox Muslims to mean that God made someone else look like Jesus and that this person was crucified instead. Finally, the words *"God raised Him up to Himself"* are taken to mean that Jesus was raised alive to heaven without dying. This theory of substitution has been the basic doctrine on the fate of Jesus in orthodox Islam from the time of Muhammad until now, though, as we shall see, there is apparently irreconcilable dispute on this point among Muslims even to this day. Let us consider a few quotes from commentators who hold to the orthodox view. One makes this comment on Surah 4:157:

> After this, God, Who can do any and everything He wills, raised Jesus to Himself and rescued him from crucifixion and the one who was crucified

afterwards was somehow or other taken for Christ (Maududi, *The Meaning of the Qur'an*, p. 390).

Immediately we can detect some uncertainty on the part of the commentator who says that someone else was *somehow or other* taken for Jesus. A similar sense of ambiguity is shown in this comment as well:

> It was not Jesus who was executed but another, who was miraculously substituted (how and in what way is another question, and is not touched upon in the Qur'an) for him (Maulana Abdul Majid Daryabadi, *Holy Qur'an*, Karachi: Taj Company Ltd., 1970, p. 96).

These authors speak vaguely about what really took place that day. The reason is that the expression "*so it was made to appear to them*" is ambiguous and none of the commentators is therefore able to make dogmatic statements about its interpretation. Nevertheless, while the whole theory of substitution has a vague foundation, we intend to assess it on another ground altogether—and that is the wide range of serious moral implications that arise from it.

THE MUSLIM THEORY OF SUBSTITUTION

First, the suggestion that God transformed another man's appearance to make him look like Jesus immediately implies that the Supreme Being does not consider it fraudulent to misrepresent one man as another. We consider it a felony to forge a signature on a check or to impersonate another person. Surely this theory imputes such guile to God and makes him guilty of doing something fraudulent.

We cannot accept the reply so often ventured that God can do what He likes and that He was merely giving a demonstration of His power. We know that God has the power to do anything He wishes, but, just as holy men do not exercise their power to rob, pillage, assault and destroy, so the God who shows himself Holy and righteous (Isaiah 5:16) takes no delight in wickedness and under no circumstances will He or can He show His power by doing something which is morally wrong. In our view this suggestion that God changed the features of a bystander to look like Jesus is nothing less than blasphemy and attributes actions to God which are considered reprehensible when committed by men. Christians believe in the absolute honesty and justice of God and therefore must reject this suggestion.

Some Muslim writers and traditionists have been acutely aware of the shortcomings of a theory which claims that God was the cause behind the agonizing death of an innocent bystander and they have suggested that it was Judas Iscariot who was made to look like Jesus. In this way they hope to minimize the obvious fallacy of the theory for it was this man who betrayed Jesus and, if he can be identified as the victim, the charge that an innocent bystander was victimized falls away. There is no evidence either in the Qur'an or in any pre-Islamic book to back up this suggestion. Necessity though, is the mother of invention. (The *Gospel of Barnabas* makes Judas the victim after the *wonderful God acted wonderfully* in transforming him to look like Jesus.)

Others say Judas, or another bystander, looked like Jesus and was crucified by mistake. Those who make this suggestion are trying to avoid both difficulties—the misrepresentation by God and the execution of an innocent victim. This claim must be rejected, however, on at least two counts. First, the mother of Jesus and a few of His closest disciples stood at the foot of the cross—surely they would have recognized the error. Second, the Qur'an says it was made to appear to the Jews that they had crucified Jesus and these words imply that the substitution came about as a result of a deliberate act of God to effectively cause it.

Second, we must ask whether the substituted victim was made to think he was Jesus as well as look like Him. Surely another man would have raged from the cross that he was not Jesus and that a mistake had been made. Instead we read that the man crucified had something to say when he saw the mother of Jesus and his closest disciple at the foot of the cross:

> He said to his mother, "Woman, behold, your son!" Then he said to the disciple, "Behold, your mother" (John 19:26-27).

Who else but Jesus could have spoken these words? One only has to read through the serene statements made by Jesus before the High Priest and the Roman Governor Pontius Pilate to see immediately that the very man tried and executed could be none other than Jesus Christ Himself.

Third, if God chose to raise Jesus to heaven, why was it necessary for Him to satisfy the Jews by victimizing an innocent bystander? We cannot see what purpose was being served in this action. Why allow an innocent man (one at least innocent of the alleged crime of Jesus) to suffer an agonizing death purely so that the people could be satisfied in thinking that they had crucified Jesus? We Christians believe in a God of eternal wisdom—but for our part we can see no wisdom at all in this.

Fourth, if the man who was crucified was made to look like Jesus, surely no one can be blamed for thinking it really was Jesus. All His disciples certainly believed it was He for they preached the crucifixion of Christ wherever they went. For three years they had followed Jesus and to what end—a deception by the Almighty which they proclaimed for the rest of their lives and, for many, at the expense of their lives? Can one really believe such a thing?

The substitution theory implies that God is callous and dishonest and that He cares little for the death of an innocent bystander or for the grief of the closest disciples or one of His prophets. The theory is contradictory with the nature of God as presented in the Gospel narratives in which the God of eternal love spared not His own Son but gave Him up for us all that He might reconcile us to Himself.

"HAZRAT ISA IS DEAD!" — A MODERN ALTERNATIVE

Ever since Christian missionaries began serious evangelism among Muslims in the last century, many Muslims have sought an alternative to the substitution theory. Whereas the Qur'an states that Jesus was no more than a messenger like those who had passed away before Him (Surah 5:75), His virgin birth, ascension and return make Him obviously far more than a messenger and decidedly unique among men. These doctrines seem to support the Christian belief that He is the Son of God far more than the Muslim belief that He was just a prophet.

After all, the other prophets were born naturally and died naturally and therefore, these Muslims have reasoned, if Jesus was just like them He must be reduced to their level and be shown to have lived an ordinary life and to have died naturally at the end of it. Therefore some Muslims have proposed an alternative theory—*Hazrat Isa* (Jesus), they say, *is dead.* They allege that He died a natural death some years after His alleged ascension to heaven.

During 1978 a huge controversy raged in South Africa over the proposed distribution of a book entitled *The Message of the Qur'an* which is an English translation and commentary on the Qur'an by Muhammad Asad. The debate centered on this comment on the relevant verse to the crucifixion, Surah 4:157:

> Nowhere in the Qur'an is there any warrant for the popular belief that God has "taken up" Jesus bodily, in his lifetime, to heaven (p. 135).

Many orthodox Muslim publications in South Africa, such as *The Majlis* and *The Muslim Digest*, are strongly opposed to this interpretation and devoted whole issues to exhaustive proofs in favor of the substitution theory. They challenged those Muslims who advocate the alternative theory to come into the open and publicly identify themselves. None had the courage to do so. One of them, who protected his anonymity by hiding behind the *nom de plume* "Special Correspondent," wrote an article in the September 1978 issue of the *Al-Qalam* on the subject entitled *Is the Question "Hazrat 'Isa Alive or Dead," Part of Iman?* In the article this very interesting statement occurs indicating a frank admission of confusion on the real meaning and interpretation of Surah 4:157:

> The event of the "raf" (ascension) and "wafat" (death) of Hazrat Isa (A.S.) belong to those verses of the Qur'an which are called the "Mutashabihat" the true interpretation of "which is known only to Allah" (Qur'an 3.7, p. 15).

The Islamic Council of South Africa eventually declared that it rejected Asad's views and that it subscribed to the beliefs held by the overwhelming majority of the Muslims of the world that Jesus was taken alive to heaven and that He would return to earth (*The Muslim Digest*, Oct./Nov. 1978, p. 3).

While we do not hold to the substitution theory, we Christians do believe that it is the only reasonable one that can be drawn from the vague statements of the Qur'an. We reject the alternative theory that Jesus died a natural death many years later as being unworthy of serious consideration for the following reasons:

1. *Origin*. This theory is of fairly recent origin. In early Islam all the traditions that arose, although often confusing and contradictory at times, supported the substitution theory in one form or another.

2. *Cause.* The alternative theory has arisen not from a sincere study of the sources and evidences available in the Qur'an and Hadith but purely as a negative reaction against Christian beliefs.

3. *Credibility.* The testimony of history is set against any idea that Jesus lived on earth beyond the age of 33. There is no evidence to support any theory that His earthly life and ministry continued after the time of His recorded crucifixion and ascension to heaven. (The substitution theory is consistent with the evidence of history in this respect.) Furthermore, the Bible and the Qur'an both plainly state that Jesus was sent expressly to Israel (Matthew 15:24 and Surah 61:6), and He could not therefore have continued a lengthy ministry elsewhere as is sometimes suggested.

The Christian Church spread rapidly after the ascension of Jesus to Heaven. Surely if Jesus was still alive in Israel, conducting His prophetic ministry, this phenomenal spread would never have occurred. It was opposed on many grounds but never on the assumption that Jesus was still alive on earth.

We are constrained to ask those who promote this theory to tell us when Jesus died, where His death occurred, and how it happened. Until such facts are presented to us we can only dismiss it as a fallacy based not on factual evidence but more on Islamic interests.

Finally we must say it appears to militate against the teaching of Surah 4:157 as well. It is suggested by those who promote it that the words "God took him to Himself" mean that at the end of His natural life some years later, God exalted Him spiritually to Himself. For two reasons this escapist interpretation must be rejected. First, the Arabic word *rafa'a* principally implies a bodily ascension and, second, the action of God is set in immediate contrast to the attempt of the Jews to crucify Jesus. The clause surely is an explanation as to *why* they did not kill Him—at that moment God raised Him to Himself. It is introduced with a deliberate "but"—implying that what follows was the immediate action of God to prevent the crucifixion of Christ. We feel that the sensible interpretation that can be drawn from the words quoted in Surah 4:157 is that God took Jesus alive to heaven.

Teachings of
Islam

THE ISLAMIC SWOON AND ITS AHMADIYA ORIGIN

Many Muslims are acutely conscious of the inherent weaknesses of the various interpretations of Surah 4:157 and in desperation have decided that the best policy is to steer clear of the Muslim theories and attack the Christian standpoint instead.

One such Muslim is Ahmed Deedat of Durban, South Africa. In 1975 co-author John Gilchrist held a symposium with him in Benoni, South Africa, on the subject, *Was Christ Crucified?*, and, having read his booklet of the same title, pleaded with him to confine himself to a sound exposition of the Qur'anic attitude to the crucifixion. Instead he merely repeated the contents of his booklet, attacking the biblical narratives instead. He tried to prove that Jesus had not died on the cross but had come down alive in a *swoon* and that He had later recovered His health. The only way he could press this theory on his audience was to expediently overlook the wealth of evidence in the Bible that Jesus died on the cross.

In *Christianity Explained to Muslims* in the chapter on "The Historicity of the Crucifixion," Lewis Bevan Jones discusses the Ahmadi view:

> The Muslim professes not to believe in the death of Jesus, at least *that is the view of the preponderating orthodox party* [italics added]. The modern nationalist, on the other hand, asserts…that it was not on the cross that He died.

> We have here an amazing feature in Islam: the vast majority of the Muslim people have always held, and do still hold, that God, in the phrase of the Qur'an "took up" Jesus to heaven, so that He escaped death that day at the place called Golgotha. But now, *over against this centuries-old traditional belief, the Ahmadis have propounded the view that Jesus after all did die and that a natural death, at some other time and place* [italics added]. Both parties seek support for their opinions in such verses of the Qur'an as refer to the subject. We are required, therefore, to examine rather closely the particular language used at these places.

> The relevant passages are:

> "The peace of God was on me the day I was born, and will be the day I shall die *(amutu)*, and the day I shall be raised to life" 19:34.

> "And the Jews plotted, and God plotted. But of those who plot God is the best. Remember when God said, 'O Jesus, verily I will cause thee to die…

and will take thee up...to myself and deliver thee from those who believe not.' "

"And for their (Jews) saying, 'Verily we have slain the Messiah, Jesus the son of Mary, an Apostle of God'—yet they slew him not, and they crucified him not, but they had only his likeness. And they who differed about him were in doubt concerning him: no sure knowledge had they about him but followed only an opinion; and they did not really slay him, but God took him up...to Himself. And God is Mighty, Wise" 4:159.

(Jesus speaks) "I was a witness of their actions while I stayed among them: but since Thou has taken me to Thyself...Thou has Thyself watched them and Thou art witness of all things" 5:117 (Lewis Bevan Jones, *Christianity Explained to Muslims*, Calcutta, India: Baptist Mission Press, 1964, pp. 75, 76).

Jones then goes on to explain the orthodox view, that Jesus did not die, but was taken up to heaven. Then he offers comment on the swoon theory, which he calls the rationalist view:

In more recent times Muslim rationalists have been busy trying to reconcile these conflicting statements in the Qur'an, and the Ahmadis are persuading themselves that they have at length found a more correct interpretation of the Arabic. The meaning they have put upon these passages is not only a repudiation of the traditional view in Islam, but a shrewd blow aimed at the very foundation of the Christian faith.

Thus, according to Mirza Ghulam Ahmad of Qadian, "Jesus did not die upon the cross but was taken down by his disciples in a swoon and healed within forty days by a miraculous ointment called in Persian *marham-i-'Jsa*, 'the ointment of Jesus.' He then travelled to the east on a mission to the ten lost tribes of the children of Israel, believed by Ahmad to be the peoples of Afghanistan and Kashmir, and finally died at the age of 120, and was buried in Kahn Vau Street, in Srinagar, the capital of Kashmir."

It will be noticed that the Mirza makes nothing of the statement in the Qur'an to the effect that confusion prevailed as to who was actually crucified (see p. 77). Instead, he puts forward this notion *which has no support whatever in the Qur'an*, that Jesus merely swooned on the cross and was revived. But this idea was not his own invention, even though his imagination undoubtedly was. He borrowed it, and in considerable detail, from the west (ibid., pp. 82, 83).

The swoon theory has no biblical basis but is contrary to Muslim beliefs as well. The author of the article in the *Al-Qalam* previously referred to stated that whatever a Muslim might believe about the ascension and return of Jesus, one thing could not be disputed—the Qur'an denies that Jesus was ever crucified. To *crucify* obviously means to *affix to a cross* and therefore the Qur'an obviously denies that Jesus was ever put on a cross. Deedat's theory suggests that He was, however, and to get around this difficulty he constantly maintains that to crucify means to *kill* on a cross and that if a man does not *die* on the cross, he cannot be said to have been crucified!

This peculiar line of reasoning is an attempt to reconcile the swoon theory with the Qur'anic denial of the crucifixion. Deedat alleges that if it is proved that Jesus came down alive from the cross, this shows he was never crucified! In his booklet he says *even if Jesus was taken to the cross—he was not crucified* (p. 33). If the word *crucify* only means *to kill on a cross*, we are at a loss to find an alternative verb to describe the mere act of *impaling on a cross.* (Even though Deedat claimed he was proving that Jesus was not crucified, the *Benoni City Times* the Friday after the symposium summed up his theory very neatly: "He was crucified but did not die, he argued.")

There are many Muslim writers who have been unable to resist the temptation and have adopted Deedat's view, having tried to attack the biblical basis of the crucifixion on the grounds that the texts of the Gospels can be distorted and perverted into giving the impression that Jesus survived the cross. Examples are A.D. Ajijola in his book *The Myth of The Cross* (Lahore: Islamic Publications Ltd., 1975), Ulfat Aziz-us-Sammad in her book *A Comparative Study of Christianity and Islam* (Lahore: Sh. Muhammad Ashraf, 1976) and W.J. Sheard in his booklet *The Muth of the Crucified Saviour* (Karachi: World Federation of Islamic Missions, 1967). The latter author, however, has exposed the whole fallacy of the theory and has frankly admitted that the texts of the Bible cannot, by any fair means of exegesis, yield this interpretation. He says in his booklet on page 1:

> The only way open to a seeker of truth is to read between the lines in the various verses of the Gospels in order to be able to find out the truth (W.J. Sheard, *The Myth of the Crucified Saviour*, Karachi: World Federation of Islamic Missions, 1967, p. 1).

Sheard knew that the plain teaching of the Bible is that Jesus died on the cross and that he must come to this conclusion by a fair, impartial and objective study of the Scriptures. But Sheard, like Deedat, Ajijola and others, was not interested in reading the lines to find meaning; his interest lay between the lines.

Where does this theory come from? As Jones states, the theory is not of recent origin:

> (The swoon theory) was advanced over a century ago by the German rationalist Venturini, who wrote a romance in which he suggested that, since death by crucifixion is a very slow process, Jesus when taken down from the cross after some six hours was not in reality dead, but in a swoon. Having been laid in a cool cavern He was revived by the application of healing ointments and strongly scented spices. Dr. Paulus and the still more famous Schleiermacher lent their support to this extravagant theory, but it was ridiculed by no less a person than the skeptic Strauss (Jones, *Christianity Explained*, p. 82).

He states concerning Ahmad, who adopted this theory:

> However, the point to bear in mind is that Ghulam Ahmad sought in this way not only to deny the historicity of the Resurrection, but to proclaim that Jesus is dead. And in this all Ahmadis are simply repeating what he gave out (ibid., p. 84).

Perhaps if the average Muslim were aware that it is the basic belief of the Qadianis who belong to the *Ahmadiya Movement* founded by Mirza Ghulam Ahmad, he would give it no credibility at all. The Ahmadiya branch of Islam is considered by many Muslims to be outside the fold of the true Muslim faith. This is because some of its doctrines run against traditional Islam, although they are similar on most points. The most prominent differences occur in doctrines that would better support Islam against Christianity. This is due to the fact that the main characteristic of the Ahmadiyas or Qadianism is their strong stand against the Christian faith. It is not Christians or most Muslims who believe it, it is mainly a dogma of *Qadianism*. Consider this quote from the one-time President of the Ahmadiyah-Anjuman-Ishaat-I-Islam of Lahore which follows numerous evidences of the Sheard-type to show that Jesus came down alive from the cross:

> All these facts point conclusively to the truth of the statement made in the Holy Qur'an that Jesus was not killed, nor did he die on the cross, but was likened to one dead and thus escaped with his life, afterwards dying a natural death, as is affirmed by the Holy Qur'an (Moulvi Muhammad Ali, *Muhammad and Christ*, Lahore: Ahmadiah Anjuman-I-Ishaet-I-Islam, 1921, p. 141).

The same writer, in his commentary on the Qur'an, makes the following comment on Surah 4:157:

> The word does not negate Jesus being nailed to the cross but it negates his having expired on the cross as a result of being nailed to it...The circumstances relating to the crucifixion, far from showing that Jesus died on the cross, clearly proved that he was taken down alive (Maulvi Muhammad Ali, *The Holy Qur'an*, pp. 241, 243).

In the Ahmadiya textbook on the life and status of Jesus we read a similar statement:

> It does not seem legitimate to doubt the historicity of the fact that Jesus was put on the cross, but exception can be taken to the details in the Gospel account and it can be established that he did not die on the cross (Khwaja Nazir Ahmad, *Jesus in Heaven on Earth*, p. 185).

It is clear that Deedat has been promoting a Qadiani theory to Christians and Muslims. A perusal of Deedat's booklet shows that if he did not borrow his arguments chiefly from those in Ahmad's book, they are similar to the Qadiani author.

A modern Muslim writer in a recent book rejects the whole swoon theory as a "baneful attempt...to strike a new historical trend...to the effect that Jesus was put up on the crucifix, was released half dead, met with slow ultimate death, and was buried in some obscure place in Kashmir" (S.M.B. Alam, *Nuzul-e-Esa: The Descension of Jesus Christ*, p. 46). His reasons and writings should be examined by all Muslims today.

The Qadianis want us to believe that both the Bible and the Qur'an support the swoon theory in defiance of their plain statements to the contrary. The Bible says Jesus *was* crucified and killed (Acts 2:23) while the Qur'an says he *was not* (Surah 4:157). The following examines the Islamic view of the swoon theory as expressed by Ahmed Deedat, a follower of the Ahmadiya position.

AHMED DEEDAT'S "WAS CHRIST CRUCIFIED?"

The following is a reply to some of Deedat's major points set out on pages 31 and 32 of his booklet *Was Christ Crucified?* and also to his *Resurrection or Resuscitation* and *Who Moved the Stone?*

THE ISLAM
DEBATE

Point 1. Jesus was reluctant to die. Throughout the Gospels we find that Jesus displayed remarkable fortitude in the face of impending death. He went up to Jerusalem knowing beforehand that He would be crucified (Luke 18:31-34), and when the Jews came to arrest Him one night in a garden near the city, He calmly walked forward, knowing all that was to befall Him (John 18:4). He went precisely where He knew they would look for Him (John 18:2) and without resistance gave Himself over to them, even though He could have called on more than 12 legions of angels to deliver Him (Matthew 26:53). Instead of being reluctant to die, He was determined to give up His life.

He calmly took all the insults and injuries heaped on Him the following day and, without any sign of fear or protest, gave Himself over to be crucified. As He was taken out of Jerusalem He showed more concern for the women of the city and their children than for Himself (Luke 23:28) and on the cross cared only for those around Him (John 19:26-27). Indeed, instead of finding that He was reluctant to die, we discover in the gospel narratives that He set his face toward the cross and, although He had many opportunities to avoid it, He did not seize them but went on, determined to redeem men from their sins (Luke 9:22, 51; 18:31).

The only reluctance He showed was when He fell on His face in the garden and pleaded: "My Father, if it be possible, let this cup pass from Me, nevertheless, not as I will, but as Thou wilt" (Matthew 26:39). This plea arose not from a fear of the cross. Christ's words reflect the agony facing Him, not His reluctance to carry out the Father's will. The pain was real; true love reflects pain. Our life cost Christ His, but He chose it. If Christ had been afraid, it would have been supremely manifested in His greatest moment of agony—on the cross.

Up to that time Jesus had enjoyed the full presence and fellowship of His Father and now He was to be handed over to sinners. Nothing ever motivated Jesus but the will and good pleasure of His Father (John 14:31), and He had never known the presence or effect of sin in His life. Jesus had only one supreme dread—to be forsaken of His Father and to be found in the realm of sin and at the mercy of sinners. To redeem the world, it was necessary that He should be made sin for us (2 Corinthians 5:21) and endure the consequences of our iniquities. Jesus showed a godly fear of sin and its effects—a holy fear most men lack, to their eternal peril. At the prospect of the *spiritual sufferings* that awaited Him He recoiled, but as His love for sinners was stronger than His fear of dying for our sins, He sought strength to endure the agonies that lay before Him.

Points 2 to 4. *He beseeched God for help, God "heard" His prayers, the angel strengthened Him.* These three points are coincidental and can be treated as such.

One finds little logical progression of thought in Deedat's argument that an angel was sent to comfort Jesus and that God was going to save Him (p. 13). If so, surely God would have taken Him away immediately. What sort of "comfort" or "strengthening" could the angel have given Him if God's hand was only to be revealed after hours of indescribable agony and torture to the point of death on the cross?

First, such pain and suffering would have been unnecessary and God's deliverance would have come about after a tragic delay. Second, it could have been no comfort to Jesus to know that He faced the horrors of crucifixion only to be delivered at the point of death. Furthermore, if Jesus was taken down alive from the cross because He was so close to death that all thought He was already dead, we cannot see how God "saved" Him or where He even intervened.

The whole argument is strained against the logical progression of the events in the Gospels. The truth of the whole matter is that Jesus was physically at the breaking point at the prospect of suffering for sin. He had just told His disciples that His soul was exceedingly sorrowful— even unto death (Mark 14:34). God heard the prayer of Jesus and the angel gave Him strength to proceed and endure the cross and death and so fulfill His mission to redeem sinners from sin, death and hell.

To save Jesus from dying, while at the point of death after hours of agony on the cross, would have been an untimely and senselessly delayed deliverance accompanied by a lengthy period of painful recovery from the horrific ordeal. To save Him from death by resurrecting Him in perfect health is sensible and also in line with the biblical account of the crucifixion.

Points 5 and 6. *Pilate finds Him "not guilty" and his wife sees a dream to save a "just man."* These two points were advanced in support of point 12 which will be dealt with later.

Point 7. *On the cross for only three hours.* This is not true as Jesus was on the cross for six hours. Deedat quoted Jim Bishop's book *The Day*

THE ISLAM
DEBATE

Christ Died elsewhere in his booklet, but ignored him on page 289: "Jesus willed himself to die." Jesus said:

> No one takes [My life] from Me but I lay it down of My own accord. I have power to lay it down and power to take it again; this charge have I received from My Father (John 10:18).

We see this proved in the sequence of events which surround His death. A man who was crucified would normally expire after many hours of hanging limp on the cross with his body sagging and his head drooping. Jesus, however, was nowhere naturally near the point of death. When He knew in His eternal spirit that He had fully accomplished His work of salvation, however, He cried out, "It is finished," and He bowed His head and gave up His spirit (John 19:30). Herein lies the key to His death. For all its horrors the cross could not sap His strength. But in perfect dignity He deliberately bowed His head and consciously exercised His power to lay down His life. He willed Himself to die. Three days later, by the same power, He raised Himself from the dead.

Point 8. *The other two were still alive.* This argument falls away in the light of what has just been said. These two men were suffering as criminals and could not give up their lives as Jesus could. Jesus willed Himself to die, they could not.

Point 9. *Encyclopaedia Biblica says, "Was alive when spear was thrust."* On page 3 of his booklet Deedat claimed that he was advancing evidence from *the Bible itself* to refute the doctrine of the crucifixion. Here, however, he has been forced to refer to an external source. The account of an eyewitness, in any event, must always be preferred to any other. The account of the eyewitness is based on fact whereas the latter comment is based on speculation at best. And the account of the eyewitness, the apostle John, is that Jesus was already dead when the spear was thrust (John 19:33, 34).

Point 10. Deedat claims that *Jesus' legs were not broken.* The decision by the soldiers not to break the legs of Jesus is conclusive proof that He was already dead. Dr. Pink observes that:

> Trained executioners as these Roman soldiers were, it is quite unthinkable that they would make any mistake in a matter like this. Pilate had given orders for the legs of the three to be broken, and they would not dare to disobey unless they were absolutely sure that Christ were dead already.

Infidels expose themselves to the charge of utter absurdity if they claim that Christ never died, and was only in a swoon. The Roman soldiers are witnesses against them! (Arthur W. Pink, *Exposition of the Gospel of John*, Grand Rapids, MI: Zondervan Publishing House, 1945, p. 248).

Point 11. *Thunder, earthquake and eclipse within three hours.* These served rather to enhance the claim that Jesus was not accidentally crucified but was in fact suffering and dying for the sins of others. There was no eclipse. The sun's light was miraculously darkened for the whole period of the second three hours while Jesus hung on the cross. And it is no coincidence that the darkness was gone the moment Jesus died. The darkness was a sign from God that sin was being thoroughly accounted for that day.

Point 12. *Pilate marvels on hearing about His death.* Deedat further claims that although Pilate was surprised to hear from the centurion that Jesus was dead after only a few hours, he made no effort to verify the statement, caring not whether Jesus was alive or dead.

On the contrary, the very fact that Pilate consulted the centurion who presided over the crucifixion is proof that he was very much concerned about the death of Jesus. For he would have been in a lot of trouble if Jesus had come down alive from the cross. Already he had delivered Him to be crucified to placate the Jews and ensure that his own status as Governor of Judea would be unaffected. If Jesus had survived the cross, those Jews who sought His death would have been all the more incensed. Pilate could have been accused of being inefficient in the execution of the sentence and could have lost his position as Governor.

The very fact that Pilate consulted the centurion is plain proof that he determined to leave nothing to chance. For of all the people who were connected with the crucifixion of Christ, the centurion assuredly would have been the last to make any mistake about the death of Jesus. If he had been mistaken, he would probably have forfeited his own life. When the apostle Peter some time later escaped from prison in the same city, the sentries were executed (Acts 12:19). Again, when another jailer supposed that Paul and Silas had escaped from prison as well, *he drew his sword and was about to kill himself* (Acts 16:27) until he discovered they had not. He preferred to die by suicide than by execution. Death was usually the penalty for allowing prisoners to escape.

Point 13. Another of Deedat's claims is that the *Jews doubted Jesus' death*. The Jews did not doubt His death, but rather they feared the disciples would remove His body. One only has to consider what the Jews actually said to Pilate after the burial of Jesus:

> Sir, we remember how that impostor said, while He was still alive, "After three days I will rise again" (Matthew 27:63).

The Jews did not doubt that Jesus was dead. This is obvious from the fact that they spoke of what Jesus had said while He was *still alive*. These words plainly imply that He had since died. In any event the prophecy they were recalling was one where Jesus had said that after He was *killed*, He would be raised on the third day (Luke 9:22).

Point 14. *Placed in a roomy sepulchre*. There is no evidence in the Bible that Jesus was ever placed in a large tomb which was sufficiently ventilated for Him to recover from His wounds. Once again Deedat has resorted to an extra-biblical source (Jim Bishop's book again) and it is based, like the last one, on 20th-century speculation, with no historical evidence.

Point 15. *Stone had to be moved*. Deedat has recently made a big issue of the stone which sealed the tomb by publishing a booklet entitled *Who Moved the Stone?* In it he suggests that the stone was moved by two disciples of Jesus who were Pharisees—Joseph of Arimathea and Nicodemus (p. 10). But in his booklet *Was Christ Crucified?* he suggests it was a "Super-Woman" (p. 25), implying that it was Mary Magdalene. There is no evidence of any form to support these extreme presumptions.

Once again Deedat has departed from and contradicted the very source on which he claims to base his arguments, namely, the Bible. The Scriptures plainly state that an angel of the Lord descended from heaven and came and rolled back the stone (Matthew 28:2).

Point 16. *Always in disguise*. The theory that Jesus was continually in disguise also finds no support from the Scriptures or any place else. The Bible states that after His resurrection His body bore the nature that the righteous will bear in heaven. He was able to transcend all earthly limitations and could appear or vanish at will. He could suddenly appear in a locked room (John 20:19) and could reveal Himself or conceal His identity at will.

Points 17 to 19. *Jesus and Mary's reaction*. Jesus did not forbid Mary to touch Him after his resurrection because it would hurt as Deedat claims (p. 26). Rather, Christ told Mary that He had not yet ascended, implying a time for touching would come later. There is no scriptural support for Deedat's claims. For Christ later encouraged the disciples to touch Him to evidence His *physical* resurrection.

Points 20 to 21. *The disciples were terrified as He ate food with them.* The disciples were struck with fear because Jesus had suddenly appeared in their midst in a room which was totally barred to anyone outside. This Jesus could do with a resurrected body, but to achieve this after recovering from swooning would be impossible. He ate food to prove that He was still a physical being despite His ability to transcend the limits of the physical realm.

Points 22 to 23. *Never appears to the Jews and took only short trips because of His weak, swooned condition.* Jesus was interested in showing Himself to His disciples (Acts 10:41) and we find, in fact, that He did this in no small measure. There were many who witnessed his resurrection. Paul says of Him:

> He appeared to Cephas, then to the twelve. Then He appeared to more than five hundred brethren at one time, most of whom are still alive, though some have fallen asleep. Then He appeared to James, then to all the apostles. Last of all, as to one untimely born, He appeared also to me (1 Corinthians 15:5-8).

It must be remembered that all the disciples were Jews. There are those who say (and this is probably what Deedat was referring to) Jesus never appeared to non-believers but only to His followers. That is not true. He appeared to both Paul and James, His brother. They did not become believers until after His resurrection. The resurrection was one of the pieces of evidence that convinced both men of Christ being the eternal Son of God.

To suggest that Jesus took only short trips is not the case. Jesus appeared to disciples in Galilee some 60 miles from Jerusalem—a journey Jesus could have accomplished in those days only if He had risen in excellent health from the dead. No one recovering from "swooning" could have achieved this.

Point 24. Another obvious biblical oversight is Deedat's claim that *Jesus never said "I was dead and now I am alive."* In this point Deedat exposes his ignorance of the Bible for he obviously does not know that the words of Jesus are not only recorded in the four Gospels but also in the Book of Revelation. In this book we find that Jesus said the *very words* which Deedat denies that He had ever said. Jesus said to John:

> Fear not, I am the first and the last, and the living one. I died, and behold I am alive for ever more (Revelation 1:17-18).

Point 25. *German scientists say Jesus' "Heart never stopped."* For the fourth time Deedat has matched a minority 20th-century speculation against an historical eyewitness account of the death of Jesus. The majority of medical evidence does not support Deedat's conclusion (See *The Resurrection Factor* by Josh McDowell.)

Every one of Deedat's 25 points has been soundly refuted. In conclusion we need only say that he has shown how utterly futile the swooning theory is. It has no valid foundation and is to be rejected by all who wish to know what really happened to Jesus Christ.

Consider the following rebuttal to the swoon theory as well. These are some key points presented in *Evidence That Demands a Verdict.*

First, Christ did die on the cross, according to the judgment of the soldiers, Joseph and Nicodemus.

> *J.N.D. Anderson* remarks of the hypothesis that Jesus did not die: "Well... it's very ingenious. But it won't stand up to investigation. To begin with, steps were taken—it seems—to make quite sure that Jesus was dead; that surely is the meaning of the spear thrust in His side. But suppose for argument's sake that He was not quite dead. Do you really believe that lying for hour after hour with no medical attention in a rock-hewn tomb in Palestine at Easter, when it's quite cold at night, would so far have revived Him, instead of proving the inevitable end to His flickering life, that He would have been able to loose Himself from yards of graveclothes weighted with pounds of spices, roll away a strone that three women felt incapable of tackling, and walk miles on wounded feet?" (J.N.D. Anderson, "The Resurrection of Jesus Christ," *Christianity Today*, March 29, 1968, p. 7. Used by permission).

Second, Jesus' disciples did not perceive Him as having merely revived from a swoon. The skeptic, David Friedrich Strauss—himself certainly no believer in the resurrection—gave the deathblow to any thought that Jesus revived from a swoon. Here are his words:

It is impossible that a being who had stolen half-dead out of the sepulchre, who crept about weak and ill, wanting medical treatment, who required bandaging, strengthening and indulgence, and who still at last yielded to his sufferings, could have given to the disciples the impression that he was a Conqueror over death and the grave, the Prince of Life, an impression which lay at the bottom of their future ministry. Such a resuscitation could only have weakened the impression which he had made upon them in life and in death, at the most could only have given it an elegiac voice, but could by no possibility have changed their sorrow into enthusiasm, have elevated their reverence into worship (David Friedrich Strauss, *The Life of Jesus for the People*, Vol. I, 2d ed. London: Williams and Norgate, 1879, p. 412).

Third, those who propose the swoon theory also have to say that Jesus, once He had revived, was able to perform a miracle of wiggling out of the graveclothes which were wound tightly about all the curves of His body and leave without disarranging these at all. Merrill C. Tenney explains the graveclothes:

In preparing a body for burial according to Jewish custom, it was usually washed and straightened, and then bandaged tightly from the armpits to the ankles in strips of linen about a foot wide. Aromatic spices, often of a gummy consistency, were placed between the wrappings or folds. They served partially as a preservative and partially as a cement to glue the cloth wrappings into a solid covering....John's term "bound" (Gr. *edesan*), is in perfect accord with the language of Luke 23:53, where the writer says that the body was *rolled*...in linen....On the morning of the first day of the week the body of Jesus had vanished, but the graveclothes were still there.... The wrappings were in position where the head had been, separated from the others by the distance from armpits to neck. The shape of the body was still apparent in them, but the flesh and bone had disappeared....How was the corpse extricated from the wrappings, since they would not slip over the curves of the body when tightly wound around it? (Merrill C. Tenney, *The Reality of the Resurrection*, Chicago: Moody Press, 1963, p. 116, 117. Used by permission).

Fourth, Christ would have had to push away the stone, overpower the guards and then escape unnoticed.

"Those who hold this theory," says *James Rosscup*, "have to say that Christ, in a weakened condition, was able to roll back the stone at the entrance of the tomb—a feat which historians say would take several men—step out of the sepulchre without awaking any one of the soldiers (if we assume for argument's sake that they were asleep, and we know they were certainly not!), step over the soldiers and escape" (James Rosscup, Class Notes, La Mirada, CA: Talbot Theological Seminary, 1969, p. 3).

Fifth, if Jesus had merely revived from a swoon, the long walk "... to a village named Emmaus, about seven miles from Jerusalem" (Luke 24:13), would have been impossible.

Sixth, if Jesus had merely revived from a deathlike swoon, He would have explained His condition to the disciples. Remaining silent, He would have been a liar and deceiver, allowing His followers to spread a resurrection proclamation that was really a resurrection fairy tale.

Paul Little comments that such a theory requires us to believe that:

> Christ Himself was involved in flagrant lies. His disciples believed and preached that He was dead but became alive again. Jesus did nothing to dispel this belief, but rather encouraged it (Paul E. Little, *Know Why You Believe*, Wheaton: Scripture Press Publications, Inc., 1967, p. 26. Used by permission).

John Knox, the New Testament scholar, quoted by Straton, says:

> It was not the fact that a man had risen from the dead but that a particular man had done so which launched the Christian movement.... The character of Jesus was its deeper cause (Hillyer H. Straton, "I Believe: Our Lord's Resurrection," *Christianity Today*, March 31, 1968, p. 3. Used by permission).

Jesus would have had no part in perpetrating the lie that He had risen from the grave if He had not. Such an allegation is unreservedly impugned as one examines His spotless character.

Finally, if Christ did not die at this time, then when did He die and under what circumstances?

This is an important question. No alternative explanation with any historical merit or evidence exists anywhere. As great as Jesus' impact before His death, it defies credibility to believe that no one knows when or where He died.

WHAT WAS THE SIGN OF JONAH?

Toward the end of his booklet, *Was Christ Crucified?* and in a subsequent publication, *What Was the Sign of Jonah?* Deedat raises two further objections to the crucifixion of Christ as it is recorded in the Bible. Both his objections arise from the following statement which Jesus once made to the Jews:

> An evil and adulterous generation seeks for a sign; but no sign shall be given to it except the sign of the prophet Jonah. For as Jonah was three days and three nights in the belly of the whale, so shall the Son of man be three days and three nights in the heart of the earth (Matthew 12:39, 40).

Since Jesus died on a Friday afternoon and was raised on the following Sunday morning, Deedat questions how such a short period could be said to cover *three days and three nights.* The answer is simply that this is a colloquialism, a typical Jewish idiom. We do not speak in such terms today but we often find a period of time in the Bible spoken of in terms of days and nights. In Matthew 4:2 we read that Jesus fasted *forty days and forty nights* and the same is said of the time Moses spent on Mount Sinai in Exodus 24:18. Such expressions imply that the period referred to covered a portion of the stated number of days and nights. So *three days and three nights* did not mean a period of 72 hours exactly but rather a portion of three days. In the case of the burial of Jesus we find that three days were indeed involved—Friday, Saturday and Sunday.

In Esther 4:15-5:1, we read that Esther proclaimed a fast for three days, night and day, but completed the fast on the third day, that is, after only two nights. The pattern is identical to that which we find in the case of the burial of Jesus. He spoke of being raised *on the third day* (Matthew 20:19), as well as predicting that He would be buried for *three days and three nights* (Matthew 12:40). Obviously, therefore, only a portion of three days was being considered.

More proof of this is found in the reaction of the Jews after the death of Jesus. They recalled His saying "after three days I will rise again" (Matthew 27:63) but, instead of waiting till two full days had passed the Roman governor *on the day after* the crucifixion ordered that the tomb be made secure immediately. They knew that Jesus' statement did not mean that a full 72 hours would have to pass, but rather that the event could be expected at any time on the third day after the crucifixion. Therefore they asked that the tomb be sealed *until the third day*

THE ISLAM
DEBATE

(Matthew 27:64). Jesus said He would rise *after three days* but, knowing what this meant according to the idioms of their language, the Jews were only concerned to have the tomb secured *until the third day*. (For further explanation of the "three days and three nights" time frame, see *The Resurrection Factor*, p. 121-123.)

The second objection Deedat raises is that, as Jonah was alive during his sojourn in the stomach of the fish, so the prophecy must be taken to mean that Jesus would be alive while he was in the heart of the earth. Deedat quotes Jesus as saying *As Jonah was...so shall the Son of man be* in his booklet on the Sign of Jonah (p. 6) and implied that this meant that as Jonah was alive, so would Jesus be alive. The similarity Jesus raised, however, is plainly stated in the prophecy to be the *time factor* and not the condition He would be in (i.e., whether alive or dead). Let us consider a similar statement made by Jesus on another occasion:

> As Moses lifted up the serpent in the wilderness, so must the Son of man
> be lifted up (John 3:14).

Here we have the same pattern: *As the serpent...so must the Son of man be*, and once again Jesus draws an analogy. In this case He is comparing the occasion when Moses lifted up a brass serpent on a pole to His pending crucifixion. As the resemblance with Jonah was confined to the time factor, so this one is restricted to the actual lifting up of the impaled object on a fashioned piece of wood. Here, however, we can see the contradiction that it leads to. For in this case the brass serpent never was alive. It was dead when it was made, dead when it was lifted up, and dead when it was taken down. If we were to follow Deedat's line of argument, we would be forced to conclude that this meant that Jesus would be dead even before He was nailed to the cross.

Jonah was alive throughout his ordeal whereas the serpent was a dead object at all times while it was raised in the camp. Clearly these analogies do not go so far as to cover the question of life or death. They are obviously confined to the specific similarities referred to—the three-day time period and the lifting up respectively.

Finally let us consider one other statement made by Deedat to the effect that there is *no clearer statement of Jesus throughout the Gospels* about His pending crucifixion than the sign of Jonah and that it was *the only sign* He was prepared to give the Jews *(Was Christ Crucified?, p. 33)*. We not only entirely agree with this statement, but we believe it negates the swoon theory completely and proves that Jesus actually died on the cross and rose again from the dead.

Jesus had performed many signs which the Jews could not deny. He had healed the sick, cleansed lepers, opened the eyes of the blind, and raised the dead, among other things. Despite all these proofs, however, the Jews still were not satisfied. Other prophets had performed similar marvels. What sign did Jesus have that outweighed them all to prove that He was the Messiah? In reply Jesus gave them only one sign—the sign of Jonah.

Now if Jesus was taken down from the cross at the point of death in a swoon and survived only because He was as good as dead, and managed through clandestine meetings with His disciples and various disguises to gradually recover, what sign could this be? If Deedat's contentions are to be taken seriously, we must conclude that Jesus escaped death entirely by chance and recovered according to a natural process. No miracle manifests itself here. There is no sign in this.

On the contrary, if Jesus died on the cross and three days later raised Himself to life again, then we have indeed a sure sign—conclusive proof that all His claims were true. Other living prophets have raised dead men to life but *Jesus alone raised Himself from the dead* and that to eternal life, for He ascended to heaven and has been there alive for nearly 20 centuries. Here we discover the full import of the sign of Jonah and we can clearly see why Jesus singled it out as the only sign He was prepared to give to the Jews.

So we see that Deedat's final argument in favor of the swoon theory is in fact the very strongest evidence against it, and that it testifies conclusively in favor of the oft-stated proclamation in the Bible that Jesus rose from the dead.

MUSLIM CONFUSION ABOUT THE CRUCIFIXION

The Qur'an is quite ambiguous on the subject of death of Jesus Christ (Abdul-Haqq, *Christ in the New Testament and the Quran*, Evanston, IL: no pub., 1975, p. 18).

We have seen thus far not only how true this statement is, but also what confusion has been caused among Muslims through the vagueness

THE ISLAM
DEBATE

of the crucifixion denial in the Qur'an. The ambiguity in the Qur'an on this point is so great that the theories suggested are considerably different from one another.

> There is no doubt that this variety of versions resulted from the lack of clear wording in the Qur'an with regard to the last days of Christ's human life on earth (Iskander Jadeed, *The Cross in the Gospel and the Qur'an*, no pub. n.d., p. 11).

Some Muslims have sincerely admitted that they have serious problems resolving the puzzling statements in Surah 4:157 about the fate of Jesus and the strange manner in which it was made to appear to the Jews that they had indeed crucified Him. The great commentator on the Qur'an, Razi, was constrained to make the following comment on the Qur'anic teaching about the destiny of Jesus:

> What Mohammed here tells us in the heaven-inspired Qur'an, we must simply accept as the Word of God, surrounded as it is with difficulties, and it is the Lord alone that can give thee true direction (Quoted in Abdul-Haqq, *Christ*, p. 19).

It surely seems more sensible to conclude that the difficulties here spoken of militate against believing the Qur'an, and that the confusion in the Muslim world has been caused by denial in the Qur'an of actual history—the crucifixion of Jesus Christ.

The evidence for this fact is so strong that many Muslims have appreciated that the actual crucifixion of Jesus cannot be seriously denied, but, to avoid contradicting the Qur'an altogether, they have tried one way or another to reconcile it with the statement in the Qur'an that Jesus was not killed by the Jews.

EVIDENCE IN THE BIBLE FOR THE CRUCIFIXION
AND RESURRECTION

We have shown why the Qur'anic denial of the crucifixion of Christ should be rejected. Now let us examine proof in favor of the biblical record of His death and resurrection.

We are fortunate in that God has preserved evidence that Jesus Christ did in fact die for the sins of men on a cross and rise for their salvation.

In the Bible we discover prophecy after prophecy out of the mouths of true prophets to the coming crucifixion of the Christ. We shall consider just a few passages where the crucifixion is foretold.

In the *Zabur*, the Psalms of David, we find one Psalm where the events of the crucifixion are foretold in minute detail. It begins with these words: *My God, my God, why hast thou forsaken me?* (Psalm 22:1). And we find in the *Injil* that these are the very words which Jesus spoke on the cross (Matthew 27:46). The Psalmist then prophesies in these words:

> They have pierced my hands and feet—I can count all my bones— they stare and gloat over me; they divide my garments among them, and for my raiment they cast lots (Psalm 22:16-18).

It was a common practice in Roman crucifixions for soldiers to nail the hands and feet of the victim to the cross and then to divide his clothing between them. These words were written a thousand years before Christ— long before crucifixion was ever used—and yet we can see quite clearly His crucifixion foretold. That these words refer to him specifically is clear from the riddle "they divide my garments among them and for my raiment they cast lots." Why were lots cast for the victim's raiment if the rest of his clothes were divided between the soldiers? The reason is clearly given in the record of the *Injil:*

> When the soldiers had crucified Jesus they took his garments and made four parts, one for each soldier; also his tunic. But the tunic was without seam, woven from top to bottom; so they said to one another, "Let us not tear it, but cast lots for it to see whose it shall be" (John 19:23, 24).

In his prophecy David also records that the victim complained that all his bones were out of joint and that his tongue was cleaving to his jaws (Psalm 22:14-15), agonies which scientists have shown to be typical of the effects of crucifixion. Likewise the prophet also records that those passing by the victim would mock at him and wag their heads, saying, *"He committed his cause to the Lord, let him deliver him, let him rescue him, for he delights in him"* (Psalm 22:8). This is precisely what the Jewish leaders cast in the face of Jesus as they passed by His cross:

> He trusts in God; let God deliver him now, if he desires him (Matthew 27:43).

The rest of the Psalm outlines the agonizing death of the victim on his cross, and yet immediately speaks of his return to his brethren to address them—a clear reference to the resurrection of Christ.

The prophet David (*Dawud* in Arabic) foretold in plain language the crucifixion of Jesus and *foresaw and spoke of the resurrection of the Christ* (Acts 2:31). It is one thing to record such an event when it is part of history, but when a prophet of such standing is able to foretell it centuries before it takes place, we must conclude that he was only able to do so *because God Himself revealed it to him beforehand.* Here is one of the strongest evidences in favor of the crucifixion of Christ, indeed one which cannot ultimately be denied.

David elsewhere predicted that the legs of Jesus would not be broken on the cross (Psalm 34:20)—a very significant prophecy, as the soldiers broke the legs of the two robbers crucified with Jesus but did not break His legs (John 19:32-36).

The last prophecy we shall consider is that of the prophet Isaiah who not only predicted the crucifixion as well but also gave the reasons for it:

> He was wounded for our transgressions, he was bruised for our iniquities …All we like sheep have gone astray; we have turned every one to his own way: and the Lord has laid on him the iniquity of us all (Isaiah 53:5-6).

These words tell us quite clearly that Jesus died not as a martyr but as a sacrifice for the sins of men and for their salvation. The prophecy has numerous factual predictions relating to the crucifixion as well. It foretells that Jesus would not be crucified alone but together with wrongdoers (i.e., the two thieves who were crucified with him):

> He poured out his soul to death, and was numbered with the transgressors (Isaiah 53:12).

Not only so, but we know that this passage refers to the actual crucifixion of Jesus Christ for He plainly told His disciples on the night before this event that this whole prophecy referred to Him:

> I tell you that this scripture must be fulfilled in me, "And he was reckoned with the transgressors," for what is written about me has its fulfillment Luke 22:37).

Numerous other features of the prophecy were fulfilled in the crucifixion of Christ, some of which were that He was making himself an *offering for sin* (v. 10), that He would rise from the dead and *see the fruit of the travail of His soul and be satisfied* (v. 11), and that He would make *intercession for the transgressors* (v. 12), which Jesus did when He prayed for His murderers in these words: *Father, forgive them, for they know not what they do* (Luke 23:34).

Of special interest is another prophecy which had a unique fulfillment in the death of Christ. We read:

> They made his grave with the wicked and with a rich man in his death (Isaiah 53:9).

How could His grave have been made with the wicked if He was buried in the distinguished tomb of a rich man? The answer is that, whereas all victims of crucifixion were thrown into a pit for the wicked when they died, a rich man named Joseph obtained leave from the Roman governor to bury Jesus in his own tomb which he had hewn out of a rock (Matthew 27:60).

Jesus Christ was crucified for the sins of men and rose from the dead for their salvation. The prophets who went before Him predicted these facts and the apostles who followed Him gave the same unanimous testimony on the grounds of incontrovertible facts of history to which they were witnesses.

THE RESURRECTION

Because of the interpretation of the crucifixion by Islam, the resurrection does not receive a great deal of attention. This is not because it is seen as insignificant by Muslims, but rather because if true it would deny Islamic truth. This is one reason Muslims go to great lengths to explain away the crucifixion.

> The Resurrection of Christ is not, strictly speaking, an issue with Muslims. The orthodox, as we have seen, believe that He did not die, so that for them there can be no question of His having risen again. As for the Ahmadis, they follow the lead of the founder of their sect, who in order to establish his own claims made it his business to assert that Jesus was dead. But so far as the crucifixion is concerned we have noted that he adopted the baseless theory that Jesus merely swooned on the cross and was revived, only to die later. In this way he denied also the historicity of the Resurrection (Bevan Jones, *Christianity Explained*, p. 153).

THE ISLAM
DEBATE

For in-depth evidence on the resurrection, we would suggest Chapter 10 of *Evidence That Demands a Verdict, The Resurrection Factor,* both by Josh McDowell; *Who Moved the Stone,* by Frank Morrison, or *Testimony of the Evangelists, Examined by the Rules of Evidence Administered in Courts of Justice,* by Simon Greenleaf.

Three specific historical facts shall be briefly mentioned here.

First, the tomb was empty. To this day, no adequate explanation has been offered for this fact, other than the biblical account.

Second, the attitude of the knowledgeable disciples following the alleged resurrection affirms its validity. Two specific contrasts must be noted. One, from sorrow to joy. One must explain this away. Second, from fear to boldness. There must be an explanation as to why men at one time were afraid of death and then later were transformed into men over whom death had no hold.

Third, one must explain away the existence of the Church and changed lives down through history, all of which point to the resurrection as the reason for this transformation.

The crucifixion and death of Jesus is inseparably linked to His resurrection through the empty tomb. Down through history, men and women have always pointed to the empty tomb and the appearances of Jesus as the rock of their faith, and they are right in doing that. Islam is aware of this too. For if Jesus was not taken up to heaven before His crucifixion as the Muslims claim—a claim for which there is no evidence—then He must have been crucified *and* resurrected. These are two events which are linked by history, and are the only reasonable explanations in light of the evidence, both biblical and non-biblical.

ISLAMIC SECTS

One of the criticisms leveled against Christianity by Islam is that Christianity's fragmentation into denominations illustrates the fact that it cannot be completely true and is corrupted. If this were not true, then there would not be so many "different" interpretations on various issues. The fact is that Islam suffers from the same credibility problem. Two points surface: One, differing opinions do not remove the possibility of ascertaining the truth, whether it be Christian or Islamic. Second, unity is not uniformity and splintered sects from any group only take on significance in view of a standard or central teaching of the main group. These issues concern the *reliability* of the teaching. In the case of Islam, the question becomes which sect or division is the most reliable and trustworthy representation of Islam? But the issue between Islam and Christianity is not one of reliability but of *validity*, namely, which one of the two is true to the facts?

The two greatest divisions within Islam are the Sunnis and the Shi'ites. Often the Sunnis are considered as the orthodox group and the Shi'ites as one of the sects. Obviously, the Shi'ites would disagree. It is really not correct to call the Shia a sect. It is a major branch of Islam. True, it is much smaller than the Sunni branch, but the literal term "sect" might not be accurate for two reasons.

1. It implies that the Shi'ites are either a group *within*, or an offshoot *of* the Sunni faith. This is not true.

2. The term "sect" would seem by connotation to equate the Shi'ite faith with any number of the smaller splinter groups of Islam. This they are not.

Islam became divided at infancy into two major schools of thought.

Shi'ites

The Shi'ite sect has historical roots that are traced back to shortly after Muhammad's death. The Shi'ites believe that the rightful ruler to follow Muhammad was his son-in-law, Ali, who eventually became the fourth Caliph to succeed Muhammad. They believe only descendants of Muhammad had the right to succeed him.

The following offers a good introduction to the Shi'ite sect:

> The Shi'a constitute the only important schism in Islam. Unlike the Kharijites, who rebelled against the Ijma' of the Community at the practical level, the Shi'a have, over the centuries, evolved a doctrine of Divine Right (both with regard to religion and political life) that is irreconcilable with the very spirit of Ijma'....

> Thus, we see that Shi'ism became, in the early history of Islam, a cover for different forces of social and political discontent. The southern Arabs used it

as a facade to assert their pride and independence against the Arabs of the north. In the Iraqi mixed population, it claimed the services of the discontented Persians and contributed to the rise, during the 'Abbasid period, of an extreme Persian cultural, nationalistic movement known as the Shu'ubiya....The fundamental religious impulse was derived from the violent and bloody death of Husayn, 'Ali's son from Fatima, at Karbala' at the hands of government troops in the year 671, whence the passion motive was introduced. This passion motive combined with the belief in the "return" of the Imam gives to Shi'ism its most characteristic ethos. Upon this were engrafted old oriental beliefs about Divine light and the new metaphysical setting for this belief was provided by Christian Gnostic Neoplatonic ideas (Fazlur Rahman, *Islam*, Chicago: University of Chicago Press, 1979, pp. 170-172).

Today the Shi'ites completely dominate Iran; their most prominent leader there is the Ayatollah Khomeini.

There are a number of divisions among the Shi'ites themselves. The two most common are the twelvers and the seveners (Ismailis). The former, being the largest group, holds the first 12 caliphs after Muhammad are the only legitimate leaders (descendants) or imams. The seveners hold to only seven. The twelvers believe that eventually the final imam will return before the last judgment, and that he is simply in hiding for the moment. Another name for this imam is the "Mahdi."

Sunnis

Along with the caliphate controversy, conflict raged on another front, that of law and theology. Through this conflict emerged four recognized, orthodox schools of Islamic thought. All four schools accepted the *Qur'an* (Koran), the *Sunna*, or the practice of the Prophet as expressed in the *Hadith* (traditions), and the four bases of Islamic Law *(Shari'a)*: the *Qur'an*, the *Hadith*, the *Ij'ma'* (consensus of the Muslim community) and the *Qi'yas* (use of analogical reason). These four groups came to be called the Sunnis.

The requirements of a caliph are:

1. He must be righteous.

2. He must be male.

3. He must be adult.

4. He must be a member of the tribe of Quraish.

5. He must be sane.

However, the Sunnis do not put a strong emphasis on any one caliph or leader or any family group. They rely on the Qur'an, and, on matters not specifically expressed, seek the view of the community as a whole.

Noss explains:

> The rapid expansion of Islam confronted Muslims with other crucial, and even more complex, decisions concerning Muslim behavior. Situations early appeared in areas outside of Arabia where the injunctions of the Qur'an proved either insufficient or inapplicable. The natural first step in these cases was to appeal to the *sunna* (the behavior or practice) of Muhammad in Medina or to the Hadith that reported his spoken decisions or judgments. In the event that this proved inconclusive, the next step was to ask what the sunna and/or consensus of opinion *(Ijma)* of the Medina community was, in or shortly after the time of Muhammad. If no light was yet obtainable, the only recourse was either to draw an analogy *(Qiyas)* from the principles embodied in the Qur'an or in Medinan precedents and then apply it, or to follow the consensus of opinion of the local Muslim community as crystallized and expressed by its Qur'anic authorities.

> The Muslims who took this way of solving their behavioral problems were, and are to this day, called Sunnites (Noss, *Religions*, p. 530).

The majority of the Islamic world today is Sunni.

In *Islam: A Survey of the Muslim Faith*, George Fry and James King comment on the Sunnis:

> As a common noun, *sunnah* means "norm" or "customary practice"; when capitalized, it refers to the deeds and words of the Prophet, which have binding force on Muslims. This prophetic *Sunnah* is embodied in a book (the Qur'an), in the comments and deeds of the Prophet (as embodied in the *hadith*), and in *shari'ah* law as it has emerged throughout the ages. The Sunnites, whose name indicates their acceptance of this body of material, regard the first four caliphs—the so-called rightly-guided caliphs—as an expression of divine will, they read the Qur'an literally and put it at the center of their faith (theirs is not a priestly creed which puts a human mediator between them and God); they do not tend to look for great dimensions in history, in the Qur'an or in any human personality. As the central body of Muslims, dominant in North Africa, Turkey, Syria, Palestine, and the Arabian Peninsula, they tend to receive a good press because most

books written about Islam by Westerners are written from a Sunnite point of view (Geroge C. Fry and James R. King, *Islam: A Survey of the Muslim Faith*, Grand Rapids, MI: Baker Book House, 1980, p. 113).

As mentioned in the brief history, a conflict has raged between the Shi'ites and the Sunnis since their split. Most recently this has come to be of international interest as their conflict is played out on the stage of world politics.

This Shi'ite-Sunni controversy has been a focal point of world attention since we saw the militant Shi'ite sect topple the once-believed unshakeable regime of the Shah of Iran. The same militant Islamic fundamentalists were responsible for the assassination of President Anwar Sadat of Egypt.

Fry and King comment on these sects as well as others:

> Much of the material that might be surveyed here is not esoteric, but a good deal of it is of considerable interest to non-Muslims, either because it reflects certain issues which have loomed as significant within the House of Islam (the history of the Christian church is likewise dotted with points of controversy) or because it helps to explain issues that are very much in the news today:
>
> (1) In the *mid-seventies, Sunnite-Shi'ite disruptions contributed to civil war in Lebanon.* More recently, at the end of the decade, there was a resurgence of Islamic fundamentalism in Iran, inspired by Shi'ite leaders, which was instrumental in overthrowing a ruler thought to be invulnerable and producing striking changes in the cultural and social structure of a great country.
>
> (2) The extreme cultural conservatism which Westerners who work in Saudi Arabia encounter can be traced to the eighteenth-century *Wahhabi movement,* which succeeded in establishing the strictest of moral codes on the peninsula.
>
> (3) *The Sufi movement has taken the West by storm.* Many American cities now have Sufi centers; college bookstores display Sufi material which is eagerly read by young people. The Sufi order in the West attracts large crowds from all over the country to its meetings; Sufism is more respectable in New York City than in many parts of the Middle East! An examination of the major Muslim sects can thus shed some light on the books that our children are reading, as well as on the price we are paying for oil (Fry and King, *Islam,* p. 112).

Besides the conflict involving Iran, Iraq, Saudi Arabia, the Soviet Union (who are warned about the militant Muslim fundamentalists) and other Arab countries, the controversy also stands at issue in recently besieged Lebanon where Beirut is portioned off into Sunni and Shi'ite sections.

Sufis

In any strong, legalistic, religious system, worship can become mechanical and be exercised by rote, making God seem transcendent. Such an impersonal religion often motivates unsatisfied believers to react. Such is the case with Islam, as the Sufis, the most well-known Islamic mystics, have developed over the years in response to orthodox Islam and to the often loose and secularist view of Islamic leadership during some of its early days under the *Ummayad* and *Abbasid* dynasties. Muhammad himself was a mystic. This helped Sufism to progress parallel with legalism. Many Sufis are also Sunnis.

> Despite the claims of the Law, another aspect of Islam has been almost equally important for the rank and file of the faithful—this is Sufism: mysticism, as it is usually translated.

> The Sufis are those Muslims who have most sought for direct personal experience of the Divine. While some of them have been legalists of the most fundamentalist stamp, their emphasis on direct religious experience has more often led the Sufis into tension with the legalists, and their attitude toward the Law has ranged from patronizing irony to outright hostility (Williams, *Islam*, p. 136).

The Sufis are the most mystical of the Islamic believers. Fry and King comment:

> We have followed through many aspects of Islam the distinction suggested by two critical Arabic words, *batin* and *zahir*, inner and outer meanings, esoteric and exoteric knowledge. But we have yet to say anything about what is perhaps the most important reflection in Islam of the inner, esoteric dimension of thought, the great mystical tradition of Sufism. There are several possible etymologies for this term, which—in some circles at least—is by now almost a household word. The one most usually accepted, however, is (a) derivation from the Arabic word *suf*, wool, referring to the coarse, much-patched garment that the Sufi mystics may wear. Other terms for Islamic mystics which one may hear are *dervish* or *fakir* (both of which suggest poverty), *qalandar* (a wandering dervish who flouts public opinion), and *pir, sheikh,* or *murshid* (dervish masters) (Fry and King, *Islam*, p. 120).

THE ISLAM
DEBATE

They continue:

> The Sufi movement, so popular today in America and Europe, had its beginning in the Middle East very early in Islamic history as a protest against the growing intellectualism of Islamic thought in Baghdad and elsewhere. The Sufis encouraged a relationship to God that was based on profound trust and that expressed itself in glowing, deeply felt love. There are some important links between the Sufis and the Shi'ites, for both groups preach a radical, antiestablishment form of Islam, reflecting the intense commitment of each group to spiritual values and the haunting sense that each group feels about in some way being "left out" (ibid., p. 120, 121).

On the emergence of the Sufis, Noss states:

> Millions of Muslims had within themselves the natural human need to feel their religion as a personal and emotional experience. Islam had no priests, then or now, ordained and set apart for a life dedicated to the worship of God and the pursuit of holiness, and yet everyone knew that Muhammad had been a true man of God, wholly dedicated to his mission, who in the period before the revelations came had retired at times from the world to meditate in a cave. It was thus that he had become an instrument of God's truth.

> It was the popular yearning for the presence among them of unworldly men dedicated to God, asceticism, and holiness that encouraged the eventual emergence of Islamic mysticism (Noss, *Religions*, p. 535).

Ahmadiya

As Sufism is the mystical sect of Islam, the Ahmadiya is the rationalist sect. Recent in origin, the following gives a brief historical backdrop.

> In the modern period two important sects have arisen in Islam: Babism *(q.v.)*, which, as the Baha'i Faith, has formally gone outside Islam, and the Ahmadiya, a sect founded by Mirza Ghulam Ahmad at the turn of the 20th century. He began by writing books against the Christian missionaries in defense of Islam but in 1879 began to claim that he was the promised Mahdi and the Messiah in the village of Qadian in the Punjab, India. Over against the general Muslim belief that Jesus was not actually crucified but was raised to heaven and will reappear on earth, Mirza Ghulam Ahmad claimed that Jesus, after escaping from crucifixion, went to Kashmir and died in Srinagar (*Encyclopaedia Brittanica*, p. 667).

The Ahmadiya are not believed to be true Muslims by many. They are declared to be a non-Islamic sect in Pakistan.

In their teaching the Ahmadiya are strongly militant against Christianity.

Aside from discounting the crucifixion they also deny the virgin birth of Christ, and His sinless nature. In fact, the sect seeks to discredit any type of superior or supernatural status to Christ, which might elevate Him above Muhammad.

Kharijites, Mu'tazilites, Wahhabis

These three groups existed more as fragmented movements than exclusive sects. The Kharijites were a small group whose emphasis was on their refusal to compromise with their excessively radical judgments of Islam and they believed that any such compromise had to be severely dealt with. They also adhere to "free will."

The Wahhabis were a strong, militant, puritanical group. They survive today mainly in Saudi Arabia and Nigeria, and are an extreme fundamentalist wing of the Sunnis.

The Mu'tazilites were more a school of philosophy, rationalist in nature, and a group which fell away during the conservative recovery in Islam and in the early Middle Ages. They were greatly influenced by Greek thought.

In any case, the Islamic criticism of Christianity's various denominations loses its impact when compared to the diversity of Islamic sects. Muslims often forget that the same "tests" of validity they apply to Christianity have no meaning unless they are also applied to their own beliefs.

THE DEBATE

took place in August, 1981, in Durban, South Africa.

THE TOPIC
was the question:
Was Christ crucified?

THE PARTICIPANTS
were Josh McDowell and Ahmed Deedat, the president of the Islamic Propagation Centre in Durban, South Africa.

The debate, a transcript of which appears on the following pages, was divided into three parts:

Opening arguments, 50 minutes.

Rebuttals by each, 10 minutes.

Closing statements, 3 minutes.

CHAPTER THREE

TRANSCRIPT OF THE DEBATE

OPENING ARGUMENT

Ahmed Deedat

Mr. Chairman, ladies and gentlemen. On the subject of crucifixion, the Muslim is told in no uncertain terms, in the Holy Qur'an, the last and final revelation of God, that they didn't kill Him, nor did they crucify Him. But it was made to appear to them so. And those who dispute therein, are full of doubts. They have no certain knowledge; they only follow conjecture, guesswork. For of a surety, they killed Him not.

Mr. Chairman, ladies and gentlemen. Could anyone have been more explicit, more dogmatic, more uncompromising, in stating a belief than this? The only one who was entitled to say such words is the all-knowing, omniscient Lord of the universe.

The Muslim believes this authoritative statement as the veritable Word of God. And as such, he asks no questions, and he demands no proof. He says, "There are the words of my Lord; I believe, and I affirm." But the Christian responds in the words of our honorable guest. In his book, Josh McDowell with Don Stewart in *Answers to Tough Questions* on pages 116 and 117, states the Christian's attitude toward this uncompromising statement of the Muslim. He says, "A major problem

THE ISLAM
DEBATE

with accepting Mohammed's account is that his testimony is 600 years after the event occurred, while the New Testament contains eyewitness, or first-hand, testimony of the life and ministry of Jesus Christ."

In a nutshell, the Christian asks how can a man a thousand miles away from the scene of the happening of the crucifixion and 600 years in time away from the happening know what happened in Jerusalem? The Muslim responds that these are the words of God Almighty. And therefore, as such, God knew what had happened. The Christian naturally reasons that, had he accepted this book, the Qur'an, as the Word of God, there would have been no dispute between us. We would all have been Muslims!

We have eyewitness and earwitness accounts of these happenings which are stated for us in the Holy Bible, more especially in the gospels of Matthew, Mark, Luke and John. Now, the implication of this crucifixion is this: it is alleged that Jesus Christ was murdered by the Jews by means of crucifixion 2,000 years ago. And as such, the Jews are guilty of the murder of Jesus Christ. We Muslims are told that they are innocent because Christ was not killed, nor was He crucified. And as such, I am given the (mandate) by the Holy Qur'an to defend the Jews against the Christian charge. I'm going to defend the Jews this afternoon, not because they are my cousins, but simply because justice must be done. We have our points of difference with the Jews—that is a different question altogether. This afternoon, I will try my very best to do justice to my cousins, the Jews.

Now, in this argument, this debate, this dialogue, I am actually the defense counsel for the Jews, and Josh McDowell is the prosecuting counsel. And you, ladies and gentlemen, are the ladies and gentlemen of the jury. I want you to sit back, relax and at the end of this, give judgment to yourself, to your own conscience, whether the Jews are guilty or not of the charge as alleged by the Christians.

Now, to get to the point, as the defense counsel for the Jews, I could have had this case against the Jews dismissed in just two minutes— in any court of law, in any civilized country in the world, simply by demanding from the prosecuting counsel the testimonies of these witnesses, Matthew, Mark, Luke and John. And when they are presented, in the form of sworn affidavits, as we have them in the gospels, I could say that, in their original, they are not attested. And the proof—you get any authorized King James Version of the Bible, and you'll find each and every

Transcript of
the Debate

affidavit begins: "The Gospel according to St. Matthew, the Gospel according to St. Mark, the Gospel according to St. Luke, the Gospel according to St. John." I'm asking, ladies and gentlemen of the jury, what is this "according...according...according"? Do you know what it means? It means Matthew, Mark, Luke and John didn't sign their names. It is only assumed that these are their work. And as such, in any court of law, in any civilized country, they would be thrown out of court in just two minutes.

Not only that, I can have this case dismissed twice in two minutes in any court of law in any civilized country. I said *twice* because one of the testators in the Gospel of St. Mark, chapter 14, verse 50, tells us that at the most critical juncture in the life of Jesus, all His disciples forsook Him, and fled. *All.* If they were not there, the testimony of those who were not there to witness what happened will be thrown out of court. I said, twice in two minutes, in just 120 seconds flat, the case would be over. In any court of law, in any civilized country in the world.

But where is the fun of it? You have come a long way from far and wide, after all the threatening rains. And now, if we say the case is closed and go home, where is the fun of it? To entertain you, I will accept those documents as valid, for the sake of this dialogue, and we are now going to put these witnesses into the box for cross-examination. And I want you to see where the truth lies.

The first witness that I'm going to call, happens to be St. Luke. And St. Luke has been described by Christian authorities as one of the greatest historians. As a historical book, the Gospel of St. Luke is unique. Now, we get St. Luke, chapter 24, verse 36. I'm going to tell you what he has said—what he has written in black and white. He tells us that it was Sunday evening, the first day of the week, when Jesus Christ walked into that upper room, the one in which He had the Last Supper with His disciples. This is three days after His alleged crucifixion. He goes in, and He wishes His disciples, "Peace be unto you." And when He said, "Peace be unto you," His disciples were terrified. Is that true? We're asking you. I would like to ask Him, why were the disciples terrified? Because when one meets his long-lost master, his grandfather, his guru, his Rabbi—we Eastern people embrace one another; we kiss one another. Why should His disciples be terrified? So Luke tells us they were frightened, because they thought He was a spirit.

I'm only quoting what he said. And you can verify in your own Bible at

THE ISLAM
DEBATE

home. They were frightened, they were terrified because they thought He was a spirit. I'm asking Luke, did He look like a spirit? And he says no. I'm asking all the Christians of the world again and again, of every church and denomination, this master of yours, did He look like a spirit? And they all say no. Then I say, why should they think that man is a spirit when He didn't look like one?

And everyone is puzzled—unless Josh can explain. Every Christian is puzzled. Why should they think the man is a spirit when He didn't look like one? I will tell you. The reason is because the disciples of Jesus had heard from hearsay that the Master was hanged on the cross. They had heard, from hearsay, that He had given up the ghost. In other words, His spirit had come out; He had died. They had heard from hearsay that He was dead and buried for three days. All their knowledge was from hearsay, because as I said at the beginning (Mark, chapter 14, verse 50), your other witness says that at the most critical juncture in the life of Jesus all His disciples forsook Him and fled. *All!* They were not there.

So, all the knowledge being from hearsay, you come across a person who you heard was dead for three days. You assume that He's stinking in His grave. When you see such a person, naturally, you're terrified. So Jesus wants to assure them that He's not what they're thinking. They are thinking that He has come back from the dead. A resurrected, spiritualized body, so He says—I am only quoting what Luke says—He says, "Behold My hands and My feet." Have a look at My hands and My feet, that it is I, Myself. I am the same fellow, man, what's wrong with you? Why are you afraid? He says, "Handle Me and see. Handle Me and see. For a spirit has no flesh and bones, as you see me have."

A spirit; indefinite article "a." A spirit, any spirit, has no flesh and bones, as you see me have. So, if I have flesh and bones, I'm not a spirit; I'm not a ghost; I'm not a spook. I am asking the English man—the one who speaks English as his mother tongue—since I have flesh and bones, I'm not a spirit; I'm not a ghost; I'm not a spook. I say, is that what it means in your language?

I say, you Afrikaner, when a man tells you that, does it mean that he's not what you are thinking? That is, he is not a spirit, he is not a ghost, he is not a spook. And everybody responds "yes." If a man tells you a spirit has no flesh and bones, it means it has no flesh and bones. As you see, I have these things, so I'm not what you're thinking. You are thinking that I was dead, and I have come back from the dead and am resurrected. If a spirit has no flesh and bones, in other words, he's telling you that the body you are seeing is not a metamorphosed body. It is not a translated body; it is not a resurrected body. Because a resurrected body gets spiritualized.

Who says so? My authority is Jesus. You say, "Where?" I say Luke, you look again—chapter 20 in verse 36. What does he say? You see, the Jews were always coming to Him with riddles; they were always asking Him, "Master, shall we pay tribute to Caesar or not? Master, this woman, we found her in the act. What shall we do to her? Master..." Again and again. Now, they come to Him and they ask Him, it says, "Master," Rabbi in the Hebrew language, "Master, we had a woman among us, and this woman, according to a Jewish custom, had seven husbands." You see, according to a Jewish custom, if a brother of a man dies and leaves no offspring, then the man takes his brother's wife to be his own wife. And when he fails, the third brother does likewise, and the fourth and the fifth and the sixth, and the seventh.

Seven brothers had this woman as a wife, but there was no problem while on this earth because it was all one by one. Now, they want to know from Him that at the resurrection, in the hereafter, which one is going to have her, because they all had her here. In other words, there will be a war in heaven, because we believe that we will all be resurrected simultaneously. All together, at one time. And these seven brothers wake up at the same time, and they see this woman and every one would say, "My wife! My wife!" and there would be a war in heaven between the brothers for this one woman.

So they want to know from Him which one is going to have her on the other side. Luke, chapter 20, verse 36. Check it out. In answer to that, Jesus said about these resurrected men and women, "Neither shall they die anymore." In other words, "Once they are resurrected, they will be immortalized." This is a mortal body. It needs food, shelter, clothing, sex, rest. Without these things mankind perishes. That body will be an immortalized body. An immortal body, no food, no shelter, no clothing, no sex, no rest. He says neither shall they die anymore. For they are equal unto the angels.

In other words, they will be angel-ized. They will be spiritualized; they will be spiritual creatures; they will be spirits! For they are equal unto angels and the children of God. Such are the children of the resurrection—spirit! He said, "A spirit has no flesh and bones, as you see Me have." In other words, "I'm not resurrected." And they believed not for joy and wonders—Luke 24 again. What happened then?

We thought the man was already dead, perhaps stinking in His grave. And they believed not for joy—overjoy—and they wonder what happened? So He says, "Have you any broiled fish and a honeycomb here, meat—something to eat?" And they gave Him a piece of bread and He took it and ate it in their very sight. To prove what? I'm asking ladies and gentlemen of the jury, what was He trying to demonstrate? What? "I am the same fellow, man; I am not what you are thinking; I have not come back from the dead."

This was Sunday evening after the alleged crucifixion.

Let's go back. What happened in the morning? Your other witness, John, chapter 20, verse 1, tells us that it was Sunday morning, the first day of the week, when Mary Magdalene went to the tomb of Jesus. I'm asking John, why did she go there? Or, let's put another of your witnesses on the stand, Mark, chapter 16, verse 1. Mark, tell us—why did Mary go there? And Mark tells us, "She went to anoint Him." Now, the Hebrew word for anoint is *massahah* from which we get the word *messiah* in Hebrew and *masih* in Arabic. The root word for both Arabic and Hebrew is the same. *Massahah* means to rub, to massage, to anoint.

I'm asking, do Jews massage dead bodies after three days? And the answer is no. I say to you Christians, do you massage dead bodies after three days? Do you? The answer is no. We Muslims are the closest to the Jew in our ceremony of law. Do Muslims massage dead bodies after three days? The answer is no. Then why would they want to go and massage a dead, rotten body after three days? Within three hours, you know that rigor mortis sets in, the hardening of the cells, the rotting of the body, fermentation from within. In three days' time the body is rotten from inside. Such a rotting body when you massage it falls to pieces.

Why would she want to go and massage a dead, rotten body unless she was looking for a live person? You see, according to your witnesses, from my reading, she must have seen signs of life in the limp body as it was being taken down from the cross. She was about the only woman who, with Joseph of Arimathea and Nicodemus, had given the final rites to the body of Jesus. All His other disciples had forsaken Him and fled. They were not there. So if this woman had seen signs of life, she was not going to shout, "There, He's alive! He's alive!"—to invite a sure death.

Transcript of
the Debate

Three days later, she goes in, and she wants to anoint Him. And when she reaches the sepulchre, she finds that the stone is removed. The winding sheets are inside. So, she starts to cry. I'm asking, why was the stone removed and why were the winding sheets unwound? Because for a resurrected body you won't have to remove the stone to come out. For the resurrected body, you don't have to unwind the winding sheets to move. This is the need of this physical body. This mortal body. Because a poet tells us, "The stone walls do not a prison make nor iron bars a cage." For the soul, for the spirit, these things do not matter. Iron bars or walls. It's the need of His physical body. Jesus Christ, according to the Scriptures, was watching her from wherever He was, not from heaven, but from this earth.

Because this tomb, if you remember, was privately owned property belonging to Joseph of Arimathea. This very rich, influential disciple had carved out of a rock a big, roomy chamber. Around that chamber was his vegetable garden. Now, don't tell me that this Jew was so generous that he was planting vegetables five miles out of town for other people's sheep and goats to graze upon.

Surely he must have bought his laborers quarters. Or for people who looked after his garden, or perhaps his country home where he went with his family for holidays, on the weekends.

Jesus is dead and He watches this woman. He knows who she is and He knows why she's there. And He goes up to her. He finds her crying. So He says, "Woman, why weepest thou? Whom seekest thou?" I'm asking, doesn't He know? Doesn't He know? Why does He ask such a silly question? I'm telling you, this is not a silly question. He's actually pulling her leg, metaphorically. She, supposing Him to be the gardener—I'm only reading you evidence as it is given. She, supposed Him to be the gardener—I am asking, why does she suppose He's a gardener? Do resurrected bodies look like gardeners? Do they? I say, why does she suppose He's a gardener? I'm telling you, because He's disguised as a gardener. Why is He disguised as a gardener? I say, because He's afraid of the Jews. Why is He afraid of the Jews? I say, because He didn't die. And He didn't conquer death. If He had died, and if He had conquered death, there's no need to be afraid anymore. Why not? Because the resurrected body can't die twice. Who says so? I say the Bible. What does it say? It says it is ordained unto all men, once to die, and after that, the judgment. You can't die twice.

THE ISLAM
DEBATE

So, if He had conquered death, there would be no need to be afraid. He's afraid, because He didn't die. So she, supposing Him to be the gardener, says, "Sir, if you have taken Him hence, tell me where have you laid Him to rest?" To relax, to recuperate, not where have you buried Him. "So that I might take him away." *I* alone—one woman—a frail Jewess. Imagine her carrying away a corpse of 160 pounds, at least, not 200 like me. A muscular carpenter—supposed to be a young man in the prime of His life, at least 160 pounds. And another 100 pounds' worth of medicines around Him, John, chapter 19, verse 39. That makes Him 260.

Can you imagine this frail Jewess carrying this bundle of a corpse over 260 pounds, like a bundle of straw, like a super-woman in the American comics? And take Him where? Take Him home? Put Him under a bed— what does she want to do with Him? Does she want to pickle Him? What does she want to do with a rotting body. I ask you?

So Jesus—the joke has gone too far—says, "Mary..." The way He said "Mary," she recognized that this was Jesus. So, she wants to grab Him. I'm asking why. To bite Him? No! To pay respect. We Eastern people do that. She wants to grab Him. So Jesus says, "Touch Me not." I say, why not? Is He a bundle of electricity, a dynamo, that if she touches Him she will get electrocuted? Tell me, why not? I say because it hurts. You give me another reason why not. "Touch Me not for I am not yet ascended unto My Father." Is she blind? Can't she see the man is standing there beside her? What does He mean by "I'm not gone up" when He is here? He said, "I am not yet ascended unto My Father." In the language of the Jew, in the idiom of the Jew, He's saying, "I am not dead yet."

The problem arises: who moved the stone? How could she get to Him; who moved the stone? And the Christians are writing books upon books. One is Frank Morrison, a rationalist lawyer. He writes a book of 192 pages and he gives six hypotheses. At the end of the 192 pages, when you are finished, you still haven't got the answer. Who moved the stone? And they're writing books upon books: who moved the stone? I can't understand why you can't see the very obvious. Why don't you read your books? These gospels, you have it in black and white in your own mother tongue. This is an anomaly that you read this book in your own mother tongue.

The Englishman in English, the Afrikaner in Afrikaans, the Zulu in Zulu. Every language group has got the book in their own language. And each and every one is made to understand the exact opposite of what he is reading. Exact opposite. Not just merely misunderstanding.

I want you to prove me wrong. I'm telling you…I'm only quoting word for word exactly as your witnesses have said it. Preserved it for us in black and white. I'm not attributing motives to them. I'm not saying that they are dishonest witnesses. I'm telling you. Please read this book of yours once more. Remove the blinders, and read it again. And tell me where I'm not understanding your language. You Englishmen, or you Afrikaners, you Zulu. You come back to me and if you feel that at the end of the talk, our honored visitor has not done justice to the subject, you call me—to your Kingdom Halls or to your school hall or anywhere you want to discuss it further with me. I am prepared to come.

Who moved the stone? I'm asking. It's very simple—they're talking about 20 men required. It is so huge, it needed a superman from America to move it. One and a half to two tons. I'm telling you, please read Mark and Matthew and he tells you that Joseph of Arimathea alone, put the stone into place. One man—alone. One man! If one man can put it into place, why can't two persons remove it, I ask you?

Now, all those happenings—you know that this was prophesied. It was ordained. And all the stories about what happened afterward—I'm telling you that Jesus Christ had given you a clear-cut indication of what was going to happen. And that's also preserved in black and white in your testimony in the Gospel of St. Matthew, another of your witnesses, chapter 12, verses 38, 39 and 40. The Jews come again to Jesus, with a new request.

Now they say, "Master, we would have a sign of Thee." We want You to show a miracle to convince us that You are the Messiah we are waiting for. You know, something supernatural like walking on the water, or flying in the air like a bird. Do something, man, then we will be convinced that You are a man of God—the Messiah we are waiting for.

So Jesus answers them. He says, "An evil and adulterous generation seeketh after a sign. But there shall be no sign given unto it, except the sign of the prophet Jonah. For as Jonah was three days and three nights in the belly of the whale, so shall the Son of Man be three days and three nights in the belly of the earth." The only sign He was prepared to give them was the sign of Jonah. He has put all his eggs in one basket. He didn't say, "You know blind Bartimaeus, I healed him. You know that woman with issues who had been bleeding for years. She touched Me and

THE ISLAM
DEBATE

she was healed. You know, I fed five thousand people with a few pieces of fish and a few pieces of bread. You see that fig tree. I dried it up from its very roots." Nothing of the kind. "This is the only sign I will give you, the sign of Jonah." I'm asking, what was that sign?

Well, go to the book of Jonah. I brought the book of Jonah for you—one page by God—it is only one page in the whole Bible. This is the book of Jonah. Four short chapters. It won't take you two minutes to read it. It's hard to find the book because, in a thousand pages, to find one page is difficult. But, you don't have to go there. If you went to Sunday school, you will remember what I'm telling you. I'm telling you that Jonah was sent to the Ninevites. You know, God Almighty told him, "Go to Nineveh," a city of 100,000 people. He was to warn them that they must repent in sack-cloth and ashes; they must humble themselves before the Lord. Jonah was despondent because these materialistic people—worldly people—"They will not listen to me. They will make a mockery of what I have to tell them." So instead of going to Nineveh, he goes to Joppa. That's what this one-page book tells you. He went to Joppa and was taken aboard a ship—he was going to Tarshish. You don't have to remember the names.

On the way, there's a storm. And according to the superstitions of these people, anyone who runs away from his master's command, who fails to do his duty, creates a turmoil at sea. So, they begin to question in the boat, who could be responsible for this storm. Jonah realizes that as a prophet of God, he is a soldier of God. And as a soldier of God, he has no right to do things presumptuously on his own. So he says, "Look, I am the guilty party. God Almighty is after my blood. He wants to kill me, so in the process He's sinking the boat, and you innocent people will die. It will be better for you if you take me and you throw me overboard. Because God is really after my blood."

They say, "No, man, you know, you are such a good man. Perhaps you want to commit suicide. We won't help you to do that. We have a system of our own of discovering right from wrong," and that is what they call casting lots. Like heads or tails. So, according to the system of casting lots, Jonah was found to be the guilty man. And so they took him, and they threw him overboard.

Now I'm going to ask you a question. When they threw him overboard, was he dead or was he alive? Now, before you answer, I want you to bear in mind that Jonah had volunteered. He said, "Throw me." And when a man volunteers, you don't have to strangle him before throwing, you don't have to spear him before throwing, you don't have to break his arm or limb before throwing. You agree with me?

The man had volunteered. So when they threw him overboard, what does your common sense say? Was he dead or was he alive? Please, I want your help. Was he dead or was he alive? Alive. You get no prize for that— it was too simple a question. And—astonishingly the Jews say that he was alive, the Christians say he was alive and the Muslims say he was alive. How much nicer it would be if we would agree on every other thing.

We all agree that he was alive when he was thrown into that raging sea. And the storm subsided. Perhaps it was a coincidence. A fish comes and gobbles him. Dead or alive? Was he dead or was he alive? Alive? Thank you very much.

From the fish's belly, according to the book of Jonah, he cries to God for help. Do dead men pray? Do they pray? Dead people, do they pray? No! So he was alive. Three days and three nights the fish takes him around the ocean. Dead or alive? Alive. On the third day, walking on the seashore, I'm asking—dead or alive? Alive. What does Jesus say? He said, "For as Jonah was." Just like Jonah. "For as Jonah was, so shall the Son of Man be," referring to Himself. How was Jonah—dead or alive? Alive. How was Jesus for three days and three nights in the tomb according to the Christian belief? How was He? Dead or alive? Dead.

He was dead according to our belief. In other words, He's unlike Jonah. Can't you see? He says, I shall be like Jonah and you are telling me— there's one thousand two hundred million Christians of the world—that He was unlike Jonah. He said, I will be like Jonah, you say He was unlike Jonah. If I was a Jew, I would not accept Him as my Messiah. I am told in the Qur'an that Jesus was the Messiah. I accept. He was one of the mightiest messengers of God—I accept. I believe in His miraculous birth. I believe that He gave life to the dead by God's permission. And He healed those born blind and the leper by God's permission. But if I was a Jew, according to the sign that He has given, He failed. Jonah is alive—Jesus is dead. They are not alike. I don't know in what language you can make them alike—that they are like one another. So the clever man, you know, the doctor of theology, the professor of religion, he tells me that I don't understand the Bible.

Your Bible, I don't understand. Why don't I understand the Bible? He says, "You see Mr. Deedat, Jesus Christ is emphasizing the time factor." Note, He uses the word "three" four times. For Jonah was three days and three nights, so shall the Son of Man be three days and three nights. He uses the word "three" four times.

In other words, He's emphasizing the time factor—not whether He was dead or alive. I'm telling you that there is nothing miraculous in a time factor. Whether the man was dead for three minutes or three hours or three weeks, that's not a miracle.

The miracle, if there is one at all, is that you expect a man to be dead and he's not dead. When Jonah was thrown into the sea, we expect him to die. He didn't die, so it's a miracle. A fish comes and gobbles him—he ought to die. He didn't die, so it's a miracle. Three days and three nights of suffocation and heat in the whale's belly. He ought to die; he didn't die. It's a miracle; it's a miracle because you expect a man to die and he didn't die.

When you expect a man to die, and if he dies, what's so miraculous about that? I ask you, what's miraculous about that? If a gunman took a gun and fired six shots into the heart of a man and he dies, is that a miracle? No. But if he laughs it off, if he is still alive and walking with us and if, after the six shots tear his heart to pieces, he laughs: ha ha ha ha--- he's alive. So we say it's a miracle. Can't you see? The miracle is when we expect a man to die and he doesn't die. When the man who is expected to die, dies, it's no miracle.

We expect Jesus also to die. For what He had been through, if He died, there is no miracle. There's no sign. If He didn't die, it's a miracle—can't you see? So He says, "No, no. It is the time factor." Drowning men clutch at straws—drowning women do the same. He says, "No, it's the time factor." I say, did He fulfill that? He says, "Of course, He fulfilled that." I say, how did He fulfill it? Look, it's very easy to make statements. *How* did He fulfill it? I say, watch. When was He crucified, I ask you? The whole Christian world says on Good Friday. Britain, France, Germany, America, Lesotho, Zambia—in South Africa we have a public holiday—every Christian nation commemorates Good Friday. I am asking, what makes Good Friday good?

So the Christian says, "Christ died for our sins. That makes it good." So He *was* crucified on the Good Friday. He says, yes. Yes. I say, when was He crucified—morning or afternoon? So the Christian says in the afternoon.

How long was He on the cross? Some say three hours, some say six hours. I say, I am not going to argue with you. Whatever you say, I accept. You know, when we read the Scriptures, they tell us that when they wanted to crucify Jesus, they were in a hurry. And they were in such a hurry that Josh tells us in his book, *The Resurrection Factor*, that within some 12 hours, there were six separate trials. Six trials He went through.

These things only happen in films. These sort of things—six trials in 12 hours from midnight to the next morning and on, only take place on films. But I believe whatever you tell me. Whatever you tell me, I accept. So the Jews were in a hurry to put Him up on the cross. Do you know why? Because of the general public. Jesus was a Jew. The general public loved Him. The man had healed the blind and the lepers and the sick and had raised the dead. He had fed so many thousands of people with bread and fish. He was a hero, and if they discovered—the general public—that their hero's life was in danger, there would have been a riot.

So, they had a midnight trial. Early in the morning they took Him to Pilate. Pilate says, "He is not my kettle of fish—take Him to Herod." Herod says, "I'm not interested—take Him back to Pilate. And hurry, hurry, hurry." And they held six trials within 12 hours. Six. As if they had nothing else to do, but I believe what you tell me.

They succeeded in putting Him up on the cross, according to your witnesses. According to your witnesses. But as much as they were in a hurry to put Him up, they were in a hurry to bring Him down. You know why? Because of the Sabbath. Because at sunset on Friday, at six o'clock, the Sabbath starts. You see the Jews count the days, night and day, night and day. We Muslims count our days, night and day, night and day. Not day and night. We count night and day. Six o'clock, our day begins in the evening.

So, before sunset, the body must come down because they were told in the book of Deuteronomy that they must see to it that nobody is hanging on the tree on the Sabbath day. "That thy land be not defiled which the Lord thy God giveth thee for an inheritance." So quickly, quickly, they brought the body down and they gave Him a burial bath, and they put a hundred pounds of medicine around Him. And they put Him into the sepulchre. Not a grave—a sepulchre. A big, roomy chamber above ground. So it's already evening. From three o'clock in the afternoon, for whatever you do, the details are given in Josh's book. Burial baths normally take more than an hour. You read the details about how the Jews

THE ISLAM
DEBATE

give a burial bath to the dead. That takes more than an hour itself. But let's say they succeeded in doing all these things in a hurry, hurry. You know they were in a hurry. Six trials in 12 hours. Now they put Him into the sepulchre.

By the time they put Him in, it's already evening. So watch—watch my fingers. Friday night He's supposed to be in the grave. Watch my finger. Saturday day, He still is supposed to be in the grave. Am I right? Saturday night, He still is supposed to be in the grave. But Sunday morning, the first day of the week, when Mary Magdalene goes to the tomb, the tomb was empty.

That's what your witnesses say. I am asking—how many days and how many nights? You remember, I said, supposed, supposed, supposed... You know why? Because the Bible doesn't say actually when He came out. He could have come out Friday *night*. The Bible doesn't say how He came. So, Friday night, Saturday day, Saturday night. I'm asking, how many days and how many nights? Please, if you can see, if your eyes are not defective, tell me how many? How many do you see? Right! Two nights and a day. Look at this. Is it the same as He said, for as Jonah was three days and three nights, so shall the Son of Man be three days and three nights? Three and three. Look at this: two and one. Please tell me now it means the same thing.

I want to know what you are reading. I want to know what you are reading in your own book! The man is telling you that what is going to happen will be like Jonah. And the sign of Jonah is a miracle. And the only miracle you can attribute to this man, Jonah, is that we expected him to die and he didn't die. Jesus—we expect Him also to die. If He died, it is not a sign. If He didn't die, it is a sign.

Mr. Chairman, ladies and gentlemen of the jury. Can you see, the people have been programmed. We all get programmed from childhood. When I went to America, and spoke at the University in San Francisco, I said you people are brainwashed. I told them, "You are brainwashed." Of course, I could afford to talk to them—the American will take it. He is the almighty. You know, great guy. He can take it. So I said, "You people are brainwashed." So one American, a professor, interjected, "No, not brainwashed—programmed." I said, "I beg your pardon—programmed." So, Mr. Chairman, ladies and gentlemen, I hope, by the time this meeting is over, you will be re-programmed into reading the book as it is, and not as you are made to understand.

Transcript of
the Debate

Thank you very much, ladies and gentlemen.

Josh McDowell

Ladies and gentlemen, good afternoon. Mr. Deedat, and the wonderful people of this city, and this country of South Africa, I am thankful for the opportunity to be a part of this symposium on Islam and Christianity's view of the crucifixion and the resurrection.

In preparation for this, I didn't realize that I would be dealing with so many different theories on the crucifixion from the Islamic viewpoint. I found out, first of all, that the majority of the Muslims throughout the world hold to the substitutionary theory. That in Surah number 4, in the Qur'an, a substitute, another person, was placed in Christ's position on the cross—that Jesus was removed and taken to heaven.

In other words, it was someone else. But then, I found such a diverse opinion among Muslims. Some Muslim writers say that it was a disciple of Jesus who was placed on the cross in His stead. Another Muslim writer, Tabari, quoting Ibn Ishaq, said it was a man by the name of Sargus, or Sergius, who was placed on the cross. Another Muslim writer by the name of Baidawi, said it was a Jew named Titanus who was placed on the cross. Another, Ath-Tha-'labi, says it was a Jew named Fal Tayanus, who was placed on the cross. And still another Muslim writer, Wahb ibn Munabbah, said it was a Rabbi of the Jews, Ashyu, who was placed on the cross.

Then, others feeling that it might be a little unfair to put an innocent man there, say, well, it must be Judas Iscariot who was placed on the cross. Now, Mr. Deedat might be able to correct me, but I do not believe there is any evidence whatsoever in the Qur'an for that. There are in some of the sects, earlier than Islam, references to that. But I always wondered, why did God have to have a substitute? Why couldn't He have simply taken Jesus then?

Others will say—and this is not what the majority of Muslims believe—that Jesus died a natural death some years after the crucifixion and the alleged resurrection. In other words, "Hazrat Isa," Jesus is dead! This is a more recent development in Islam. And I'm always wary of recent developments.

THE ISLAM
DEBATE

It was started mainly by a man by the name of Venturini, who said Jesus really didn't die on the cross—He just swooned or passed out, then was put into a tomb and resuscitated. This is also the theme of the Ahmadiyas, a radical sect of Islam. One of their main doctrines, established by their founder and allegedly their prophet, Mirza Ghulam Ahmad, it is a part of the doctrine of Qadianism.

Some will say to be crucified means to die. Therefore, Jesus wasn't crucified because He did not die on the cross. I'm not quite sure how they got that definition. What I need to do is this: present the facts to you, as I have been able to document them in my books, and then let you, as fair-minded, intelligent people, make up your minds. The background for the points I'm going to make is that when I was in the University, I wanted to write a book against Christianity. I wanted to refute it intellectually. The last thing I wanted to do was become a Christian. But after two years of research and spending a lot of money and time, I discovered facts—not only facts that God has stated in His Holy Word, the Bible, but facts that are documented in sources in history. Men and women, these are some of the facts that I found as I tried to refute Christianity and I couldn't.

The first fact I found is that Jesus was not afraid to die. In fact, He predicted His own death and resurrection. He said, "Behold, we are going up to Jerusalem." He said to His disciples, "The Son of Man is going to be delivered up to the death. And they will deliver Him to the Gentiles to mock and to whip and to crucify Him. And on the third day He will be raised up" (paraphrased from Matthew 17:22-23).

In another place He began to teach them that He had discovered many things. And then He said He'd be rejected by the elders and the chief priests and the scribes, He would be killed, and He added that after three days, He was to rise again (Matthew 20:18, 19).

In Matthew 17, Jesus said to them, "The Son of Man is going to be delivered into the hands of men; and they will kill Him, and He will be raised again on the third day.

The second thing I learned as I studied the life of Jesus Christ is that Jesus was willing to die. In Matthew 26, He said, "My Father, if it is possible, let this cup pass from Me." But what a lot of people leave out is the context of what Jesus said. He said, "Yet not as I will, but as Thou wilt, Father" (Matthew 26:39).

Transcript of
the Debate

Now Jesus did not hide Himself. He is very clear about where He is. It says in John 18 that He went to the place where they usually found Him. He didn't want to hide from the authorities. He knew what was going to happen. In John 18, verse 4, it says, "Jesus therefore, knowing all the things that were going to come upon Him." He knew it! And He was ready for it. In Matthew Jesus says, "Don't you understand, I could call on twelve legions of angels to protect Me?" But He said, "I want *Your* will, Father," and God answered His prayer and let Him fulfill "the will of the Father." Jesus said in John 10: "The Father loves Me because I lay down My life that I may take it up again. No one has taken it away from Me, but *I* lay it down on My own initiative." You have to remember—Jesus being the God-Man, came as God the Son, the eternal Word, to take the sins of the world upon Himself. The Holy Bible (1 Corinthians 5:21) says that He, God, made Jesus sin for us, and, if you can, imagine the agony that the eternal Word, the Son, was going through at that time.

The third fact that I learned is that the Jews were not guilty of the crucifixion of Jesus Christ. I was very surprised, Mr. Deedat, that you needed to be the defender of the Jews. There are Muslims and Christians that have gotten that distorted all through history. Jesus said in Matthew 20, verses 18 and 19, "We are going up to Jerusalem; and they will condemn Me to death, and will deliver Me over to the Gentiles, to mock and whip and crucify Me." Jesus said, "I *lay down* My life." If anyone was guilty, Jesus was. He said, "I have the power to lay it down, I have the power to take it up."

Also, Mr. Deedat, I feel that both you and I are responsible, because the Bible says, "For all have sinned and fall short of the glory of God" (Romans 3:23). It was our sins that drove Jesus Christ to the cross.

The fourth fact that I learned is that the Christians are called to an intelligent, intellectual faith—not a blind faith. I was quite surprised when I read in the little booklet, *What Was the Sign of Jonah?*, by Mr. Ahmed Deedat, that over one thousand million Christians today blindly accept that Jesus of Nazareth is the Christ. I'm a little confused, because really, Mr. Deedat, you read from the Qur'an and you said you accept it, you don't need facts, you don't need any evidence. You simply accept it and then you're saying that Christians, because they accept what God, Yahweh, has revealed through the Holy Bible, that Jesus *is* the Christ, that because we accept that, we do it blindly. I'm amazed, because in the Muslim book, the Qur'an, it states that one of the titles given to Jesus is "al-Masih." I believe it is referred to 11 times that way. The Muslim translator of the Qur'an into English, Yusuf Ali, translates the Arabic here

THE ISLAM
DEBATE

as "Christ" in the English translation. So, why are we accused of being blind in accepting Jesus as the Christ?

In my country, one of the greatest legal minds that ever lived—the man who made the university of Harvard famous—was Dr. Simon Greenleaf. He became a Christian through trying to refute Jesus Christ as the Eternal Word and the resurrection. Finally, after trying to do it, he came to the conclusion that the resurrection of Jesus Christ is one of the best established events of history, according to the laws of legal evidence administered in the courts of justice.

C.S. Lewis, the literary genius of our age, was the professor of medieval and renaissance literature at Oxford. He was a giant in his field. No one could question his intellectual capabilities. He became a believer in Jesus Christ as his Savior and Lord when he tried to refute the reliability of the New Testament and he couldn't. And he said, "I was one of the most reluctant converts, but I was brought to Jesus Christ because of my mind."

Lord Caldecote, the Lord Chief Justice of England, a man that held the highest offices that anyone could hold in the legal systems of England, said, "…as often as I have tried to examine the evidence for Christianity, I have come to believe it as a fact beyond dispute."

Thomas Arnold was the headmaster of a major varsity and university for 14 years. He is an historian and the author of the famous three-volume series, the *History of Rome*. He said, "I know of no one fact in the history of mankind which is proved by better and fuller evidence than the resurrection of Jesus Christ."

Dr. Verner von Braun, the German scientist—the man who immigrated to my country—was one of the creators of the American Space Program. He said he never really became a scientist until he came to know Jesus Christ personally as Savior and God.

The fifth fact that I discovered was the historical accuracy of the Christian Bible. The Christian New Testament is exceptional in its reliability and trustworthiness and survival down through history. It is unrivaled in manuscript authority. A manuscript is a hand-written copy over against a printed copy. Men and women, of the Christian New Testament alone, there are more than 24,000 manuscripts. Not versions of the Bible, Mr. Deedat, manuscript copies. Men and women, the number two book in all of history in manuscript authority and literature, is Homer's *Iliad*, with 643. The number two book in the whole of history in manuscript authority.

Then, Sir Frederick Kenyon was a man who was second to no one in the ability and the training to make authoritative statements about manuscripts of literature in history. The former curator and director of the British Museum, he said, "The last foundation for any doubt that the Scriptures have come down to us as they were written now has been removed. Both the authenticity and the general integrity of the books of the New Testament may now be regarded as finally established."

The point: there are some people who do not have an historical perspective of literature, who try to make an issue out of the fact that the writers of the four accounts of the gospel, Matthew, Mark, Luke and John, never signed their names. Please, men and women, we need to go back through history and see how they did it then.

First of all, the manuscripts were so well-accepted as being authoritative, with everyone knowing who wrote them, they did not need names placed on them. You might say it was the writers' way of not distracting from the purpose of making Jesus Christ the central issue. Also, the work of these authors, Matthew, Mark, Luke and John, went through the apostolic age. They went through the test of the apostolic period of the first century to confirm their accuracy, authenticity and reliability. Other people, through limited reading and absence of any type of research, say that the documents of Matthew, Mark, Luke and John are hearsay because the writers were not eyewitnesses of the events surrounding the crucifixion and resurrection of Jesus Christ.

The people who say that will often appeal to Mark 14:50. They say that within two minutes they could dismiss the argument because Jesus' followers all left Him and fled. So therefore, everything was hearsay. Men and women, this line of reasoning ignores common sense in the facts of the case. For example, read just the next four verses. It says this: "And Peter followed Him." You see, they left Him in a group, but they came back individually—immediately, Mr. Deedat.

Verse 4 says: "And Peter followed Him at a distance." He went right into the courtyard of the high priest. And he was sitting there with the officer. Can you imagine? With the officers, and warming himself. In Mark 14, it says, "And Peter was below, in the courtyard." Men and women, if you have studied the Scriptures, you'll realize that Mark, in his gospel, was writing down all the eyewitness accounts of Peter. Peter was right there. Then we go to John 18, verse 15: "And Simon Peter was following Jesus, and so was another disciple. Now that disciple was known to the high priest and entered with Jesus into the court of the high priest." John 19:26, "When Jesus therefore saw His mother, and the disciple whom He loved standing nearby, He said to His mother, 'Woman, behold your son.' " They were eyewitnesses. They were there.

About being permissible in a court of law. In most legal situations, you have what can be referred to as an ancient document rule. Now, you have to go to law to substantiate these things. Dr. John Warwick Montgomery is a lawyer and dean of the Simon Greenleaf School of Law, and a lecturer at the International School of Theology and Law in Strasburg, France.

He said that the application of the ancient document rule to the documents of the New Testament (especially the four gospels)—this is a head of a law school speaking—"Applied to the gospel records, and reinforced by responsible lower (textual) criticism, this rule would establish competency in any court of law."

The greatest eyewitness testimony is not found in the gospels. It is found in I Corinthians, the epistle by the apostle Paul, chapter 15, and was written in A.D. 55 to 56. I have yet to find a reputable scholar who would deny that. Paul says (now it's 20 years earlier, right after his conversion—he had met with the leaders. He had met with James, the brother of Jesus in Jerusalem), that the tradition was passed on to him that there were over 500 eyewitnesses of the resurrection. If you take that into a court of law, give each eyewitness just six minutes, that would make 3,000 minutes of eyewitness testimony, or 50 hours of eyewitness testimony.

However, that's not the key point here. That was the tradition handed down to him, what he had examined personally. But Paul says then, the majority of them are still alive right now. Not when the tradition was passed down, but right now. Men and women, Paul was saying, "If you don't believe me, ask them."

Also, many people overlook the fact that when the message of Jesus Christ was presented by the apostles and disciples, and the New Testament was shared, present in the audience were hostile and antagonistic witnesses. If they would have dared to depart from the truth of what was said, there were hostile witnesses to correct them immediately. In a court of law that is referred to as the principle of cross-examination. They did not dare to depart from the truth. Also, apart from the Bible, you have several extra-biblical secular sources.

One, a man by the name of Polycarp, was a disciple of the apostle John. He writes in his works, going back almost 2,000 years ago, "So firm is the ground upon which these gospels rest, that even the heretics themselves would not undermine it." They had to start from what was presented and then develop their own heresy. Because even then, they could not say, Jesus didn't say that. Jesus didn't do that then...they couldn't do that. So, they had to start with what He said, and develop their own heresy.

The conclusion of many scholars is a tremendous confidence in the Christian Bible. Mr. Millar Burrows was on the staff of Yale University, one of the most prestigious universities in my country. He said, "There is an increase of confidence in the accurate transmission of the text of the New Testament itself." Dr. Howard Vox, a researcher and archaeologist, said, "From the standpoint of literary evidence, the only logical conclusion is in the case where the reliability of the New Testament is infinitely stronger than any other record of antiquity."

The sixth fact that I discovered was that Christ *was* crucified. What does the historical, reliable record show? It is clear, not only from the Christian's biblical historical record, but also from secular sources, which are documented in the back of my book, *Evidence That Demands a Verdict*, that He not only predicted His death by crucifixion, but that He was actually crucified. Jesus said that He would be whipped and delivered over to be crucified. And then, in John 19:17, 18, "They took Jesus therefore, and He went out, bearing His own cross, to the place called the Place of a Skull....There they crucified Him, and with Him two other men, one on either side, and Jesus in between."

Let's follow through what actually happened. First of all, it points out that Jesus was whipped by the Romans. What did that mean? The Romans would strip a person down to the waist and would tie him in the court-yard. Then they would take a whip that had a handle about a foot and a half long. At the end of the handle, it had four leather thongs with heavy, jagged bones or balls of lead with jagged edges, wound into the end of the straps. A minimum of five. They would be different lengths. The Romans would bring the whip down over the back of the individual and all the balls of lead or bone would hit the body at the same time, and they they

THE ISLAM
DEBATE

would yank the whip down. The Jews would only permit 40 lashes. So they never did more than 39 so they wouldn't break the law if they miscounted. The Romans could do as many as they wanted. So, when the Romans whipped a Jew, they did 41 or more out of spite to the Jews. And so he had probably at least 41, if not more, lashes.

There are several medical authorities that have done research on crucifixion. One is a Dr. Barbet, in France, and another is Dr. C. Truman Davis, in the state of Arizona in my country. He is a medical doctor who has done meticulous study of the crucifixion from a medical perspective. Here he gives the effect of the Roman flogging:

"The heavy whip is brought down with full force again and again across (a person's) shoulders, back and legs. At first, the heavy thongs cut through the skin only. Then, as the blows continue, they cut deeper into the subcutaneous tissues, producing first an oozing of blood from the capillaries and veins of the skin, and finally spurting arterial bleeding from vessels in the underlying muscles. The small balls of lead first produce large, deep bruises, which the others cut wide open. Finally, the skin of the back is hanging in long ribbons, and the entire area is an unrecognizable mass of torn, bleeding tissue."

Other sources I have documented said that sometimes the back is literally opened up to the bowels within. Many people would die just from the whipping.

After the whipping they took Jesus out to the execution area and drove spikes into His wrists and His feet. It says that late that Friday afternoon they broke the legs of the two thieves hanging with Jesus, but they did not break His legs. Now, why did they break someone's legs? When you are prostrate on the cross, or hanging there, they bent the legs up underneath and drove the spike through here. When you died by crucifixion, often what would happen is you would die from your own air. The pectoral muscles would be affected and you could not let your air out. You could take it in, but could not let it out.

And so, you'd hang there and suffocate; you would push up on your legs to let the air out, and then come down to take it in. When they wanted to bring about the death immediately, they broke their legs and they couldn't push up, and they would die. Jesus' legs were not broken. As the Holy God, revealing His Holy Word in the Bible, points out, Jesus had died. Men and women, if they had broken His legs, He would not have been our Messiah. He would not have been the Eternal Word, because God, Yahweh in the Old Testament, prophesies in Psalms that His legs would not be broken. His bones would not be broken. Men and women, He was fulfilling what God, Yahweh, had already revealed would take place.

The next fact that I discovered was that Christ was dead. That's the seventh fact that I discovered. Men and women, in John 19:30, Jesus willed Himself to die. That's why He didn't take so long. He came to die. He said, "I lay My life down." And in John 19, He said, "It is finished," and He bowed His head and He gave up the Spirit. He willed Himself to die. Now, in John 19, verse 34 (Mr. Deedat, in his booklet, has referred to it as *Evidence That Jesus Was Not Dead*), you have reference to the blood and water.

He was on the cross and they'd already acknowledged Him being dead, but they thought they'd give a parting shot, as you would say. They took a spear, and thrust it into His side. Eyewitness accounts said blood and water came out separated. Mr. Deedat, in his book, appealed to this phenomenon as evidence that Christ was still alive. He supports this in his writing, by an appeal to an article in the *Thinker's Digest*, 1949, by an anesthesiologist. I was able to acquire medical research by various people in this area.

I have time to share just two of the findings. First, from a scholastic viewpoint: many medical and university or varsity libraries that once carried this journal, no longer do so. It is considered by many in the medical field to be not only out of date, but behind the medical times.

Second, from a medical viewpoint: A wound of the type inflicted on Jesus, if the person were still alive, would not bleed out the wound opening, but bleed into the chest cavity, causing an internal hemorrhage. At the aperture of the wound, the blood would be barely oozing from the opening. For a spear to form a perfect channel that would allow the blood and serum to flow out the spear wound is next to impossible. The massive internal damage done to a person under crucifixion, and then being speared in the heart area, would cause death almost immediately, not even including what happens with the details of a Jew's burial.

At the State of Massachusetts General Hospital, over a period of years, they did research on people who died of a ruptured heart. Normally, the heart had 20 cc's of pericardial fluid. When a person dies of a ruptured heart, there is more than 500 cc's of pericardial fluid. And it would come out in the form of a fluid and clotted blood. Perhaps this is what was viewed at that time.

The Jewish burial would have been a final death blow. Mr. Deedat says in his book, page 9, in *What Was the Sign of Jonah?* that they gave the Jewish burial bath, plastered him with 100 pounds of aloe and myrrh. Now, going through whipping, where the back is almost laid open, having your arms and feet pierced, being put on a cross, having a spear thrust in your side, being taken down and then plastered with 100-some pounds of spices of cement consistency—it would call for a greater miracle than the resurrection to live through that.

Then, the severe discipline of the Romans. Pilate was a little amazed, and I would have been too, that Christ had already been dead, or that they had come and asked for the body. So, he called a centurion in. And he said, "I want you to go and confirm to me that Jesus is dead." Now men and women, this centurion was not a fool. He was not about ready to leave his wife a widow.

The centurion would always check with four different executioners. That was Roman law. There had to be four executioners. They did that so in case one man was a little lax, the other one would catch him in it. And you would never have all four lax in signing the death warrant. Discipline was severe with the Romans.

For example, when the angel let Peter out of jail in Acts 12 in the New Testament, Herod called in the guard and executed them all—just for letting one man out of jail. In Acts 16 in the Christian New Testament, the doors had been opened up in the jail for Paul and Silas, their chains had been loosened, and the moment the guard saw they were freed, he pulled out his own sword to execute himself. And Paul said, "Wait a minute!" You see, that guard knew what would happen. He would rather die by his own sword, than be executed by the Romans.

Then Christ was dead. Flavius Josephus, the Jewish historian, records that when he went into Jerusalem in A.D. 70 when Titus was destroying it, he saw three of his friends being crucified. They had just been put up there. They had been whipped and everything. He went to the commander of the guard and he said, "Please release them." Now, you have to understand, Flavius was the name given to Josephus by the Roman Emperor who had brought him into his own family. That's why he had influence as a Jew. And you know, immediately, the Roman guard captain took the three men down from the cross and still, men and women, two of the three died. They'd just been put up there and they were removed quickly. Crucifixion was that cruel.

The Jews knew that Jesus was dead. In Matthew 27 they went to the Roman leader and said, "Sir, we remember that when He was still alive..." In other words, what is He now? Dead! "When He was still alive He said, 'After three days I am to rise again.' " I believe Mr. Deedat has his books saying that the Jews realized they'd made a mistake. He really wasn't dead, so they thought they wouldn't make a second mistake, so they go and get a guard unit put there. Well, the Jews themselves said He was already dead. "We just want to make sure no one takes His body so there won't be any deception." The Jews have been accused of a lot of things, but very seldom have they ever been accused of stupidity. They knew He was dead.

The next fact I discovered was the burial procedure of the Jews. Some people say they were hurrying because of the Sabbath coming, and they had to carry Him back. Men and women, I checked this out in detail. And I documented in my *Resurrection Factor* book that the burial procedure was so important they could even do it on the Sabbath. They didn't have to worry about the Sabbath coming up. They didn't want the body to hang on the cross once the Sabbath began, but they could take their time burying Him. They would put spices around the body—in this case, 100 pounds of aromatic spices—along with a gummy, cement substance.

They would stretch the body out or straighten it out. They'd take a piece of linen cloth 30 centimeters wide. They would start to wrap the body from the feet. In between the folds, they put the cement consistency and the spices. They wrapped the body to the armpits, put the arms down, started below the fingers again, wrapped to the neck, and put a separate piece around the head. In this situation, I would estimate an encasement of 117 to 120 pounds.

The next fact that I discovered is that they took extreme security precautions at the tomb of Jesus Christ. One, it says that they rolled a large stone against the tomb. Mark says the stone was extremely large. One historical reference going back to the first century says that 20 men could not move the stone. Now, I think it was exaggerated a little bit there. But he was making a point about the size of the stone. Two engineering professors, after they heard me speak on the stone, went to Israel. As non-Christian engineering professors, they calculated the size stone needed to roll against a four-and-a-half to five-foot doorway of the Jewish tombs. They wrote me a well-documented letter, and said it would have to have a minimum weight of one and a half to two tons.

Mr. Deedat, in his books, makes an issue that one man, or two at the most, rolled the stone against the entrance. Therefore, one or two men could roll it back. It says Joseph of Arimathea rolled the stone against the entrance. Don't force on the Bible or the Qur'an anything you would not force in conversation today. For example: when I came to the stadium the other day to look it over, I said to one of the people that brought me here, "How did all these chairs get here?" He said, "Mr. Deedat brought them." Mr. Deedat, did you bring all 700 of these chairs personally, yourself? No! They were brought by many people. I could go away from here saying Mr. Deedat put on this symposium. But I think there were some others that helped make all the arrangements.

History says Hitler invaded France. Now, maybe he would have tried it in France alone, but I don't think he would try it in South Africa alone.

There could have been a number of people that helped Joseph of Arimathea. Plus, you find when you go back and research it out that the tombs had a trough going up the side. They placed the stone there. They had a block. Then, men and women, my seven-year-old daughter could roll it, because you simply pull up the block, letting the stone roll down the front and lodge itself against the entrance of the tomb.

Then, a security guard was put there. The Jews wanted one. They went to the Romans and said, give us a guard unit. The Greek word was *kustodia*. Men and women, a *kustodia* was a 16-man security unit. Each man was trained to protect six square feet of ground. The 16 men, according to Roman history, were supposed to be able to protect 36 square yards against an entire battalion and hold it. Each guard had four weapons on his body. He was a fighting machine, almost the same as was true of the Temple Police.

Next, a Roman seal was placed on the tomb with a Roman insignia. That seal stood for the power and the authority of the Roman Empire. The body of Christ was encased with 100 and some pounds of cement and aromatic spices. A one-and-a-half to two-ton stone was rolled against the entrance; a 16-man security unit was placed there, and a Roman seal. But something happened. It's a matter of historical record: after three days, the tomb was empty.

I don't have to debate that. Mr. Deedat agrees the tomb was empty. So, I won't waste any time here.

The sign of Jonah—I'm so glad you brought that up. The sign of Jonah—won't take too much time there because I don't think it's necessary in this sense. Whenever you study something, you study it in the language and the culture of that day. Now, you go back to the Jewish language, and the Jewish culture of *that* day. Not today—not South African, not Indian, not American. The Jewish-Israelite culture of that day.

Let's see what three days and three nights mean. In Esther, chapter 4, in the Old Testament of the Christian Jewish Bible, it says there was a fast for three days and three nights. But then, it went on, and it says they completed the fast on the third day. You see, in Jewish language, "after three days and three nights," meant "to the third day" or "on the third day." Jesus said in Matthew 12:40 He would be buried for three days and three nights.

In Matthew 20, Jesus said He would be raised up *on* the third day—not *after* the third day. The Jews came to Jesus, and they said in Matthew 27, verse 63, "Sir...that deceiver said 'After three days I am to rise again.'" So, they asked for a Roman guard. Now watch the language here. "Therefore, give orders for the grave to be made secure until the third day," not *after* the third day. They knew what Jesus said, three days and three nights, meant *until* the third day, "lest His disciples come and steal Him away."

Friday before six o'clock they had three hours to bury Him. It took less than an hour. The Jewish reckoning of time in the Jewish Talmud and the Babylonian Jerusalem Talmud (the commentaries of the Jews), said any part, an "onan"—any part of the day is considered a full day. On Friday before six o'clock by Jewish reckoning, any minute was one day and one night. From Friday night at six o'clock to Saturday at six o'clock, was another day and another night.

Men and women, from Jewish reckoning—not ours—any moment after six o'clock Saturday night is another day, another night. We do the same thing in my country. If my son was born one minute before midnight on December the 31st, on my income taxes to my government, I could treat my son with the same time principle as having been born at any time during that one full year—365 days and 365 nights.

THE ISLAM
DEBATE

When the Roman guards failed in their duty, they were automatically executed. One way they were executed was they were stripped of their clothes and burned alive in a fire started with their own clothes. The seal was broken. Men and women, when that seal was broken, the security forces were thrown into finding that man or men, and when they were found, anyone breaking that seal was condemned to crucifixion upside down.

The stone was removed, men and women, and I'll ask Mr. Deedat to check it out carefully. The revealed Word of God in the Christian New Testament, in the original Greek (as the Qur'an is in Arabic, the New Testament is in Greek), points out that a one-and-a-half- to two-ton stone was rolled up a slope, away from not just the entrance, but away from the entire tomb, looking like it had been picked up and carried away. Now, if they wanted to tip-toe in, move the stone over, and help Jesus out, why all the efforts to move a one-and-a-half to two-ton stone up away from the entire sepulchre? That guard unit would have had to have been sleeping with cotton in their ears and with earmuffs on not to have heard that one.

Then, Mary went to the tomb in John 20. Mr. Deedat says that she went there to anoint the body and that the word "anoint" means "to massage." Well, let me tell you, if that's true—it's not—but if it *were* true, and that's the way the Muslims do it, it would have killed Jesus. If I went through crucifixion, had my hands and feet pierced, my back laid open to the bowels, 100 and some pounds put around me, I wouldn't want anyone to massage me. The word "anoint" means "consecrated." As Mr. Deedat brought out in his book, the priests and kings were anointed when being consecrated to their office. When He said, "Touch Me not," Mr. Deedat says it means, "I am hurting—don't touch Me." Well, read the next phrase, Mr. Deedat. It says, "Do not touch Me, because I haven't yet ascended to the Father."

That's why they're not to touch Him because "I haven't ascended to the Father." And then He says, "Now, go tell My disciples I am ascending to the Father." A little bit later, He says, "You can touch Me. Grab My feet." Why did He do that? Oh, men and women, this is one of the most beautiful things. In the Old Testament, at the tabernacle, the Jewish high priest would take the sacrifice into the Holy of Holies. And the people would wait outside, because they knew if God did not accept their sacrifice, the priest would be struck dead.

They would wait for the high priest to come back. And when the high priest walked back out, everybody shouted with joy! Because they said, "God has accepted our sacrifice." Jesus said, "Don't touch Me...I've not ascended to the Father." Jesus, between that time and when the others grabbed hold of Him and touched Him, ascended to God the Father, presented Himself as a sacrifice, and, ladies and gentlemen, if Jesus had not come back, if He had not permitted the others to touch Him, it would have meant His sacrifice had not been accepted. But I thank God He came back and said, "Touch Me." It's been accepted.

As for the spiritual-physical body of Jesus Christ, I think, Mr. Deedat, you need to first study our Scriptures. I think you need to read just as I did to study *your* scriptures. You need to read 1 Corinthians 15:44, 51. The explanation of the glorified, imperishable body. It was a spiritual body, and yet, it had substance. He could walk through a door; He could appear in their presence. He didn't need food, but He took food. Otherwise, they would have said, "You're merely a spirit." No. He had what the Bible called the resurrected, glorified, incorruptible body. And if I were in that room and I knew I'd seen Him crucified, buried and everything else, and all of a sudden, with the doors locked, He appeared in the midst of the group, I think I'd be a little frightened, too. Men and women, Jesus Christ is raised from the dead! Thank you.

THE ISLAM
DEBATE

<small>REBUTTALS</small>

Ahmed Deedat

Mr. Chairman, and ladies and gentlemen of the jury. The crux of the problem—the clear-cut statement by Jesus Christ, is the mistake that the disciples were making in thinking that He had come back from the dead. By assuring them that "a spirit has no flesh and bones, as you see Me have." This is King's English, basic English. And one does not need a dictionary or a lawyer to explain to you what it implies.

Throughout the length and breadth of the 27 books of the New Testament, there is not a single statement made by Jesus Christ that "I was dead, and I have come back from the dead." The Christian has been belaboring the word resurrection. Again and again, by repetition, it is conveyed that it is proving a fact. You keep on seeing the man, the man's eating food, as though He was resurrected. He appears in the upper room—He was resurrected. Jesus Christ never uttered that word that "I have come back from the dead," in the 27 books of the New Testament, not once.

He was there with them for 40 days. And He never uttered that statement. He is proving again and again that He was that same Jesus, the one who had escaped death, so to say, by the skin of His teeth. Because He was ever in disguise. He never showed Himself openly to the Jews. He had given them a sign. "No sign shall be given unto it except the sign of Jonah." No sign, but this. And He never went back to them to the temple of Jerusalem, to tell them, "Here I am." Not once. He was ever in hiding. Now, we will not belabor the things that have passed.

The points were, that Jesus was *not* reluctant to die. He had actually come for this purpose. Now, *my* reading of the Scriptures tells me that not only was He reluctant, but He was preparing for a show-down with the Jews. You see, at the Last Supper, He raises the problem of defense, telling His disciples, "As you remember, when I sent you out on your mission of preaching and healing, I told you that you were not to carry anything with you. No purse, no sticks. No staff. Did you lack anything?"

And they said "No, we lacked nothing." But now, I tell you, He tells them, "Those of you who have no swords must sell their garments and buy them." You must sell your garments and buy swords. I'm asking you, what do you do with swords? You peel apples? Or you cut people's throats? What do you do with swords? So one of them said, "Master, we have two already." And He said, "That is enough."

And He takes His disciples—11 of them. Judas had already gone to betray Him. Eleven disciples and Himself, and they walk to Gethsemane. And at Gethsemane—read the book, read your gospels—and it'll tell you that Jesus put eight men at the gate. I'm asking you, why should He go to Gethsemane in the first place? And why put eight at the gate, telling them, "Tarry ye here, and watch with Me."

He means, stop here, and keep guard. Guarding what? What was there to guard in Gethsemane? A courtyard, olive press, empty place. What were they, the disciples, to guard five miles out of town at Gethsemane? Then He takes with Him, Peter, and the two sons of Zebedee. At least two of them had swords. And He makes an inner line of defense and He tells *them*, "Tarry ye here, sit ye here, and watch with Me. While *I* go and pray yonder... *I* alone go and pray beyond." I'm asking you, why did He go to Gethsemane? Why did He go there—to pray? Couldn't He have prayed in that upper room, while there at the Last Supper? Couldn't He have gone to the temple of Jerusalem, a stone's throw from where they were? Why go five miles out of town? And why put eight at the gate? And why make an inner line of defense?

And He goes a little farther, and falls on His face, and He prays to God. "Oh, my Father... if it be possible, let this cup pass from Me." Meaning, remove the difficulty from Me, but not as I will, but as Thou wilt. In the end, I leave it to You. But I want You to save Me. And, being in agony, He prayed more earnestly, and His sweat was as if it were great drops of blood falling down to the ground. Is this how one man, a person goes to commit suicide? Is this how the person who is ordained from the foundation of the earth, for the sacrifice, is this how He behaves, I ask you?

That He is sweating, it says, being in an agony, He prays more earnestly, and His sweat was as if it were great drops of blood falling down to the ground. And the Lord of Mercy sends His angel, says the Bible. An angel came to strengthen Him. I say, in what? In the belief that God was going to save Him. What does the angel come to strengthen Him in? To save Him. And in everything that happened from there onward, you can see God planning His rescue. Look. The fact was that the prophecy He had made was that He would be like Jonah—and we are told that He was

THE ISLAM
DEBATE

unlike Jonah. He didn't fulfill. Jonah is alive, Jesus is dead.

Then, Pontius Pilate—he marveled when he was told that Jesus was dead because in his knowledge, he knew no man can die within three hours on the cross. Because this crucifixion was to be a slow, lingering death. This was the real purpose of crucifixion. It was not getting rid of an anti-social character, like a firing squad, or hanging, or impaling a person. It was a slow, lingering death.

And the bones were not broken—says the Bible. It was a fulfillment of prophecy. Now, the bones of an individual—of a dead person—whether you break them or not, is of the least consequence. If the bones were not broken, the only time it can help anybody, is if the person was alive. So you see, for 2,000 years now, it's a programming, a continuous programming. And Paul has put the whole gamut of religion on one point: on this death and resurrection, because he tells us, 1 Corinthians, chapter 15, verse 14, that "if Christ is not risen from the dead, our preaching is in vain; our faith is in vain." Useless! You haven't got a thing!

So now, like drowning men clutching at straws, the Christian must, by hook or by crook, prove that somehow crucifixion killed the man, so we can earn salvation. Now, we would like you, Mr. Chairman, ladies and gentlemen of the jury, to read this book once more, and the testimony, word for word. If you examine the prophecies—what Jesus says, and the way He behaves—they are conclusive proof that Christ had not been crucified.

Josh McDowell

I'm not sure that I heard, but did you say, "Nowhere in the 27 books of the New Testament did Jesus ever say He was 'dead and now alive' "? May I read to you from the book of Revelation, chapter 1, verse 18? He said, "I am the living one. I was dead, and behold, I am alive forevermore." Also, Mr. Deedat, He appeared to the Jews. The whole New Testament Church was started with Jews. He appeared to the Jewish antagonist, the apostle Paul, when he was Saul of Tarsus.

But men and women, the greatest thrill to me, when it comes to the resurrection and Christ as my Life and Savior, is that God Yahweh has promised, when a man enters into that relationship through asking Christ to forgive him, who died for our sins, was buried and raised again on the third day, that God, the Holy Spirit, enters that person and changes them. And one of the greatest evidences is my own life. After I came to the point where I acknowledged Jesus Christ as my Savior and Lord, surrendered my will up to Him, and trusted Him, men and women, in about six months to a year, or a year and a half, the major areas of my life were changed.

First, I developed a desire to live a holy and godly life. Second, I started to experience a peace and genuine joy—it wasn't because I don't have conflict—it's in spite of conflict, the peace that God gives through Jesus Christ. Third, I gained control over my temper. I almost killed a young man my first year in a university. I was constantly losing my temper. After I trusted Jesus as Savior and Lord, I would catch myself arising to the crisis of losing my temper, and it was gone!

Not only my friends noticed it, but my enemies did a lot sooner. And only once now, in 22 years that I have had a personal relationship with God Yahweh, the Father, through His Eternal Word, the Son, only once have I lost my temper. He has given me a supernatural strength over it.

The greatest area, men and women, that I'm thankful I can share here, is the very love of God. In this sense: My father was the town alcoholic. I hardly ever knew my father when he was not drunk. My friends in school would make jokes about my father making a fool of himself. I lived on a farm and I'd go out to the barn and see my mother lying in the gutter in the manure—the bathroom of the cows—beaten so badly by my father, my mother couldn't get up and walk.

We would have friends over. I'd take my father, tie him up in the barn, and park the car up around the side, and tell my friends he had to go on an important business trip, so I wouldn't be embarrassed. I'd take him into the barn where the cows would have their little calves. I'd put his arms through the boards, and tie them. I'd put a rope around his neck and pull his head all the way over the backboard, and tie it around the feet, so if he shuffled his feet, he would kill himself.

One evening, two months before I graduated from high school, I came home from a date. When I went into the house, I heard my mother crying profusely. And I said, "What's wrong?" She said, "Your father has broken my heart. And all I want to do is live until you graduate, then I just want to die."

Do you know, two months later, I graduated. And the next Friday, the 13th, my mother died. Don't tell me that you can't die of a broken heart. My mother did, and my father broke it. There was no one I could have hated more. But men and women, when I came into this relationship with God Yahweh, through His Eternal Son, the Lord Jesus Christ, after a short period of time, the love of God took control of my life, and He took that hatred and turned it upside down.

So much so, I was able to look my father square in the eyes and say: "Dad, I love you." And the neatest thing is, I really meant it! I transferred to another varsity or university. I was in a serious car accident with my legs, arm and neck in traction. I was taken home. My father came into my room. He was very sober because he thought I was almost dead. He asked me this question: "How can you love a father such as I?" I said, "Dad, six months ago, I despised you. I hated you." Then I shared with him how I'd come to the conclusion seen so clearly, that God Yahweh, the Father, had manifested Himself to us, humanity through the Eternal Word, His Son. And then He had died for our sins, that's the anguish He went through, Mr. Deedat.

If you could imagine all the sins in the world—just your sins and my sins would be enough. But all the sins in the world are upon the Son. The anguish that was involved. And I said, "Dad, I asked Christ to forgive me. I asked Him to come into my life as Savior and Lord." I said, "Dad, as the result of that, I have found the capacity to love and accept not only you, but other people just the way they are."

I can look at you, Mr. Deedat, and say, "I honestly love you...God has given me a love for you...I love you so much, I would love to have you come to know Jesus Christ as Savior and Lord." And my father finally just said, "Son, if your God can do in my life what I have seen Him do in your life, then I want to know Him personally."

Right there, my father just prayed something like this: "God, if You're God, and Christ is the Eternal Word, Your Son, if You can forgive me and come into my life and change me, then I want to know You personally."

Men and women, my life was basically changed in six months to a year, to a year and a half. And there are still many areas for God to change. But then, take my father. His life was changed right before my eyes. Mr. Deedat, it was like somebody reached out and turned on a light bulb. Do you know, he only touched whiskey once after that. He got it to his lips, and that was it. He didn't need it anymore. Fourteen months later, he died. Because three-fourths of his stomach had to be removed, as a result of 40-some years of drinking. But do you know, ladies and gentlemen, in that 14-month period, scores of businessmen in my home town and the surrounding area committed their lives to the living God, through the Eternal Word, Jesus Christ, because of the changed life of one of the town's drunks.

My wife, Dottie, puts it this way. She says, "Honey, because Christ was raised from the dead, He lives. And because He lives, He has the infinite capacity through the Holy Spirit to enter a man or woman's life, and change them from the inside out." That is why the resurrected, living Christ said in one of the 27 books of the New Testament, "I was dead, now I am alive." He can say, "I stand at the door of your life and knock. If anyone hears My voice and opens the door, I will come in."

CLOSING STATEMENTS

Ahmed Deedat

Mr. Chairman and ladies and gentlemen of the jury. Man is coward by nature. From the beginning of Adam, you remember, passing the buck. It's not me, it's the woman; and the woman, it's not me, it's the serpent. Man is coward by nature. And we want somebody else to carry the burden for us. We want somebody else to take the medicine when we are sick. We want somebody else's appendix to be removed, when ours is rotten. This is man in general.

But this is not what Jesus Christ said. He wanted you to take up your own cross—get yourself crucified. Listen! He says, "He is not of Me who does not take his cross and follow Me." Take up your cross and follow Me. In other words, get yourself crucified. No, no, no. No, He didn't mean that. What He meant was, that as I carry My responsibility, you carry yours. As I pray, you pray. As I fast, you fast; as I'm circumcised, you be circumcised; what I do, you do. You carry your own responsibility.

This is what He meant. Now, that is the Islamic system! This is what Islam teaches. You see, the system that saves you after years of alcoholism, after years of pinching 10 cents from the collection plate, you read it here, in Josh's book. He says every Sunday, the only thing he got out of church was he was putting in 25 cents and taking out 35 for milkshakes. And then, later on in life, if you study, we find the same thing is being done on a very high level of intellectualism. But we haven't got the time to go into that.

Let me end with the message of Jesus: He says, "Verily, verily, I say unto you, except your righteousness exceed the righteousness of the scribes and the pharisees, you shall by no means enter the kingdom of heaven." There's no heaven for you. This is what He says; these are His words. And what is happening is, you are not contradicting His words. This is Islam! Unless you are better than the Jews, there is no heaven for you.

He didn't say it's the blood, but your righteousness. You must be better than the Jews. You must fast, as the Jews fasted, but on a higher level; you must pray, as the Jews prayed, but on a higher level; you must give charity, as the Jews gave charity, but on a higher level. And that is Islam.

So, Mr. Chairman, ladies and gentlemen of the jury, I say that this resurrection, as has been addressed by Josh in America, under the heading, "Hoax or History," I will conclude that here are one thousand million people being taken for a ride on a cross. In Durban, every week, we have horses taking thousands of people for a ride—every horse. But here, you are being taken for a ride on the cross.

Thank you very much, ladies and gentlemen.

Josh McDowell

Mr. Deedat, nowhere in the Christian Bible revealed by God is a Christian ever commanded to be crucified. We are told to acknowledge that we are already crucified in Jesus Christ.

In Romans 8:32, God, speaking from eternity into time, says, "He who did not spare His own Son, but delivered Him up...up for us all." In my country, a young lady, who was picked up for speeding, was brought before the judge. The judge said, "Guilty or not guilty?" and she said, "Guilty." He brought down the gavel, and the judge fined her $100 or 10 days. Then, an amazing thing took place. The judge stood up, took off his robe, placed it over the back of the chair, went down in front, and paid the fine. He was a just judge. His daughter had broken the law.

No matter how much he loved his daughter, he had to say $100 or 10 days. But he loved her enough, he was willing to go down, and take the penalty upon himself, and pay it. This is a clear illustration of what God Yahweh has revealed through His Holy Word. God loves us. Christ died for us. The Bible very clearly points out the wages of sin is death. So, God had to bring down the gavel.

But, men and women, He loved us so much, He was able to set aside His judicial robe, and come down in the form of the man Jesus Christ. And go to the cross and pay the price for us. And now, He can say, "I stand at the door of your life and knock. And if anyone hears My voice, and opens the door, I will come in."

Yes, Mr. Deedat, one billion Christians are riding on the cross. We are being taken for a ride. I believe God has provided the cross as the chariot to heaven, through the shed blood of His divine Son.

Thank you very much, ladies and gentlemen, for giving me the privilege, as a person from another country, to come here, and Mr. Deedat, I am greatly indebted to you for this opportunity. And if you come to my country, we'll have dinner together. Thank you.

CONCLUSION

ISLAM AND CHRISTIANITY

Many of the Muslim beliefs come from the Bible. Much of the historical foundation for the Qur'an comes from the Old Testament. Yet even though there has been influence and there are similarities, the differences in the beliefs of the two faiths are striking.

God

Islam teaches that God is a unit and this explicitly excludes the trinity. However, it is important to realize that what Islam is rejecting concerning the trinity is *not* (may we emphasize, *is not*) the biblical view of God the Father, God the Son and God the Holy Spirit, *but* rather they are rejecting the heretical concept of the trinity being God the Father, Mary the Mother and Jesus the Son. This is blasphemy to them and, may we say, to the Christian as well.

One reason for this distorted view of the trinity is that the Arabs had no Arabic New Testament and thus had been influenced by a false Christian view.

This emphasis on the unity of God comes across in other ways. Islam teaches that God is divorced from His creation. He is so unified to Himself that He cannot be associated with creation. His transcendence is so great that He acts impersonally, even to the point of choosing those He wants for heaven.

Because God is a unit many Muslims believe that the Sunnis' position that the Qur'an is the "eternal word of God" commits the sin of associating something with God. It is for this reason the Shi'ites hold that the Qur'an is a created book.

Because of their doctrine of predestination and the fact that both evil and good came from Allah, it makes their God somewhat capricious in our view. Whatever Allah chooses becomes right; this makes any true standard of righteousness or ethics hard to discern if not impossible to establish.

This is unlike the God of the Bible who is righteous. The very word righteous means, "a standard."

The Muslim finds it difficult to divorce the concept of father from the physical realm. To them it is blasphemous to call Allah or God your Father.

In addition, while calling God "Father" is to evoke thoughts of love, compassion, tenderness and protectiveness to Christians, it is not always so to the Muslim mind. To him, a father must be strict, should not be emotional, need not express love, and is bound to his family by duty and for what his family can provide for him, not by devotion.

Allah appears to be deficient in such attributes as love, holiness and grace. One reason is that to a Muslim God is above description. For the most part Allah is defined by a series of negatives, i.e., He is not this, not that, etc. Many of the above characteristics are involved in the Muslims' 99 names for God. For the Christian, these attributes, such as grace, are rooted in the very character of God (Ephesians 2).

The Bible

As mentioned before, the Muslim holy books include the sayings of Moses, the prophets, David, Jesus and Muhammad. However, Muslims believe that all of the previous sayings have been lost or corrupted and that the Qur'an alone has been preserved free of error. It claims to supercede the previous revelations as well. Remember, the holy books mentioned in Islam are *not* exactly like our biblical Scriptures.

One would presuppose that since the teachings of Christianity and Islam are clearly different, it would follow that the practical and social consequences of the doctrine would also be vastly different. This is precisely the case. As Guillaume mentions, this is nowhere better illustrated than in the status of women:

> The Qur'an has more to say on the position of women than on any other social question. The guiding note is sounded in the words, "Women are your tillage," and the word for marriage is that used for the sexual act. The primary object of marriage is the propagation of children, and partly for this a man is allowed four wives at a time and an unlimited number of concubines. However, it is laid down that wives are to be treated with kindness and strict impartiality; if a man cannot treat all alike he should keep to one.

> The husband pays the woman a dowry at the time of marriage, and the money or property so alloted remains her own. The husband may divorce his wife at any time, but he cannot take her back until she has remarried and been divorced by a second husband. (Only after three divorces can a Muslim man not take back his wife. However, he can say, "I divorce thee" three times, which to some constitutes three divorces.) A woman cannot sue for divorce on any grounds, and her husband may beat her. In this matter of the status of women lies the greatest difference between the Muslims and the Christian world (Guillaume, *Islam*, pp. 71, 72).

One coming from a Western culture needs to realize that this stand concerning women was an improvement over the pre-Islamic conditions. Thus some Islamic communities use this as a basis for teaching that Islam is progressive and that women have equal rights.

Those from Western culture often fall in the misunderstanding that views Muslims as being debauched and sex-hungry. From the Muslim's point of view, women are protected, provided for and respected in their community.

In comparing this with the present-day decline of Western culture and its attack upon traditional morality, including women, abortion, etc., a Westerner must realize that Muslims see us in exactly the same way that many from a Western culture, including many Christians in the past, have viewed or portrayed them. A penetrating question would be, "Are women beaten, raped and mugged more in Muslim lands or in Western countries?"

The mistake the Muslim is often guilty of is identifying Western culture with Christianity (see page 30).

Jesus Christ

In Islam the person and work of Jesus Christ are not seen in the same way as in Christianity. For the Christian the resurrection of Jesus Christ as the incarnate Son of God is the vital cornerstone of faith, yet the Muslim does not hold to either of these truths—that Christ is the Son of God or that He rose from the dead. A Muslim will look at Jesus as the "Word of God" and as the "Spirit of God," but not as the Son of God. To them that is blasphemy. In fact, Muslims do not even believe Jesus was crucified; rather, many believe Judas was crucified in His place. Some, however, believe it was Christ on the cross but that He did not die.

Islam does believe Jesus was a sinless prophet although not as great as Muhammad. Many Muslims teach that Jesus was greater and more spiritual but too lofty, and that Muhammad was a practical "every man's" prophet. While Surah 3:45-47 in the Qur'an speaks of the virgin birth of Christ, it is not the same biblical virgin birth. According to Muslim belief, Jesus is certainly *not* the only begotten Son of God, and an angel—rather than the Holy Spirit—was the agency of God's power in the conception. However, the idea that Allah had a son is repugnant to them. Surah 4:171 states, "Jesus...was only a messenger of Allah...Far is it removed from His transcendent majesty that He should have a son."

John states concerning Christ, "And the Word became flesh, and dwelt among us, and we beheld His glory, glory as of the only begotten from the Father full of grace and truth. And I have seen, and have borne witness that this is the Son of God" (John 1:14, 34).

Christ's claim for His own deity and sonship are unequivocal. In John 10:30 He claims equality with the Father when He states, "I and the Father are one." For not only is the sonship of Christ important per se, but the deity of Christ is also an important point of difference between Christianity and Islam since Islam denies the doctrine of the Trinity.

Of the crucifixion, the Qur'an states in Surah 4:157, "They slew him not nor crucified, but it appeared so unto them." Most Muslims believe Judas was put in the place of Christ, and Christ went to heaven. The Bible teaches that Christ went to the cross to pay the penalty for man's sins, died, and was raised from the dead, appeared to the disciples and *then* ascended to heaven (1 Corinthians 15:3, 4).

They also reject the Bible as the only authoritative book on which to base all matters of doctrine, faith and practice. When Islam rejects the truth of the written Word of God, they are left not only different from Christianity, but opposite from Christianity on almost all counts.

BIBLIOGRAPHY

Anderson, Sir Norman. *The World's Religions*, Grand Rapids, MI: William B.
Eerdmans Publishing Company, 1976.

Anderson, J.N.D. "The Resurrection of Jesus Christ" (copyright), *Christianity
Today*, March 29, 1968, used by permission.

Boa, Kenneth. *Cults, World Religions, and You*, Wheaton, IL: Victor Books, 1977.

Davood, N.J. trans., *The Koran*, London: Penguin Books, 1956.

Holt, P.M. and Lambton, and Lewis, eds., *The Cambridge History of Islam*,
London: Cambridge University Press, 1970.

Encyclopaedia Britannica, s.v. "Islam," Chicago: William Benton Publisher, 1967.

Guillaume, Alfred. *Islam*, London: Penguin Books, 1954.

Kershaw, Max R. *How to Share the Good News With Your Muslim Friend*,
Colorado Springs: International Students Inc., 1978.

Little, Paul E. *Know Why You Believe*, Wheaton: Scripture Press Publications,
Inc., 1967, used by permission.

McDowell, Josh and Stewart, Don. *Understanding Non-Christian Religions*,
San Bernardino, CA: Here's Life Publishers, 1982.

Neill, Stephen. *Christian Faith and Other Faiths*, London: Oxford University
Press, 1970.

Noss, John B. *Man's Religions*, New York: MacMillan Publishing Company Inc.,
1974.

Payne, Robert. *The Holy Sword*, New York: Collier Books, 1962.

Pickthall, Mohammed Marmaduke. trans., *The Meaning of the Glorious Koran*,

DEBATE

New York: Mentor Books, n.d.

Rosscup, James. Class Notes, La Mirada, CA: Talbot Theological Seminary, 1969.

Straton, Hillyer H. "I Believe: Our Lord's Resurrection," *Christianity Today*, March 31, 1968, used by permission.

Strauss, David Friedrich. *The Life of Jesus for the People*, Vol. I, 2d ed., London: Williams and Norgate, 1879.

Tenney, Merrill C. *The Reality of the Resurrection*, Chicago: Moody Press, 1963, used by permission.

von Grunebaum, G.E. *Modern Islam*, Berkeley: University of California Press, 1962.

Williams, John Alden. *Islam*, New York: George Braziller, 1962.

BIBLIOGRAPHY

The Life of Muhammad

Ahmad, Barakat. *Muhammad and the Jews*, New Delhi: Vikas Publishing House, 1979.

Andrae, Tor. *Mohammed: The Man and His Faith*, New York: Charles Scribner's Sons, 1936.

Anonymous. *The Life of Mahomet, or, The History of that Imposture*, London: For the Booksellers, 1799.

'Azzam, 'Abd-al-Rahman. *The Eternal Message of Muhammad*, London: Quartet Books, 1979.

Balyuzi, H.M. *Muhammad and the Course of Islam*, Oxford: George Ronald, 1976.

Bosworth-Smith, R. *Mohammed and Mohammedanism*, London: Smith, Elder & Co., 1876.

Edwardes, Michael (Ed.). *The Life of Muhammad*, London: The Folio Society, 1964.

Gabrieli, Francesco. *Muhammad and the Conquests of Islam*, London: World University Library, 1968.

Glubb, John Bagot. *The Life and Times of Muhammad*, London: Hodder and Stoughton, 1970.

Guillaume, Alfred. *New Light on the Life of Muhammad*, Manchester, England: Manchester University Press, 1960.

_____. *The Life of Muhammad*, (A Translation of Ibn Ishaq's Sirat Rasul Allah), Karachi: Oxford University Press, 1978.

Haykal, Muhammad Husayn. *The Life of Muhammad*, U.S.A.: North American Trust Publications, 1976.

Bibliography

Irving, Washington. *Lives of Mahomet and His Successors*, Paris: Baudry's European Library, 1850.

_____. *The Life of Mahomet*, London: Everyman's Library, 1920.

Luther, A. Rauf. *Mohammad: The Divine Envoy*, Lahore: Sh. Mubarak Ali, 1979.

Margoliouth, D.S. *Mohammed and the Rise of Islam*, New York: AMS Press, 1978.

Muir, Sir William. *The Life of Mohammad From Original Sources*, Edinburgh: John Grant, 1923.

Kamal-ud-din, The Khwaja. *The Ideal Prophet*, Woking, England: The Basheer Muslim Library, 1925.

Nadwi, Abul Hasan Ali. *Muhammad Rasulullah*, Lucknow: Islamic Research and Publications, 1979.

Prideaux, Dr. Humphrey. *The True Nature of Imposture Fully Display'd in the Life of Mahomet*, London: E. Curll, 1723.

Rahman, Afzalur. *Muhammad: Blessing for Mankind*, London: The Muslim Schools Trust, 1979.

Rodinson, Maxime. *Mohammed*, England: Pelican Books, 1973.

Salmin, Muhammad Ali. *The Holy Prophet Muhammad Through Different Lights*, Bombay: The Grand Muslim Mission, 1954.

Sarwar, Hafiz Ghulam. *Muhammad: The Holy Prophet*, Lahore: Sh. Muhammad Ashraf, 1969.

Siddiqui, Abdul Hameed. *The Life of Muhammad*, Lahore: Islamic Publications Ltd., 1975.

Stobart, J.W.H. *Islam and Its Founder*, London: S.P.C.K., 1876.

Watt, W. Montgomery. *Muhammad at Mecca*, Oxford: Oxford University Press, 1972.

_____. *Muhammad at Medina*, Oxford: Oxford University Press, 1962.

_____. *Muhammad: Prophet and Statesman*, Oxford University Press, 1975.

Wessels, Antonie. *A Modern Arabic Biography of Muhammad*, Leiden: E.J. Brill, 1972.

Zafrulla Khan, Muhammad. *Muhammad: Seal of the Prophets*, London: Routledge and Kegan Paul, 1980.

The Qur'an

Ahmad, Mufassir Mohammad. *The Koran*, London: Emere Limited, 1979.

Ali, Maulvi Muhammad. *The Holy Qur'an*, Lahore: Ahmadiyya Anjuman-I-Ishaat-I-Islam, 1920.

Arberry, A.J. *The Koran Interpreted*, London: George Allen & Unwin, 1980.

Asad, Muhammad. *The Message of the Qur'an*, Gibraltar: Dar Al-Andalus, 1980.

Bell, Richard. *The Qur'an*, (2 volumes), Edinburgh: T & T Clark, 1960.

Burton, John. *The Collection of the Qur'an*, Cambridge: Cambridge University Press, 1977.

THE ISLAM
DEBATE

Cragg, Kenneth. *The Event of the Qur'an*, London: George Allen & Unwin, 1971.

_____. *The Mind of the Qur'an*, London: George Allen & Unwin, 1973.

Daryabadi, Maulana Abdul Majid. *Holy Qur'an*, Karachi: Taj Company Ltd., 1970.

Dawood, N.J. *The Koran*, London: Allen Lane, 1978.

Gatje, Helmut. *The Qur'an and Its Exegesis*, London: Routledge and Kegan Paul, 1976.

Jeffery, Arthur. *Materials for the History of the Text of the Qur'an*, New York: AMS Press, 1975.

_____. *The Foreign Vocabulary of the Koran*, Lahore: Al-Biruni, 1977.

_____. *The Qur'an as Scripture*, New York: Books for Libraries, 1980.

Katircioglu, Mahmud Muhtar. *The Wisdom of the Qur'an*, Lahore: Sh-Muhammad Ashraf, 1935.

Muir, Sir William. *The Coran: Its Composition and Teaching*, London: S.P.C.K., 1903.

Noldeke, Theodor. *Geschichte des Qorans*, Hildesheim: George Olms Verlag, 1981.

Pickthall, Mohammed Marmaduke. *The Meaning of the Glorious Koran*, New York: New American Library, n.d.

Rodwell, J.M. *The Koran*, London: Everyman's Library, 1974.

Ross, Alexander. *The AlCoran of Mahomet*, London, 1649.

Sale, George. *Preliminary Discourse to the Koran*, London: Frederick Warne & Co. Ltd., n.d.

_____. *The Koran*, London: Chandos Classics, 1922.

Sale, George with Wherry, E.M. *A Comprehensive Commentary on the Koran*, (4 volumes), New York: AMS Press, 1975.

Seale, M.S. *Qur'an and Bible* (Studies in Interpretation and Dialogue), London: Croom Helm, 1978.

Sell, Canon. *The Historical Development of the Qur'an*, London: Simpkin, Marshall, Hamilton, Kent & Co., Ltd., 1923.

Shah, Rev. Ahmad. *Miftah-ul-Qur'an*, (2 volumes), Lahore: The Book House, n.d.

Stanton, H.U. Weitbrecht. *The Teaching of the Qur'an*, New York: Biblo and Tannen, 1969.

Tisdall, W. St. Clair. *The Original Sources of the Qur'an*, London: S.P.C.K., 1905.

Wansbrough, J. *Qur'anic Studies* (Sources and Methods of Scriptural Interpretation), Oxford: Oxford University Press, 1977.

Watt, W. Montgomery. *Bell's Introduction to the Qur'an*, Edinburgh: University Press, 1970.

_____. *Companion to the Qur'an*, London: George Allen & Unwin Ltd., 1967.

Wollaston, Arthur N. *The Religion of the Koran*, London: John Murray, 1917.

Yusuf Ali. *The Meaning of the Illustrious Qur'an*, Lahore: Sh. Muhammad Ashraf, 1971.

Zafrulla Khan, Muhammad. *The Qur'an*, London: Curzon Press, 1978.

Bibliography

The Religion of Islam

Ahmad, Kurshid (Editor). *Islam: Its Meaning and Message*, Leicester: The Islamic Foundation, 1976.

Ali, Syed Ameer. *The Spirit of Islam*, London: Chatto and Windus, 1974.

Ali, Maulana Muhammad. *The Religion of Islam*, Lahore: The Ahmadiyya Anjuman Ishaat Islam, 1973.

Arnold, T.W. *The Preaching of Islam*, Lahore: Sh. Muhammad Ashraf, 1968.

De Boer, T.J. *The History of Philosophy in Islam*, New York: Dover Publications Inc., 1967.

Fry, C.G. & King, J.R. *Islam: A Survey of the Muslim Faith*, Grand Rapids: Baker Book House, 1980.

Gairdner, W.H.T. *The Reproach of Islam*, London: Young People's Missionary Movement, 1911.

Gaudefroy-Demombynes, Maurice. *Muslim Institutions*, London: Allen & Unwin, 1968.

Gibb, H.A.R. and Kramers, J.H. *Shorter Encyclopaedia of Islam*, Leiden: E.J. Brill, 1974.

Goldziher, Ignaz. *Introduction to Islamic Theology and Law*, Princeton: Princeton University Press, 1981.

Guillaume, Alfred, *Islam*, England: Pelican Books, 1971.

_____. *The Traditions of Islam*, Lahore: Universal Books, 1977.

Hughes, T.P. *Dictionary of Islam*, Lahore: Premier Book House, n.d.

Hurgronje, Snouck. *Mohammedanism*, New York: G.P. Putnam's Sons, 1916.

Jeffery, Arthur. *Islam: Muhammad and His Religion*, New York: The Library of Liberal Arts, 1958.

Klein, F.A. *The Religion of Islam*, London: Curzon Press Ltd., 1979.

Lammens, H. *Islam: Beliefs and Institutions*, New Delhi: Oriental Books Reprint Corporation, 1979.

Lippman, Thomas W. *Understanding Islam*, New York: New American Library, 1982.

Margoliouth, D.S. *Mohammedanism*, London: Thornton Butterworth Ltd., 1928.

Nasr, Seyyed Hossein. *Ideals and Realities of Islam*, Boston: Beacon Press, 1972.

North, C.R. *An Outline of Islam*, London: The Epworth Press, 1934.

Padwick, Constance E. *Muslim Devotions*, London: S.P.C.K., 1961.

Parwez, G.A. *Islam: A Challenge to Religion*, Lahore: Idara-e-Tulu-e-Islam, 1968.

Rahman, Afzalur. *Islam: Ideology and the Way of Life*, London: The Muslim Schools Trust, 1980.

Rahman, Fazlur. *Islam*, Chicago: University of Chicago Press, 1979.

Roberts, D.S. *Islam*, England: Hamlyn Paperbacks, 1981.

Roberts, Robert. *The Social Laws of the Qur'an*, London: Williams & Norgate Ltd., 1925.

THE ISLAM
DEBATE

Schacht, Joseph. *An Introduction to Islamic Law*, Oxford: Oxford University Press, 1979.

_____. *The Origins of Muhammadan Jurisprudence*, Oxford: Oxford University Press, 1975.

Tabbarah, Afif A. *The Spirit of Islam*, Beirut, Lebanon, 1978.

Tisdall, W. St. Clair. *The Religion of the Crescent*, London: S.P.C.K., 1906.

Tritton, A.S. *Islam: Beliefs and Practices*, London: Hutchinson University Library, 1966.

Von Grunebaum, G.E. *Muhammadan Festivals*, London: Curzon Press, 1976.

Watt, W. Montgomery. *What Is Islam?*, London: Librairie du Liban, 1979.

Wensinck, A.J. *Muslim Creed*, London: Frank Cass & Co., Ltd., 1965.

Zafrulla Khan, Muhammad. *Islam: Its Meaning for Modern Man*, London: Routledge and Kegan Paul, 1980.

Zwemer, S.M. *The Moslem Doctrine of God*, New York: American Tract Society, 1905.

Muslim Sects Including Shi'ite Islam

Ahmad, Mirza B.M. *Invitation to Ahmadiyyat*, London: Routledge and Kegan Paul, 1980.

Ali, Yusuf. *Imam Hussain and His Martyrdom*, Lahore: Al-Biruni, 1978.

Ayoub, Mahmoud. *Redemptive Suffering in Islam*, The Hague: Mouton Publishers, 1978.

Jafri, S.H.M. *The Origins and Early Development of Shi'a Islam*, London: Librairie du Liban, 1979.

Lavan, Spencer. *The Ahmadiyah Movement*, Delhi: Manohar Book Service, 1974.

MacDonald, D.B. *The Religious Attitude and Life in Islam*, New York: AMS Press, 1970.

al-Mufid, Shaykh. *Kitab al-Irshad: The Book of Guidance*, London: Balagha and Muhammadi Trust, 1981.

Sachedina, Abdulaziz A. *Islamic Messianism*, New York: State University of New York Press, 1981.

Seelye, Kate C. *Moslem Schisms and Sects*, New York: AMS Press, 1966.

Tabatabai, Sayyid M.H. *Shi'ite Islam*, Houston: Free Islamic Literatures, 1979.

The Crucifixion in Islam and Christianity

Books by Muslims and Christians:

Ahmad, Kwhaja Nazir. *Jesus in Heaven on Earth*, Lahore: Woking Muslim Mission and Literary Trust, 1972.

Bibliography

Ajijola, A.D. *The Myth of the Cross*, Lahore: Islamic Publications Limited, 1975.

Alam, Syed M.B. *Nuzul-e-Esa: Descension of Jesus Christ*, Delhi: Dini Book Depot, n.d.

Ali, Moulvi Muhammad. *Muhammad and Christ*, Lahore: Ahmadiah Anjuman-I-Ishaet-I-Islam, 1921.

Andrae, Tor. *Der Ursprung Des Islams und das Christentum*, Uppsala: Almqvist & Wiksells, 1926.

Ansari, F.R. *Islam and Christianity in the Modern World*, Karachi: World Federation of Islamic Missions, 1965.

Assfy, Zaid H. *Islam and Christianity*, New York: William Sessons Ltd., 1977.

Basetti-Sani, Giulio. *The Koran in the Light of Christ*, Chicago: Franciscan Herald Press, 1977.

Bell, Richard. *The Origin of Islam in Its Christian Environment*, London: Frank Cass & Co. Ltd., 1968.

Bevan-Jones, L. *Christianity Explained to Muslims*, Calcutta: Baptist Mission Press, 1964.

Brown, David. *The Cross of the Messiah*, London: Sheldon Press, 1969.

Chishti, Yousuf S. *What Is Christianity?*, Karachi: World Federation of Islamic Missions, 1970.

Frieling, Rudolf. *Christianity and Islam*, Edinburgh: Floris Books, 1978.

. Hamid, A. *Islam and Christianity*, New York: Carlton Press, 1967.

Hussein, M.K. *The City of Wrong*, London: Geoffrey Bles, 1959.

Joommal, A.S.K. *The Bible: Word of God or Word of Man?*, Johannesburg: Islamic Missionary Society, 1976.

Manjoo, Muhammad E. *The Cross and the Crescent*, Durban: Foto-Saracen, 1966.

Palacios, Miguel A. *Saint John of the Cross and Islam*, New York: Vantage Press, 1981.

Parrinder, Geoffrey. *Jesus in the Qur'an*, London: Sheldon Press, 1976.

Pfander, C.G. *The Mizan Ul Haqq, or, Balance of Truth*, London: Church Missionary House, 1867.

Pfander, C.G. & Tisdall, W. St. Clair. *The Mizanul Haqq (Balance of Truth)*, London: The Religious Tract Society, 1910.

Rahim, Muhammad A. *Jesus: Prophet of Islam*, England: Diwan Press, 1977.

Robson, James. *Christ in Islam*, London: John Murray, 1929.

Sahas, Daniel J. *John of Damascus on Islam*, Leiden: E.J. Brill, 1972.

Samad, Ulfat A. *A Comparative Study of Christianity and Islam*, Lahore: Sh. Muhammad Ashraf, 1976.

Sayous, Edouard. *Jesus Christ D'Apres Mahomet*, Paris: E. Leroux, 1880.

Shafaat, A. *The Gospel According to Islam*, New York: Vantage Press, 1979.

Shenk, D.W. & Kateregga, B.D. *Islam & Christianity*, Nairobi: Uzima Press Limited, 1980.

Tisdall, W. St. Clair. *Muhammadan Objections to Christianity*, London: S.P.C.K., 1912.

Wherry, E.M. *The Muslim Controversy*, Madras: The Christian Literary Society, 1905.

Wismer, D. *The Islamic Jesus*, New York: Garland Publishing, 1977.

Zwemer, S.M. *The Glory of the Cross*, London: Marshall, Morgan & Scott, n.d.

———. *The Moslem Christ*, London: Oliphant, Anderson & Ferrier, 1912.

Muslim Publications — Booklets and Tracts:

Anonymous. *The Truth About Jesus, the Son of Mary*, Johannesburg: Young Men's Muslim Association, 1961.

Deedat, A.H. *Resurrection or Resuscitation?* Durban: Islamic Propagation Centre, 1978.

———. *Was Christ Crucified?*, Durban: Islamic Propagation Centre, n.d.

———. *What Was the Sign of Jonah?*, Durban: Islamic Propagation Centre, 1976.

———. *Who Moved the Stone?*, Durban: Islamic Propagation Centre, 1977.

Khan, Nawab M.Y. *Christ and Mary in the Holy Qur'an*, Lahore: The Book House, n.d.

Mufassir, Sulaiman S. *Jesus, a Prophet of Islam*, Plainfield: Muslim Student's Association, 1980.

———. *Jesus in the Qur'an*, Plainfield: Muslim Student's Association, n.d.

Peerbhai, Adam. *Glory of Jesus in the Koran*, Durban: Islamic Institute, n.d.

Rosenberg, Muhammad F. *Crucifixion*, Mafeking, South Africa: Mafeking Muslim Welfare Association, 1958.

Saifuddin. *Christianity or Islam?* Karachi: Islamic Foundation, 1969.

Seepye, M.O. *Crucifixion of Christ*, Pietermaritzburg: Crecent Islamic Defence and Dissemination Service, 1963.

———. *Is the Crucifixion a Fact or Fiction?*, Pietermaritzburg: Crescent Islamic Defence and Dissemination Service, 1963.

Sheard, W.J. *The Myth of the Crucified Saviour*, Karachi: World Federation of Islamic Missions, 1967.

Christian Publications: Pamphlets and Booklets:

Abdul-Haqq, Dr. Akbar. *Christ in the New Testament and the Qur'an*, Evanston, 1975.

Gilchrist, John. *The Crucifixion in the Qur'an and the Bible*, Benoni, South

Africa: Jesus to the Muslims, 1981.

Hahn, E. *Jesus in Islam*, Vaniyambardi: Concordia Press, 1975.

Jadeed, Iskander. *The Cross in the Gospel and the Qur'an*, n.d.

_____. *Sin and Atonement in Islam and Christianity*, Basel: Centre for Young Adults, n.d.

McCoomb, E. *Did Jesus Christ Die on the Cross on Behalf of Sinners?*, Durban: (Right Guidance for Muslim Friends), 1977.

GLOSSARY

ABU BAKR — (Reign: 632-634 A.D.) The first Muslim caliph, according to Sunni Muslims. The Shi'ite Muslims reject this and instead consider the fourth caliph, 'Ali, as the first true successor to Mohammad.

ALLAH — The Supreme Being. The name of God, probably derived from the Arabic *Al-Ilah* and the Syriac *Alaha*.

CALIPH — The title given to the office of the spiritual and political leadership which took over after Mohammad's death.

FATIMA — The daughter of Mohammad and his first wife, Khadija; and the wife of 'Ali, the fourth caliph.

HADITH — The sacred sayings of Mohammad, handed down by oral tradition, for generations after Mohammad's death until finally transcribed.

HAJJ — A pilgrimage to Mecca. One of the five pillars of the Islamic faith.

HIJRAH — Mohammad's flight from Mecca to present day Medina in A.D. 622

IMAM — A Muslim who is considered by Sunnis to be an authority in Islamic law and theology or the man who leads the prayers. Also refers to each of the founders of the four principal sects of Islam. The Shi'ites accept 12 great Imams.

THE ISLAM
DEBATE

ISLAM — Literally, "submission to the will of Allah."

KA'ABA — A small stone building located in the court of the great mosque at Mecca containing the black stone (a meteorite) supposedly given to Adam by Gabriel and subsequently found by Abraham who allegedly built the Ka'aba.

KORAN (QUR'AN) — Said to be the final and complete inspired word of God transmitted to the prophet Mohammad by the angel Gabriel.

MAHDI — "The guided one." A leader who will cause righteousness to fill the earth. The Sunnites are still awaiting his initial appearance while the Shi'ites hold that the last Imam, who disappeared in A.D. 874 will someday reappear as the Mahdi.

MECCA — The birthplace of Mohammad. This city, located in Saudi Arabia, is considered the most holy city by the Muslims.

MEDINA — A holy city of Islam named for Mohammad. It was previously named Yathrib. It is the city to which Mohammad fled in A.D. 622

MOHAMMAD — The prophet and founder of Islam. Born around A.D. 570, died A.D. 632

MOSLEM (MUSLIM) — A follower of Mohammad. Literally, "one who submits."

MOSQUE — An Islamic place of worship.

MUEZZIN — A Muslim crier who announces the hour of prayer.

MULLA — A teacher of Islamic laws and doctrines.

OMAR — According to the Sunnites, the second Moslem caliph and principal advisor to the first caliph, Abu Bakr.

PURDAM — A veil or covering used by Moslem women to ensure them privacy against public observation, and to indicate their submission.

RAMADAN — The ninth month of the Muslim year, when the Qur'an was supposedly brought down to the first heaven, and now devoted to fasting.

SALAT — The Muslim daily prayer ritual. One of the five pillars of Islamic faith.

Glossary

SHI'ITES — A Muslim sect which rejects the first three caliphs, insisting that Mohammad's son-in-law 'Ali was Mohammad's rightful initial successor.

SUFIS — Philosophical mystics who have largely adapted and reinterpreted Islam for themselves.

SUNNITES — The largest Moslem sect which acknowledges the first four caliphs as Mohammad's rightful successors.

SURAHS — What the chapters of the Qur'an are called.